Riding

the

Divide

To Bill Nelson

Enjoy the adventure

Riding horses,
Relating to people,
Reminiscing about life,
Revering God's creation--
with a little theology thrown in for good measure.

Riding the Divide

Micah 6:8

By
Al Quie

Al Quie

with
Carol Pettitt

Cover design by Denis D. Hogen
Cover photo by Lynn Street
Maps by Gretchen Quie
Sketches by Denis D. Hogen
Photos by Al Quie and friends who went on the rides (unless otherwise noted)

ISBN: 0-9743886-0-2

First Printing, August, 2003

Printed in the United States of America

Dedication

To my loving wife Gretchen,
who, even though she retired her sleeping bag 30 years ago,
has continued to pray for and encourage me
in my pursuit of two more loves: horses and mountains;
and who, as an artist, mother and opera lover,
has inspired me and given depth to my life.

Contents

Prologue 9
Epigraph 13
Map of Continental Divide 14
Map of Montana Rides 15
1983 17
   1 - Finally. In the company of real, live cowboys 19
   2 - A Grizzly visit 27
   3 - Rain-soaked friends, bone-dry leader 35
   4 - 'Sure. And I used to be Lady Diana!' 45
   5 - Crushed egos on the Razor Back 55
   6 - Press coverage 65
1984 75
   7 - 'The horses will be back'–and they were 77
   8 - Exploring the Dark Horse Mine 87
   9 - Riding in circles? 93
Map of Wyoming Rides 103
1985 105
   10 - In a helpless instant: three cracked vertebrae 107
   11 - A fresh start with 'The Press' 117
1986 126
   12 - 'And what does Jesus say to *you*, Mother Theresa?' 127
   13 - The need for a horse whisperer 137
   14 - A woman on the ride 147
   15 - Dissension in the ranks 157
   16 - Much too young to die 163
   17 - A young wrangler reforms 169
1987 175
   18 - A promise to care for the 'inexperienced' 177
   19 - A leather-y miner offers her help 187

Photos of the rides. 193-224

20 - Wonderings about prayer 225

21 - Encounters with wild horses and rattlesnakes 231

22 - Altitude sickness brings an understanding of prayer. 241

23 - Spelunking becomes a spiritual experience. 253

24 - Another 'Lady Diana' experience 261

Map of Colorado Rides. 269

1988 271

25 - Learning to share one's faith 273

26 - A call to a barred owl reaps a bobcat. 283

27 - Head-over-heels down the mountain 293

28 - The legendary story of Deadman's Gulch 303

1989 309

29 - Altitude sickness strikes again 311

30 - 'Phonetically, that would be spelled K-W-E-E. Kwee.' . . 317

31 - Am I ready to go through the process of dying? 325

Map of New Mexico Rides. 333

1990 334

32 - Riding the *roads* of New Mexico. 335

33 - The landlord(s) of Hachita. 345

34 - Stories about personal encounters with Cochise 353

35 - The mysterious 'Lady in Blue' 363

1991 371

36 - Floors are not bullet-proof. 373

37 - Tragedy strikes! 383

38 - Trying to make it last. 391

Epilogue 401

End Notes 405

Acknowledgments. 413

Biographical sketches 415

PROLOGUE

July, 1931

Nettie Quie put the lid back on the pan of boiling potatoes, wiped her hands on her apron and walked to the front of the farmhouse. The screen door squeaked as she opened it to call her children. "Alice and Marjorie! Albert, Paul! Time to come in and get cleaned up…supper will soon be ready!"

She looked toward the barn and saw her nearly 8-year-old son on the family's Morgan horse, Caesar. "Albert," she called. "Will you please get the mail before you come in?"

He quickly agreed, eager to have a ride with a purpose. Besides, retrieving the mail while sitting bareback on Caesar (like the cowboys do) was a challenge to be met. He wasn't about to dismount at the mailbox because he knew, if he did, his height would prevent him from getting back on that tall horse. And that would result in a shameful quarter-mile walk back, leading Caesar.

Riding down the driveway, bordered by spruce trees and one lone pine tree, he looked up at that favorite pine. Albert loved that tree, different from the others, and taller. The pine's sturdy branches and fewer needles made it easy to climb so he could look around the countryside. Only the forbidden windmill reached higher into the sky. From a perch high in that pine his imagination, stimulated by stories from his Aunt Caroline, could run wild about "the West."

Albert pulled Caesar up close to the mailbox, reached inside for the mail, closed the box, and turned the horse around. Success!

He headed back to the barn to put Caesar away and then took the mail into the house. As he entered, Albert saw that his sister Marjorie was finishing setting the table; his father, Albert Sr., who did not need calling for a meal, was already seated. He thanked Albert for the mail, started thumbing through it and stopped. One letter caught his attention. "Nettie…children! There is a letter from Caroline!" He quickly opened it, eager to find out what was new with his sister.

Eyes filled with expectation, the children clamored for answers. "Is she coming?" "When will she be here?"

Dad Quie motioned for them all to sit around the table; he began reading:

Dear brother Albert and family,

I'm lonesome for Longfurrow Farm, so I'm planning to spend part of my vacation with you. Do you think you can stand another visit from me? This spinster aunt would like to be with the children again and tell them about a water falls she saw in the mountains.

Nettie, I will help you with the chores. It will be fun to work on the farm again, with a family I love...

"The mountains!" Albert let his mind wander, oblivious to the fact his father was still reading aloud about Aunt Caroline's travel plans and her activities at Children's Hospital in Seattle where she was head nurse.

The boy had just been reading *The Trail of the Lonesome Pine* and was intrigued by the stories of cowboys and mountain men. But Aunt Caroline's stories were better. They were more fascinating than any book or drama. And besides her vivid stories of the mountains, she had wonderful tales about life on her sister's and brother-in-law's ranch near Wolf Point, Montana.

Albert interrupted his dad, "When does it say she is coming?!"

With a smile, Dad Quie said, "You were day-dreaming again, weren't you, son?" Not waiting for an answer, he replied, "She'll be here Friday."

Friday! Could he even wait that long?

~ ~ ~

Standing at the living room window, all four children kept close watch on the road, each determined to be the first to see the family car bringing Aunt Caroline from the Dennison train depot. As Albert Sr.'s vehicle crested the top of the distant hill, the sighting was well reported to Nettie Quie, still in the kitchen making final supper preparations. "They're coming!" "They're coming!"

When the car rolled up the driveway and braked in front of the garage, all five–mother and four children–ran out of the house and eagerly and excitedly welcomed the new arrival from "the West."

The children wasted no time in trying to get their aunt to share her stories. "Tell us about the falls!" they chimed. The entire family made their way to the house, with the normally bashful Albert Jr. leading the pack. He was sometimes known to hide behind the davenport when guests came, but not this time. He did not want to miss a word. To him, nothing was more important than hearing Aunt Caroline's stories.

But his mom, dad and aunt did not agree. First a meal, chores and milking the cows. *Then* there would be time for stories. Caroline assured the pestering boy, "Oh, Albert, you would love the mountains. But, wait until later."

That evening, Albert sat with his brother Paul at their aunt's feet and the others in chairs as Caroline wove word pictures describing majestic places she'd seen. She spread her arms wide and looked upward as she described the vastness of the mountain tops. She used words like "aristocracy of space," which was not unusual for this Renaissance woman. Besides having an adventuresome spirit, she loved opera, classical music, drama, and theology.

Then came the story of the falls.

"One day I was in a new place in the Washington mountains along the Pacific Crest. I came upon a marvelous water falls, so I sat on some rocks just beyond the spray, breathing in the spaciousness and beauty along with the moist air. It was like sitting before a holy altar." But then anxiety and perplexity came into her voice.

"The next morning I woke early–it was still dark–and I made my way back to the falls. I wanted to see the sunrise from that same spot–or at least be there at first light because that's when nature seems to be at peace with God and the anxiety of 'yesterday' is gone." Her voice softened. "The hope of the new day fills my soul."

Then her voice rose in an expression of concern. "As I neared the falls, there was no sound! Alarm arose in my heart instead of the expected tranquility. Arriving at the spot of the last evening's awesome splendor of a rushing water falls, I found no water cascading down the rocks. None."

She looked around and, seeing the wide-eyed look of wonder and incomprehension in little Albert's face, she said quietly and directly to him, "I felt the same way. How could this happen?"

She waited only a few moments for the dilemma to sink in before she continued. "I went back to the lodge where I had stayed the previous night and all I could get from the people who worked there was, 'I hear that happens this time of year.'

"I hear that happens?!!" she repeated incredulously. "Is that all you have to say?!!" Then to the family gathered she explained, "I wanted some answers!

"Later in the day (the time when most people visit the falls), I returned, and it was running full force again."

She just let her story hang there and then changed the subject. "One day I thought I'd lost my way on the trail, but I guess I hadn't. Couldn't have, or I wouldn't be here to tell you about it!" Everyone laughed, but Albert pushed for more stories.

So Caroline told about the rich sunsets as she had during previous visits. "At the end of each day, I'd climb either to the top or until I could not climb anymore. I'd listen to the birds getting ready to roost and to the hush of the breeze through the trees. 'An organ breathes in every grove' of trees." Albert did not know she was quoting Thomas Hood.

"Huge clouds would climb high into the velvet sky, which turned a rich multitude of colors as the sun slipped quietly below the horizon. And brush strokes of red and yellow, even purple, splashed about the sky. There was a holiness to it."

Caroline turned to Albert, "Did you know you can gain a sense of the reality of God when you are in the mountains?

"Oh, of course you don't know that. You haven't had the chance to go there yet."

"Someday," Albert thought. "Someday I will."

Behind me lay the forests hushed with sleep;
Above me in its granite majesty,
Sphinx-like, the peak, thro' silent centuries,
Met the eternal question of the sky.
Victor at last–throned on the cragged height–
I scan the green steeps of the mountain side
Where late I toiled.

Between two silences my soul floats still
As any white cloud in this sunny air.
No sound of living breaks upon my ear,
No strain of thought–no restless human will–
Only the virgin quiet, everywhere–
*Earth never seemed so far, or Heaven so near.*1

The Continental Divide[2]

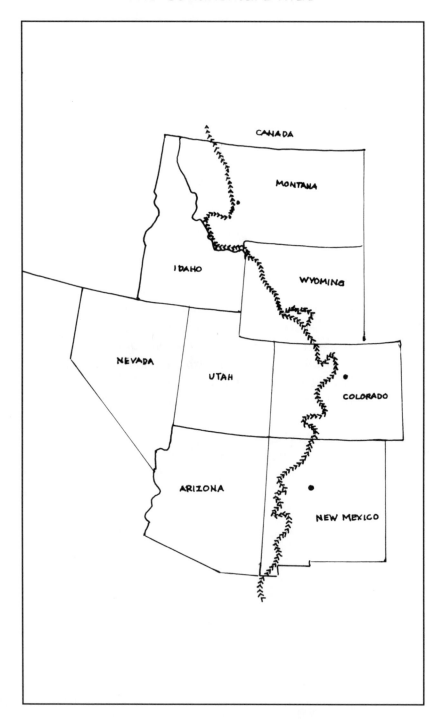

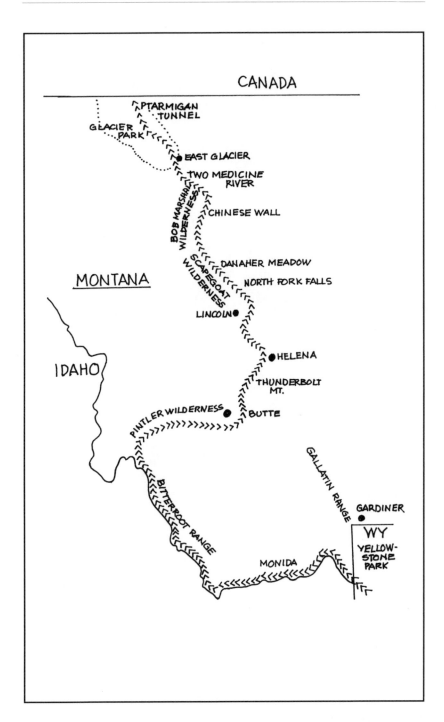

1983

Montana and Northern Wyoming

Bob Marshall Wilderness
Scapegoat Mountain
Helena National Forest
Gallatin Range
Yellowstone National Park

CHAPTER ONE

At last -- in the company of real cowboys

Saturday, June 25, 1983

Impatient, yet wanting to be patient, we wait.

The day is hot. A lot hotter than I expected as we packed our gear in the pre-dawn hours this morning.

Saying good-bye to Gretchen and to Ben's and Mike's girlfriends was difficult–for most everyone but me. Full of anticipation for this adventure, I had focused instead on making sure the horses were comfortable in their trailers, the trailers were properly hitched, and our gear was packed. I avoided the look of loneliness and concern in Gretchen's eyes. We gathered for prayer– including Grandma Hansen who is staying with Gretchen for a few days–asking the Lord for the safety of those who were heading out, and protection of those staying behind.

Not one for making lists, I did a mental perusal and hoped we were missing nothing.

As we drove along the highway toward North Dakota, I took pleasure in seeing how lush and beautiful the Minnesota country-side had become after recent rains. Unfortunately, that wasn't the case everywhere, for where good conservation practices had not been followed, the ravages of soil erosion were evident. I also saw that the corn was not as tall as it could be; it had a pale green color; I could see the clay soil showing through in spots. It hurts to see the land destroyed. Another story for another time.

~ ~ ~

It wasn't long before the rolling hills became more flat–almost making the terrain of western Minnesota indistinguishable from that of North Dakota. I felt strangely conflicted, leaving the farmlands my grandfather had come to in 1856, where my father had toiled, and where I grew up, and heading for The West, my deep love.

I have as great an anticipation now as I did at the beginning of my honeymoon with Gretchen in the Rockies in 1948. The difference is that, at the beginning of our honeymoon, there was the anticipation of what I did not know about the mountains (which I'd only heard and read about); now I have the anticipation of what I do know.

The other difference is that I was always aware that Gretchen was with me (thank goodness!) on our honeymoon in the mountains. And now, as I am in the midst of my reverie, it's as though our son Ben is not with me. Rather than sharing my thoughts with him, I am preoccupied with what this trip is all about–why I am doing this, what is motivating me, and what it will ultimately mean.

The anticipation of this undertaking is giving me a certain anxiety. The thrill of the challenge is here, but I also have some doubts about whether I am up to it and whether I can lead the men who will be accompanying me.

I've always fantasized about being a part of the West–really a part of it. As a boy, I often dreamed about tagging along with the mountain men and cowboys. I admired their ability to live and survive by themselves in the wild, depending on nothing but God's creation. Would I be closer to God if I were all alone in the mountains? I recalled that Jesus often went up into the mountains when He wanted to be alone to pray.

~ ~ ~

As we traveled along Interstate 94 in North Dakota today, I marveled at the true beauty of the Dakota prairie. I know people have called this area the "Great American Desert," and I've read about how pioneers hated having to cross the plains before they could finally get to the grandeur of the mountains. But I am thrilled with the beauty of this countryside–every part of it–whether it's cattle I see, or horses, or just the curve of the land as it was shaped by the glacier long ago. Looking off to the horizon in a wide sweep from right to left I wondered what is beyond.

I imagined what it would be like if there were no fences here. You'd be able to ride over hills and swales, not knowing where there was water, probably looking for someone who had ridden there before and who could direct you. Or maybe you'd get to know the land so well you could sense where you were likely to find water. The grass, now waving in the breeze, grows so tall here it would brush a horse's belly.

I wished there was some way I could articulate how I feel about all this so others could capture for themselves the joy of adventure, the beauty of creation and the awesomeness of God.

~ ~ ~

Mike Dudley finally caught up to us, and we caravanned the rest of the way to Medora. I guess he had gotten "lost" in his music, causing him to fall behind. Mike is a 27-year-old attorney from Wisconsin. He grew up on a farm close to ours near Northfield, so I knew about his family. His father had a great reputation as a Golden Glove boxer, they were great farmers, and the family members were wonderful believers in Jesus Christ. Mike had planned to lead a group on a trail ride in the Rocky Mountains but it didn't work out, so he asked if he could come along with me.

When we got to Medora tonight, we asked around for a place to keep our horses. There was a rodeo in town at the time so we couldn't use the rodeo grounds. We were directed to the stockyards, where there was a stream for watering the horses between the corrals and the railroad tracks.

Mike is sleeping outside in his bedroll; Ben is sleeping in the horse trailer. I will join him soon.

I forgot my sleeping bag at home–maybe I need to develop the art of making list! I will use horse blankets to stay warm, even though the narrow blankets will likely slip to the side. It'll probably be a cold night's sleep.

Having inadequate sleeping gear, though, is nothing new to me. Many times as a kid, I'd climb out the window at night, shinny down a drain pipe and sleep under the stars. Of course I'd scamper back up and into bed before dawn so my parents wouldn't catch me.

Sunday, June 26, 1983

In the morning, the moon was suspended over the buttes to the south of Medora. A herd of elk were standing like sentinels there and where I stood yawning, and two hawks were swooping by a butte a little further to the west.

At breakfast, I met a guy named Griggs who wanted to trade horses. I love to talk horses, so I took Griggs out to see my appaloosa, Spanish Bull, and his sister, Spanish Lace. Then I showed him Ben's and my two pack-horses: Goldie–a palomino I'd borrowed from my friend A.M. Lips, and Revenue–a quarter horse I'd purchased and nicknamed "Clyde" (so nicknamed because, when I was governor of

Minnesota, my Commissioner of Revenue, Clyde Allen, often carried a political load for me!)

Always interested in a good horse trade, I inquired about his horses. I was thinking Clyde might be a good horse to trade. I knew when I bought him that he was stubborn. But stubborn horses were a challenge to me. Then I began to feel uneasy talking about trading the horses I'd carefully chosen just for this trip. Common sense soon returned as I realized acquiring unfamiliar horses at this point would not be good.

I was distracted by a pickup truck with a horse trailer pulling up next to us. I could see that I didn't recognize either of the men in the truck. The driver jumped out and introduced himself–Jack Thompson. Turns out he knew my son Dan who, 13 years earlier, had spent the summer working with Jack on the ranch of N.D. Congressman Don Short. Small world.

Jack's demeanor and appearance were things I'd yearned for myself all my life. His garb. His walk. His look. He and his companion were on their way to a branding job–people working with horses to make a living. To me, this was the real West. The real live West. This was not recreation. Their horses even had the look of animals that worked for a living.

Here I was, nearly 60 years old, feeling like a little kid in the presence of real live cowboys! And yet, they were the ones who were envious of the trip we were on.

~ ~ ~

We drove from Medora to Lincoln, Montana, today (about 90 miles northwest of Helena), making it 1,138 total miles traveled. Our trip was longer than it needed to be, though–we missed our turn from Interstate 15 onto State Highway 200 north of Great Falls. We experienced lots of gravel road as we went to Power and across and back to catch 200 at Sun River.

Mike hadn't turned north on 15 out of Great Falls. Instead, he went south and cut across to 200 at Wolf Creek. I had wondered why he hadn't followed me. Perhaps he wanted to be independent. Maybe he was listening to his music again and not paying attention. Though a little concerned, I had decided not to chase after him. I seldom show people that I have a sense of responsibility for them (even when I do). Instead, I've always been one to let others learn by experience.

I guess I inherited this trait from my father. Rather than ride us about something, he'd allow experience to be the teacher. People learn better when they don't feel like someone is constantly "on" them.

So Mike probably didn't have a clue that I was concerned about him. But he knew where Lincoln was. I knew he'd get there.

We finally arrived at the ranch of Ken and Mary Faith Hoeffner, the parents of son Dan's wife, Penny Jo. Their ranch was to be our base for a couple of days as we prepared for the beginning of our ride. Ken and his son Jeff had gone to the mountains to find a lost horse, Penny Jo and her sister Jackie were at a rodeo in Augusta, and Mary Faith was busy training a young horse. Lots of activity and great to get here.

Dan had soup and sandwiches prepared for us at his and Penny Jo's home, located on another part of the ranch. Dan is my one son who actually did with his life what I only dreamed about: being a mountain man, living out doors, working with horses. I am so looking forward to spending time with him. He will be along on the first two weeks of the ride as our wrangler.

Dan is a natural at what I have to work, study, and struggle to achieve.

I remember the summer vacation we had when Dan was about 10 years old–we went fly fishing near Red Lodge. I had purchased good fly rods for my older son and a nephew. But Dan was too young, so I gave him my old casting rod with a spool reel, figuring he could entertain himself with it while the rest of us fished.

I did show him how to hook a monofilament leader on the rod, and how to put a float on it. My younger son Joel had the "job" of running around and watching people.

Soon Joel dashed to where the two older boys and I were fishing (catching nothing). "Daddy, Daddy, Dan caught a fish!" Lucky guy, I thought, and went back to fishing.

Joel soon returned, "Daddy, Daddy, Dan caught another fish!" Then I thought, maybe Dan knows something. I swallowed my ego, pulled everything in and walked near to where Dan was fishing. I stood watching him for a while, noticing how he seemed to be doing everything right.

I watched as he would cast and pull in fish after fish. I didn't know how in the world he did it, so I figured he's just gotta be where the fish are. I asked him if I could fish alongside him.

I laid mine out. Nothing. Pretty soon Dan catches another fish!

Men don't normally ask these kinds of questions, but I had to swallow my pride and say, "Dan, how do you do that?"

He said, "Well, I figure if a mosquito landed on the water, he wouldn't just lie there–he'd wiggle a little bit. So at just the right time, I wiggle the fly and the trout thinks it's alive. That's when I catch him."

"Is that right?" I responded smartly. I cast again. Still nothing. That's when I finally realized I simply do not have the natural ability that Dan does. I was dumbfounded, awestruck and truly proud of that son of mine.

It's this same son–now a man–whom I still admire. I have a longing to be around him.

~ ~ ~

After eating supper, we went through topographical maps to check the Continental Divide trails from Glacier to Lincoln.

Monday, June 27, 1983

Visited Garland's Town and Country store in Lincoln to look for a sleeping bag today. The Garlands didn't have one as long as I'd have liked–the one they had was designed for people six-foot or shorter. They said they'd order a longer one for me, but I didn't want to delay the start of my ride waiting for a sleeping bag. I'd rather be warm and a little cramped, than to have to wait.

Back at the ranch, Dan taught us more about how to pack a horse. I'd done some packing before, but it was too little and too long ago to prepare me for this ride. In just an hour and a half he showed us how to flip the mantie[3] out and lay the gear in the right place (the soft stuff like sleeping bags or tents go on the part of the canvas that will be against the horse); how to distribute the weight; how to fold everything up tight; how to hang it on the pack horse and how to tie it up right so you're not losing stuff along the way.

I learned that the higher the packs are situated on the sides of the horse, the lighter the load; and the lower the packs, the heavier the load will ride. It's also important to make the packs that will go on each side of the horse of equal weight and to balance them as you would a teeter totter–by raising one side or lowering the other through tightening or loosening the ropes.

We took a little test ride around the ranch with hay bales strapped to the pack horses. Clyde learned how to miss trees and stay behind. The packs rode perfectly. God is good.

Yes, when things go right–that's when I have a profound sense of

God's goodness. I know there are skeptics who will ask, "How can you say 'God is good' just because you've learned how to pack a horse?" But people who pack horses as a part of their everyday existence are dealing with something that is natural for them. They figured out long ago how to pack everything from kitchen stoves to dry socks on a single horse or mule. Now, they've lost the wonder of it all. I marvel at this experience. God is good.

Tuesday, June 28, 1983

We had breakfast with Dan and Penny Jo, got our gear together, loaded the horses, and talked to Mary Faith about groceries. Then we talked to Ken about the road to take from Lincoln up to Glacier. We took Highway 83 on the west side of the Bob Marshall Wilderness, and it took us 5 1/2 hours to go the 229 miles.

At East Glacier, we inquired of an old guy with a dude string where we might set up camp. He didn't know much, but told us where the Ranger Station was. After talking with the Ranger, a hiker named Terry and another rider by the name of Bruce, we learned that practically no one rides where we planned to go. Most people ride in the Park on well-groomed trails. We, on the other hand, intended to follow the Continental Divide, no matter where that would take us.

We found out, though, that there was so much snow in the northern part of Glacier this time of year that we wouldn't be able to get through Ptarmigan Tunnel. We decided we'd have to begin our ride this year at the south end of the Park, and leave Glacier Park until another year.

The Ranger told us of the Cattlemen's Association grounds six miles west of East Glacier where we found an old guy, Ben, and his son, who watched out for 500 head of cattle back in the forest. Ben had four of his own horses, plus two others. He said we could stay on the place, suggesting a spot four miles further west with a fence on three sides, a stream, and good grazing.

I put up my tent for the first time since I had purchased it four years earlier. I'd picked it up at a camping show while I was governor, dreaming of the day I'd first use it on this adventure. We cooked our first meal out, and generally got organized.

We'll stay here another day, waiting for the rest of the guys who will be joining us on this leg of the ride.

CHAPTER TWO

A Grizzly visit

Wednesday, June 29, 1983

After breakfast of bacon and eggs, son Ben and I saddled up. Mike stayed in camp while Ben and I went to scout the trail. Right outside of camp, going over a high ridge, we found Elk Calf Trail which took us to the south fork of the Two Medicine River. We followed the Two Medicine for about five miles and found a couple of trails about 100 feet higher up.

Along one of the trails I found a hatchet whose head and handle are made entirely of steel. This is truly unique. The bottom of the handle also has a wood piece riveted through it on each side. It has weathered so long, though, that the wood is rotten. But I'm keeping it. It will work fine for splitting small pieces of wood.

We came upon a trail crew just breaking camp and packing their mules. We chatted with them for a while to learn what we could and met the crew chief, Bob, who was originally from Iowa.

The snow-capped mountains looked spectacular–sometimes peeking through the clouds, sometimes in plain view. We rode along the trails for another few miles before returning to camp.

This afternoon, after peanut butter sandwiches for lunch, Ben and I took a nap while Mike packed up his mule and took about a five-mile ride. When Ben and I woke up, we saddled up–Ben on Goldie and I on Clyde–to ride to a nearby stream to go fishing.

We tied the horses to a tree and walked a ways further to the stream. After some time, I glanced up and saw a black cloud in the distance: I could see rain on the mountain side, heading our way. Three strikes at a mosquito fly was all we got, anyway, so Ben and I put our fishing gear away and headed back for the horses. Looking up at the tree where we had tied the horses, I could see only one.

Figuring it must be Clyde still there, I was ready to scold Ben: "I taught you how to tie knots! You've got to tie those knots so the horse won't get loose. You'll be left a-foot if you don't!" I was really going to read him out, but decided not to say anything, thinking he'll learn by experience. I just let it go.

As we got closer to the tree, I could see that it wasn't a bay, but a palomino that was still tied to the tree–it was Goldie!

Argh! It was *my* horse that got its knot untied! I was so thankful I hadn't taken Ben to task. I would never have been able to live that one down.

I walked the two miles back to camp, and there was Clyde, who'd found his way on the backtrail[4]. I began to wish I'd traded him to Griggs back in Medora.

But I did learn something about a horse's sense of where "home" is and how to get there. With his sense of direction, Clyde could have headed straight as the crow flies back to camp. Instead, he ran precisely in the tracks we had made on the way to the fishing hole. It's true what I've heard: you'll always find your horses in their tracks.

Tonight I cooked lentils, garbanzo beans, split peas and rice.

Thursday, June 30, 1983

It was very windy last night. Lots of noise from restless horses and the trees singing in the wind. I woke up at 5 a.m. to bad weather; it was cold and windy. I changed clothes fast in the horse trailer.

Leaving Ben in charge, I drove the five hours to Great Falls to pick up Doug Coe, his son, Jonathan, and Bill Starr, who were flying in to accompany us on the ride. Mike drove back to Lincoln to help bring horses up for Doug, Jonathan, and Bill.

Before going to the airport in Great Falls, I bought $154 worth of groceries–15 pounds of hamburger, 5 pounds of pork sausage, 8 packages of bacon, 12 loaves of bread, pancake mix, syrup, and jam. I couldn't find dried eggs, so we went without. We already had lots of freeze-dried food in camp, which Mike had brought.

What fun to see my Washington friends again. Doug said it must be love that would cause a friend to fly to Montana and ride horseback in the wilderness for two weeks. And it will likely be painful for him, too–at least for the first few days!

I was the first Congressman Doug came to visit when he started work in Washington in 1959. He joined Abraham Veriede who was involved in a ministry to government leaders, and he came to my office to meet me, apparently having heard about me and my faith. It took him a while to get the courage to come in to my office, but when he did, we prayed together.

Doug had wanted me to be active in a fellowship movement, which made me suspicious. My concern was that he wanted to use me. I was distrustful of people who might want to take advantage of my position for political, economic, or religious purposes. He rationalized that since my staff did so much work, and all in my name, why couldn't he work in the faith and spiritual realm in my name, too?

Many times we talked at length. Or perhaps it was he talking and I listening to his dream that leaders would someday be unified in the love of Christ. Still, I felt uncomfortable working with him. But one day it finally came to me: I didn't work for Doug nor would I be used by him; and he didn't work for me nor would he be used by me. We were brothers in Christ. We would work for and be used by Christ. From that day on, I was at peace with our relationship, and we have grown to be great friends.

Doug and his wife Jan have six children; Gretchen and I have five. There is much similarity in our children's ages. Doug's son, Jonathan, who is riding with us, is his youngest, and Doug loves him in a very special way.

Bill Starr had been the president of Young Life, an organization that has done so much for the spiritual strength of thousands of young people—and personally in the lives of four of our children, Jennifer, Daniel, Joel and Ben. Bill has left Young Life and is now living in Edina, Minnesota. He and Doug are very close.

~ ~ ~

We bought boots for Jonathan in Great Falls, and back in East Glacier we bought fishing gear for Doug. Bill did a good job of packing, so we didn't need to buy anything for him.

When we got back to camp late in the afternoon, we found the wind had blown the tent down, the poles were bent, and Ben was in a bad mood.

I didn't realize that leaving Ben alone all day to care for the camp and to tend the horses would be such a lonely time for him. I was insensitive to this because being alone was something I longed for, after all the years in politics and in the public eye. I was eager to be totally alone. I had never, in all my life, had the experience of being lonely when I was alone.

We straightened out the poles, turned the trailer to cut the wind and prepared for more stormy weather. The Hoeffners (Ken, Mary Faith, Jeff, and Mary Faith's mother) and Mike arrived with eight horses–a saddle horse and a pack horse for each of our three new riders, and a set for my wrangler.

The Hoeffners told me my son, Dan, had had a change in jobs and would not be able to accompany me on the ride. What a disappointment. Instead, their son Jeff will be our wrangler. He is only 17 years old. I wonder how he will do, handling the job of wrangler.

Friday, July 1, 1983

After breakfast in East Glacier, Ken, Mary Faith, and Jeff helped everyone pack, but I wanted to pack my own horse, putting into practice what Dan had taught me.

Once we were all ready, Jeff took off leading a string of pack horses. Doug, Jonathan and Bill were next with Ben following, leading Goldie, Mike leading his pack mule, and I had Clyde as my pack horse. I, the supposed leader, was the last one to leave camp. But bringing up the rear made it possible for me to take movies of "the start" with my home movie camera.

The Hoeffners transported our trailers back to Lincoln, so we were committed no matter what. There was no turning back.

About 100 yards out I came to a stream which the others had easily crossed. Spanish Bull stepped in and crossed–no problem. And then there was old Clyde. He balked at the edge of the stream. I was a little exasperated with him for having run away yesterday, so I just jerked the lead rope in an attempt to force him to come across.

In his stubbornness, he bunched up his legs and jumped to the other side of the stream. In that leap, he dislodged his pack to one side, started bucking, and kicked everything off his back!

I had an ax lying here, pots and pans lying there, and all the other riders just going on ahead.

I laughed out loud and thought to myself, "If I can't get a hundred yards without a wreck, how am I going to get to Mexico?!"

When the others realized I'd had a minor wreck, they stopped and waited as I re-adjusted Clyde's pack saddle and re-packed the load and equipment that had come loose. Good judgment comes from experience, and a lot of experience comes from bad judgment.

From then on it was ride, ride, ride. A dream is being fulfilled for me, but Bill Starr and Doug Coe are doing this simply to be with me, their friend. Jonathan Coe and Ben are here to be with their dads who had asked them to come. The love of a father for his youngest son, I guess. Mike Dudley also is fulfilling a dream. And then there's our young wrangler, 17-year-old Jeff Hoeffner, along on the ride out of obligation, wrangling his parents' horses.

We followed Elk Calf Trail and turned south along Two Medicine Creek to Baker Cabin, intending to set up camp. However, the Forest Service ranger told us we couldn't graze our horses there, so we went higher up and put up camp at Kip Creek.

~ ~ ~

All seems fine, except I did not call Gretchen when I was in East Glacier this morning. Rats! I can feel the anguish she must be experiencing, wondering what happened to me. Her "loving husband" forgot her. Now it'll be nearly three weeks before I am able to call. I could say I was too busy this morning. I was busy, but that is no excuse. I just didn't have my mind in the right place.

I've had people tell me my love for horses is so great that I put them before people, and sometimes even before my most basic needs. I recall Gretchen's frustration in the past when I would not come in to eat or go to bed because I just had to "finish with the horses."

Gretchen has always felt a twinge of jealousy toward horses. Early in our lives together I was too insensitive to realize this. Now I'm aware of it, but I still seem to let horses get in the way.

Saturday, July 2, 1983
Up at 5:30 this morning. I woke Jeff so he could help get the horses grazing. Bill woke and started the coffee over the fire I'd built in the wood stove. We had bacon and eggs and bread for breakfast; then we prepared salami or peanut butter sandwiches for lunch.[5]

Today's trek took us up Muskrat Creek to Muskrat Pass. We tried to head over to Strawberry Pass via Badger Pass, but we ran into trail after trail that was simply impossible. We finally found one that got us over to Strawberry Pass, and we set up camp where the trail branches at the East Fork of Strawberry Creek. I'm already learning: we cannot necessarily rely on the trails on the topo maps. The Forest Service has not kept them up, and some of them have evidently not been traveled for years.

Leading this expedition is heavy responsibility, but I am enjoying it. It's great to be with Ben, Doug, Bill and Jonathan. Jeff and Mike get along great. At the moment, Jeff is herding horses, Bill is reading, Doug is napping, Jon is mending his coat, Ben is whittling.

It's beginning to rain.

Sunday, July 3, 1983

It rained all night and most of the forenoon today. The rain stopped while we ate breakfast, but, as we were packing up, it started again. Our packs got soaked. I found it interesting, too, that while it was raining on us, we could look 500 feet above at the nearby mountain peak and see snow coming down.

During the rest of the day today the sun would peek out from behind the clouds–the warmth felt so good–and then the rain would start in again. It's a cold rain. Surprising how quickly the storms come and go.

We traveled along Strawberry Creek to where Clark Creek flows into the Flathead, to Bowl Creek and through to Sun River Pass. There we saw the most spectacular terrain: rugged peaks, stately pine trees, abundant flowers, rushing water, flowering meadows. If any of this was in Minnesota, it'd be a state park.

Jeff saw the first elk today. I saw two bear paw prints in the mud, so I know we are in Grizzly country.

We set up camp at the north fork of the Sun River just as another storm came up. It rained hard, and then for a while, it snowed. We got our cover up fast, though, and put all of our equipment under it.

Monday, July 4, 1983

A beautiful morning; a spectacular place for a layover day. It was our coldest day, though, and I'm not used to cold on a Fourth of July.

Our plan is to ride three days and then layover in camp on the fourth day to rest the horses and mules. They will consume more grass, also, when they are resting, which will keep their weight and stamina up.

When I got out of bed this morning, the first thing I noticed was bear tracks, including claw marks. A Grizzly had apparently looked us over sometime during the night. Its tracks showed it had come within 10 feet of us. I placed my foot (with overshoes on) in one of the tracks. The paw mark extended beyond the end of my size 14 foot! This had to have been a huge Grizzly. I wondered where he had gone, so I tracked him. The mud from fresh rains helped.

I found the Grizzly had come up to our camp, stopped and apparently just looked at us. Then he walked around to another side of our camp. I could see in the mud where he had turned again, probably looking us over. He was even closer to our camp at this point. Then his tracks showed he turned and simply walked away. Wow. I showed the tracks to the others. I realized later I could do that with joy and even bravado because the danger had passed. How would I have reacted if I had been an eye witness to the bear's visit?

Tuesday, July 5, 1983

The layover was grand. Everyone is in good spirits. We had pork sausage and eggs for breakfast, and again made salami sandwiches for lunch.

Beautiful morning as we left camp on the Sun River at 9:10 and rode up Open Creek to Kevan Mountain, then near Table and Pentagon Mountains. Unfortunately, we lost the trail in the snow and wasted two hours going up and down the mountain. Jeff and I took off from the rest, looking for the trail, and finally found our way down to Pentagon Creek, which flowed into Spotted Bear River. We went back to get the others and led them down by Switchback Pass–3-1/5 miles of switch backs, dropping 3,000 feet. It was very difficult, but I was glad we were going down rather than up.

Jonathan and Ben are especially enjoyable to have along in times of stress like this. They have the optimism of youth without the high sense of responsibility or concern for what might happen.

The trail had many logs across, and Goldie got his sling rope caught in a downed tree branch. I yelled at Ben to drop his lead rope so Goldie's pack wouldn't get caught in it too. His packs dislodged some when he jerked loose from the branch, but nothing broke and we were able to right the packs again.

We set up camp just below Pentagon Cabin. We are all bushed. Today's was a rugged trip.

Doug talked to me today about my becoming a spiritual ambassador to President Reagan. I can understand that the President could use help in this area; he is not known for being particularly religious. But I feel inadequate for the job of being a spiritual mentor to him. I suggested that someone already close to Reagan would be a better choice–someone who could report easily and briefly, and who could be trusted. Besides, I surely don't feel the call to go out to Washington again.

These are good men riding with me, and they seem to be enjoying the ride, even though it's not easy for them. Ben's back is hurting badly. Bill has leg pain, especially in the knee, but he wanted to come on the trips, anyway, so he could spend time with Doug and me. He is often in such great pain that he is white in the face.

Doug is unique–so energetic about the Lord–and his son Jon is much like him.

Jeff has good qualities, too. He is quiet, has an amiable personality, and is very capable. There was no need for me to wonder whether this 17-year-old would be able to be our wrangler. He is doing a great job.

And the horses. Spanish Bull is a peach. He and I get along so well. The same applies with Clyde, although his willfulness is trying at times. Lace is tough and holds up well. She both rides and packs well. Goldie is a steady horse.

And then there is Buford (Mike's pack mule). What a character, with a mind of his own![6] I'm enjoying watching Mike's enjoyment with Buford. He spoke to him today as though he could understand everything. Very affectionate. It's as though Buford and his horse are Mike's closest friends on this trip, as he is not "connected" to the rest of us. Coe, Starr and I have had many previous experiences. Jeff is now related since his sister is Dan's wife. But Doug is very good at trying to include Mike, and I appreciate that.

As I sit here with the Spotted Bear River rushing by, I'm able to look out at the last glows of the evening sun and see the pines pointing skyward and the rock outcropping 300 feet up in front of me. I love America. I love my family. I love my friends. I love the West, the mountains and the wilderness. But most of all I love God.

CHAPTER THREE

Rain-soaked friends, bone-dry leader

Wednesday, July 6 1983

We left camp just before 9:30 and headed up the Spotted Bear River to Spotted Bear Pass. It was a steady incline with many dead, fallen trees to get over and around. In one especially difficult place, the logs were on a steep incline, so we dismounted and led our horses over them. Clyde was great. He just followed behind Bull as I led. Some of the logs obstructing our path were 2 to 2-1/2 feet in diameter.

We spent more than nine hours on the trail today. After Spotted Bear Pass, we went by My Lake and Larch Hill where we could see, in the distance, the "Chinese Wall." It is as impressive as anyone has ever described: sheer rock cliff, 1,000 feet high, running for 15 miles. Jeff spotted a mountain goat on the wall–a big shaggy fellow. What a thrill to see. We all took turns looking through my binoculars. Farther down the wall, about two miles, we spotted elk–about 50 cows, calves, and a few young bulls.

We then made camp by a falls on Moose Creek just above a stream of water coming down from the south and no more than a mile from the Chinese Wall.

Thursday, July 7, 1983

Another layover day so Mike, Jeff, Ben, Jon, and Doug could climb the Chinese Wall. I rode Clyde south to see the tremendous sights. (I plan to ride my pack horse on layover days to give Bull a break.) Beautiful day again. We rested up well, as did the horses. Three deer came into camp tonight and stayed close. We teased Doug, who laid his lariat out on the ground hoping a deer would step into the loop.

Moose Creek is a camp to come back to.

Friday, July 8, 1983

We traveled nine miles today past Blyth Mountain, the Chinese Wall and two mountains of red rock–Haystack Mountain and Red Butte. Stopped for lunch along the west fork of the Sun River at a stony river bank. Doug initiated a rock-throwing contest. He is such a competitor! He would compete with anybody in knife-throwing, tree-climbing, you name it.

Had an interesting discussion tonight with Doug and Bill about religion and government. I have been out of the public eye for several months, now, but Doug is still working in politics, still encouraging people to be bold about sharing their faith with others.

Some in government, Doug said, are reluctant to talk about their faith because they don't know how it will be received by their constituents. Others are reluctant to share simply because they don't know how. They learn to express their political philosophies easily enough and are articulate about certain aspects of legislation they support. They can say where they stand within their political party and usually can expound on how the ethics and morality of government apply to them. But they are reticent to state they believe in Jesus Christ.

Nonetheless, Doug urges them to do so. They may not have a theological vocabulary, but they ought to just do it, and "it will come to them," he says. Doug has a real strong belief that people ought not to worry what others might think; the Spirit will give the words; just do it. It's Biblical, too.

We laughed about the time I was guest speaker–back in the early '60s–at a Governor's Prayer Breakfast in Oregon. Mark Hatfield, Oregon's governor at the time, was a good friend of Doug. I'd been told by Doug that Mark was a great man of faith, someone I could share my faith with. I was pleased, then, when after breakfast, Mark invited me to his office.

We visited about our mutual friend, Doug, a little about President Kennedy, what it was like being a follower of Christ in public service. And I waited for him to invite me to pray with him. But he didn't. I thought, "Here is this great friend of Doug Coe who knows the Lord so well, and he hasn't really talked much about that. I wonder what is wrong."

A couple of years later, I invited Mark and his wife Annette to stay with Gretchen and me when they came to Washington for the funeral of President Kennedy. It was during that visit that I found out

Mark had been wondering the same thing about me as we met in his office after that Governor's Prayer Breakfast! "Here's this Al Quie," Mark had told Doug he was thinking. "He's a great friend of Doug Coe and is supposed to know the Lord so well. Yet he hasn't really talked much about it except in his speech."

I agree with Doug: sometimes we all can be juvenile in our faith.

Doug and Bill and I also talked about how struck the church is with secular power. There were a group of church leaders who once came to Washington when Ford was president. They asked for a meeting with me prior to facing Ford. They wanted to pray before confronting the President about a stance he had taken on a particular issue. So we prayed.

But when these church leaders got to the White House, they backed down. They were intimidated by the power of government.

Not many people have the boldness of the prophets we read about in the Old Testament, or of John the Baptist, Paul, or Jesus–like the time Jesus turned over the tables of the money changers in the Temple and lashed those crooks with a whip He'd contrived from materials at hand.

~ ~ ~

Our camp tonight is set in a basin with mountains on the north and south, causing the wind to blow down the river. I'm protecting myself behind the tent as I write.

I love to just look at the pines, the mountains, the clouds–and listen to the steady sound of the water rushing over the rocks in a nearby stream. What peace. And the music of the bells on the horses gives me the security of knowing they are nearby.

The heat of the day brought out high cumulus clouds. I suspect a storm is coming.

Saturday, July 9, 1983

I was right about the storm. Mike wanted to sleep outside last night, and since I knew a storm was likely, I decided to sleep in the tent, for once, with Ben and Jonathan. Jeff also decided to sleep outside under the trees rather than under the kitchen tarp with Bill. And Doug, too, wanted to sleep under the stars. When I went to bed he was laying out his pads and sleeping bag. He even laid an axe next to his bed. In case, he said, a Grizzly came, he'd be able to defend himself!

I woke up in the middle of the night to the sound of a ruckus outside. I looked through the tent screen to find it as light as day. An enormous lightning storm was raging, lighting up the whole mountain range. The lightning came so fast it never got dark between strikes.

Soon, Jeff was heading back to camp from "sleeping under the trees." Doug, who was startled by the thunder, seemed disoriented in his sleeping bag. He quickly grabbed his axe to defend himself against this "stranger" coming out of the woods!

Thankfully Doug realized soon enough it was Jeff–not a Grizzly–coming toward him. He had just enough time to gather his stuff and move under the kitchen tarp before the rain started. He climbed back into his sleeping bag, only to notice the rain collecting in a sagging area of the tarp above him.

Secretly watching from the comfort of my tent, I saw Doug try to push the water up and out of the tarp. But the end of the tarp tucked in, and the water splashed right back on him instead! He began yelling, "I give up! I give up! Albert! Take me out of here! I don't want to be here anymore!"

I pretended to be asleep and didn't reply to Doug's pleading. Then I heard him ask Bill, "Do you think Albert knew it was going to rain, and he didn't tell us about it? After all, he's in the tent for the first time, and he's dry!"

The storm finally quieted. I had to admit at breakfast this morning that I had known about the upcoming storm. But I figured if they wanted to sleep outdoors, I'd let them have the experience! "Some friend you are," they muttered.

~ ~ ~

Even though Doug had said he was ready to give up after last night's experience, morning and daylight made things better as we all rode together. About noon, we came upon Danaher Creek where two Danaher brothers, I've read, had raised horses at the turn of the century. We could see vestiges of a cabin, bunkhouse, and barn. The brothers must have had to disassemble all their equipment and building materials and pack it on horses to get it up there.

The Danaher area is the most glorious site I've seen so far: a vast meadow, stately grove of trees, mountains on all sides–and when we rode alongside the creek, we could see the biggest trout ever in the crystal clear water. I look upon this area the same way a devout Christian would look at heaven–it is *that* beautiful. When we first came upon it, we all just stood still and drank it in.

I simply want to unpack and stay here forever. But, alas, I have to get to Mexico! (Guess I'll just have to use this spot for a layover day!)

Sunday, July 10, 1983

It rained again last night and all morning today. Miserable. We played cards, talked, ate, froze, and changed clothes to stay dry 'til we'd worn everything we had. The weather got better this afternoon, but it was cold, and it still is. So much for enjoying the Danaher on a layover day.

Monday, July 11, 1983

We left camp to go over the Dry Fork Flathead Pass. We took a wrong turn, but it wasn't our fault. We simply followed a sign pointed in the wrong direction. My senses told me the sign was pointing the wrong way, but without confidence in my intuition, we followed the sign anyway. Gradually, the trail got thinner and thinner as it headed up toward Flint Mountain. We went the entire length of the trail–2-1/2 miles–before it ran out and we were forced to turn back and get on the right trail. We contemplated turning the sign 90 degrees to point the right direction, but decided against it. It apparently had been this way for years, and we figured it must be part of the lore of finding one's way down this trail.

That wrong turn set us back quite a bit; we didn't get into camp at Canyon Creek until about 6:25 tonight. Very late.

I now regret that my desire to push forward today was so strong that I did not allow the men to stay an extra day and really experience the Danaher.

Tuesday, July 12, 1983

We rode out of camp this morning, following the Dry Fork to the North Fork Cabin where an elderly man with a magnificent white beard was living. We talked with him a little and learned he'd gotten permission from the Forest Service to reside there. He wasn't doing anything special, just living and enjoying life. I wish I could have talked to that old salt longer. A pang of jealousy hit–to be able to live alone there in the mountains, to absorb it 'til you got full.

We stopped for lunch at the North Fork Falls. I had been here in 1970 when my oldest son, Fred, and I rode with Cecil Garland up on

Scapegoat Mountain. Coming out, we stopped here at the Falls, and I climbed to the bottom. It was a tough descent for a then-47-year-old.

After hearing about that experience, Doug decided he wanted to make the climb down today. Even though I'm 59 now, I figured I could do it again. Doug will do anything I will; he likes the challenge. I went down with him, because I didn't want him to do something dangerous. The others stayed on top and rested.

We took fishing rods with us. The fishing down there was great, but we threw back all we caught. When I said it was time to go, Doug objected because he wanted to catch more fish. He wanted to stay longer, but we needed to get on; besides, having fish would just mean more to carry on the tough climb out.

Back at the top, I listened again to the roar of the water, which was almost overpowering. I looked down the gorge as the water splashed against rock precipices on its descent–it had to have been at least a 500-foot drop. There was rubble in one part as though dump trucks had backed up and unceremoniously tossed fragmented rock over the edge. With sheer rock cascading down all sides of the gorge, I wondered what in the world that rubble–tons and tons and tons of it–was doing there.

It is amazing how God has developed this landmark over time: through eons, the earth's plates have moved together to push the mountains up and create the tilt of the rocks–in seemingly unexplainable formations. Some would say it's because of "chance," but I see the hand of God in it all. There is a spiritual sense about it.

People who come here and see nothing more than the "beauty of nature," or the excitement of danger if they stand too near the edge, miss the worshipful, spiritual significance of this landmark. I guess they really don't know what they are missing.

~ ~ ~

We made it into the Hoeffner's mountain camp, a day's ride from the trailhead, this afternoon–Meadow Creek–where we'll have a lay-over day tomorrow. There were deer in camp–one white tail with a tag in the ear.

I split wood after supper tonight using the hatchet I found in the Bob Marshall Wilderness a couple of weeks ago.

Wednesday, July 13, 1983

During the night I was awakened by a blubbering, chomping sound. I wondered if the horses were outside our tents, so I got up to check it out. I found nothing, but the stars sure were enormously bright. It's amazing how clear and brilliant they are in the mountains where there is no smog or other pollution. I wonder if all stars were brighter 2,000 years ago when the wise men followed the star to find the Christ Child.

This morning I discovered the answer to last night's slobbery sounds: when I finished splitting wood last evening, I slammed the ax into the chopping block and laid my gloves over the ax handle. The gloves apparently had salt in them from my perspiration, which attracted deer–one or more of them had come into camp and gummed them to within an inch of their lives! They didn't chew them...just sucked on them. My gloves were a soggy mass.

Doug, Bill, Ben, and I went up to Meadow Lake to go fishing today. Doug caught a big fish, but–ha–mine was bigger–the biggest fish of the entire trip so far. It was fun beating Doug in this little "competition."

Bill, Doug, and I agreed to form a small Bible Study group when we get back to civilization. Bill and I will check with Bob Dunbar and Judge Paul Magnuson, and Doug will check with Sen. Bill Armstrong of Colorado for ideas about others to involve in the group. We decided we'd meet once a month, alternating between Minneapolis and Washington beginning in September. I'll ask Gretchen to have the group at our place at Marshhills, our home in Rice County, when the study group meets in Minnesota.

Thursday, July 14, 1983

We got out of camp a little after noon today and made it the rest of the way to the Hoeffner's ranch in Lincoln. It got colder as we traveled, and it began to rain. When we got to the Hoeffner's, we found out it had snowed a lot above 6,000 feet. Glad we weren't up there.

I took everyone to the 7-Up Ranch for steaks for supper tonight–Kenny, Mary Faith, Jeff, PennyJo, Dan, their little daughter Brooke, Ben, Doug, Jon, Bill, and Mike. It tasted great. I ate a 32-ounce steak. Not to be outdone, so did Doug!

Doug, Jon, Bill, and Mike are all staying at the Leepers Motel tonight. Ben and I showered at Dan's home. I've never washed off so much dirt.

~ ~ ~

It took us two weeks to go from Glacier Park to Lincoln. We all had toughened up. We learned so much about horses, packing, camping, self reliance, trails, and mountain weather.

Better yet were the relationships we developed with each other. I had wondered, going into the mountains, if there would be some special experiences with God our Creator, since I'd be in the wild–so close to His creation, where one sees little or no sign of man's impact on this earth. I can't say that this two weeks had any life-changing experience for me, but this was a significant trip because we all were thrown into close relationships with others. I believe that, unbeknownst to us, through the Holy Spirit, Christ is working through others on us. Any time we do an act of kindness to another, it is as though we are doing it unto Christ. The men on this trip were a marvelous example in their kindness to and respect for one another.

Friday, July 15, 1983

Got up at 4:30 this morning so we could get Doug, Jon, and Bill to the airport in Great Falls by 6:15. Jeff and I gave Doug our hats for souvenirs. This is the end of the trail for Jeff. Since my Washington friends will no longer be on the trip, I will no longer be using the Hoeffners' horses, and I won't need a wrangler.

In Great Falls, I finally had a chance to call Gretchen. And I remembered to do it!

If she was angry because I hadn't called her as previously promised, she didn't show it. She is such a loving person; she seldom gets upset with me. She also knows how single-minded I can be. There are times at home when I'll be reading and she'll say, "I can't stand that music. Can I turn off the radio?" I didn't even know the radio was on.

Some people have the ability to be aware of all the people and activity around them. I seem to notice this trait more in women. My brother's mother-in-law is one who had this skill in spades. I remember one Thanksgiving dinner when there was a discussion at her end of the table, one at the opposite end, and a conversation in the kitchen. She participated in all three! That takes enormous skill.

Gretchen is this way, too. And, she also recognizes I am not this way. So the fact that I didn't call her a couple of weeks ago didn't bother her. She knew I was focused on the impending ride.

After dropping my friends at the airport and talking to Gretchen, Ben and I visited the Charlie Russell Museum. I looked forward to learning more about Russell, since I always felt a closeness to him. He had such a great love for the range and for horses, and he had what seemed to be an authentic connection with American Indians in his paintings.

Because of my artist-wife Gretchen, I've learned to have a sense for feeling and color in art. She, however, does not appreciate western art–it's too macho for her!

I was disappointed in the museum, though. I thought the Cowboy Hall of Fame in Oklahoma had a better collection of Russell's paintings, as did the museum in Helena.

Of course this is all art imitating God's nature. And we have the real thing.

Ben and I got a tarp and a few other things before returning to the Hoeffners. We put pigtails[7] in my pack saddles, since I will be leading two horses at a time in the next leg of our trip.

Then we took a walk to the Blackfoot River.

CHAPTER FOUR

'Sure. And I used to be Lady Diana!'

Sunday, July 17, 1983

I have gotten some rest and had some tremendous religious and political discussions the last couple of days, as I spent this time in Butte with son Fred and his wife Mindy.

Fred had become part of the student unrest at St. Olaf College during the Vietnam War and grew politically and religiously to the opposite of how his mother and I raised him. I would describe both him and Mindy as extreme environmentalists–off to the radical left–and they both have been involved in transcendental meditation. Mindy owns a bookstore in Butte's business district.

To gain a better understanding of them, I discuss, listen, and read. They introduced me to their radical friends, as well. I think their belief systems developed out of the student unrest in the '60s. I am thankful I have the experience of knowing people, whom I love, who have this left view. They give me an understanding of why people would come to this point of view–an understanding I would not otherwise have.

There have been times in the past when I exposed myself to the different elements of society, trying to get an understanding of their points of view. I once ran a few days with a street gang in New York City; I spent time with radicals in the Watts neighborhood in Los Angeles; and I befriended people in Resurrection City after Martin Luther King was assassinated. But there is a level of trust with one's own flesh and blood that makes it easier for me to get a good grasp of their way of thinking.

Anger and frustration do seem to be steaming up in Fred as he tries to sort out the conflict of my position in politics (which he dislikes) and who I am (the father he loves and respects). We do have great love and respect for each other.

Mindy's bookstore specializes in environmental and feminist books. Surprisingly, there is not what I would call harsh, extreme revolutionary stuff encouraging the overthrow of the government. Rather, she has a good choice of books. In fact, I could hardly leave the store; I just wanted to stay there and read. She has an art gallery, too. From my perspective, she has good artistic sense. I thank God for both Fred and Mindy.

~ ~ ~

Before driving back to Lincoln, I bought groceries for the next leg of our trip–from Lincoln to Butte. Also bought an enamel coffee pot (I want to start boiling our water in case infectious bugs show up in the water), and some more silverware, as I think ours got mixed in with the Hoeffners' equipment.

Monday, July 18, 1983

After breakfast with Dan and Penny Jo, Ben, Mike, and I went to the ranger station to consult about the best route from Lincoln to Butte. We decided to start the next leg of our ride from the 7-Up Ranch, so we put the horses and all our gear in my trailer and headed there.

Once we unloaded, Ben drove my pickup and trailer to Butte so they would be there when we arrived. Since we won't be needing Goldie, Ben took him, too, and is leaving him with a rancher outside of Butte. Then he's taking a bus back to Minnesota. He surely is lonesome for his girlfriend (and hopefully future wife!), Virginia Gladder.

Now it's just Mike and I. Our personalities do not complement one another. We are both strong-willed leaders, one expedition. He's Irish, I'm Norwegian. They say every Norwegian wants to be the king.

~ ~ ~

Mike's pack mule is carrying the groceries, the kitchen, and the stove. The stove weighs only about seven pounds. Every day we have to find a dead tree that is dry enough for us to chop up for firewood. I am using Clyde and Lace to pack the rest of our gear.

We went up 7-Up Pete Trail to the 7-Up Pete Mine where we explored for a while. We then rode to Stemple Pass past Granite Butte and the lookout tower on the beginning of Helmville Trail. Fred had told me about this tower after he worked there for a year when in the Forest Service, so it was interesting for me to see it and the area.

Late in the afternoon Mike and I headed toward Marsh Creek where we found water and a meadow. Cows were grazing, and a trough fed by a spring alongside the trail make this a good place to camp.

It started raining during supper tonight, which might make some people irritable, but not me. I ponder why I like the mountains so much, even in the rain. I guess I love the challenge of finding my way. And the scenery–especially from the top of the mountains–is so beautiful. Plus, it is ever-changing from elevation to elevation. The delicate flowers are heavenly.

I also like the continuous movement of getting ready for each day: cooking, helping the horses, packing up. Seeing wild animals. It simply feels good to be outside and in the rhythm of nature.

Ah, the solitude of horses grazing. After these 16 days in the mountains, I still haven't gotten over the feeling that, for years in politics, I was fed up with too much interaction with people. I do like relating to others; it invigorates me. But it must be taken in moderation. It's kind of like loving apple pie a la mode. If you have it all the time, and stay full of it, you never have the experience of emptiness–a necessity if you want to appreciate it when you have it.

And so, I savor these times, rain or shine.

Tuesday, July 19, 1983

What a day! We left camp about 10 a.m. after filling our canteens in the Marsh Creek spring. Heading south, the trail took us across and along Nevada Creek. We climbed and climbed, reaching heights over 8,000 feet. Looking back, we could clearly see Red Mountain and Scapegoat behind us and out to the Mission Mountains 40 miles ahead. What a spectacular sight!

It was a tough day for the horses, though. Part of the time we were on a faint trail that went alongside the mountain with loose shale under foot. One slip and we'd have fallen 2,000 feet.

Also, I feel badly since I left my new-found and unique hatchet in camp by the spring where we camped last night.

Wednesday, July 20, 1983

Went down Charity Gulch, heading for Hope Creek and Uncle Ben Gulch today, but we got confused with so many logging trails, and went too far west. We finally decided to follow a trail that was heading mostly south but a little west. We climbed for three hours. It was tiring for us and the horses, except for Bull who always seems to be on the alert.

He brought me back to the present once today when he was startled by something in the distance. I looked in the direction he was staring and thought I saw the faint image of a bear running. But in a split second, I realized it was a man running through the woods at a right angle to our travel. It was a very thick woods, but I could see he was carrying a small pack in his left hand with something tan attached to it. I was going to call out, but next I saw he was also carrying a rifle. Instead of shouting words of greeting, I kept my mouth shut.

He ducked down behind a clump of three trees. I could see the hump of his back as he hid in the trees. The man was probably a poacher. If he had aimed at us, I guess I'd have had to drop down on the far side of Bull. I kept an eye on the spot 'til we got out of sight.[8]

~ ~ ~

Right before we were to stop for lunch, Clyde apparently decided he'd had enough. He simply stopped and lay down on his side. Now I was really wishing I'd sold him back in Medora. Lace instinctively tried to pull him up. Nothing doing. I unhooked his lead rope from the other horses, gave him a "little encouragement," and he jumped to his feet. In his stubbornness, he tried to buck but for some reason couldn't. He ran into one of the other horses, backed away, lay down again, and tried rolling onto his back. The packs kept him from rolling any further.

I unpacked him, got him up, gave him a spanking, and re-loaded him. Then he went OK the rest of the way.

After lunch, we started down a steep switch back, finally arriving at Charles Canyon. We then stayed on roads as we traveled into Elliston, west of Montana's capital city, Helena. Here, I could make a couple of phone calls: to Gretchen and to my friend, Montana Governor Ted Schwinden.

As we rode into town, I soon saw there were only two buildings—a SALOON that was identified with large letters, and a small store that appeared to sell a few groceries and dry goods. Well, I'd sooner go into a small store like that than a saloon, so I looked for a place to tie up the horses there. I could find only a flat bed trailer parked next to the store. I don't like to tie up horses lower than their eye level; it goes against my grain to not follow the safest procedures. But in this case, I had no choice. Besides, I figured the horses were all tired enough that they would not jerk back and run off, all in the same direction, dragging the trailer with them!

Inside the store, I looked around for a public phone and saw none. I asked the lady (who was the only person there, and who was evidently the proprietress) where I could find a public phone.

"There ain't any in town," she said curtly as she looked me over. With several days' beard growth, dirty clothes, and no bath for a number of days, I probably looked like a not-to-be-trusted dude, not a mountain man.

"May I use *your* phone, then?" I asked politely.

"There is none in the store. There's only one in the kitchen."

The "kitchen" was apparently a part of the building she used as her home, and by the way she talked to me, I could tell she didn't plan to invite me into her kitchen any time soon.

Perhaps if I told her who I was and whom I wanted to call, she might soften.

"I just finished my term as governor of Minnesota," I explained. "I'd like to use your phone to call your governor. You see, when I was at a Regional Governors' Conference I met Governor Schwinden and told him about this trip I'm taking. He said I should give him a call when we reached the point where the Continental Divide crosses Highway 12, and he'd come out and meet me."

She looked at me in a most unbelieving way, as if to say, "Ya, and I used to be Queen Elizabeth!"

I wasn't about to give up, though. "If you will let me use your phone, you can listen and see that it is Governor Schwinden I am calling."

Continuing to look at me with a skeptical eye, she led me into her kitchen. Wouldn't you know–Schwinden was out of the office for the day.

I did get through to Gretchen, though. Was it ever good to talk to her.

When I finished the call, I figured I ought to buy something from the store in return for the woman letting me use her phone. I was thankful I had thought to take my billfold out of my pack this morning and put it in my pocket. As Mike and I looked around in the store, the woman disappeared into her kitchen.

Pretty soon, people started coming into the store. And before long, most everyone from this very small town must have been there. They were all polite, pretending to shop, snatching sidelong glances, and quietly conversing among themselves. I wish I was a more gregarious person; I would have gathered them together and shared my experiences.

I can imagine their conversations after we left. "Do you suppose he really was....?"

~ ~ ~

Leaving Elliston, we traveled about a mile and a half along a road and then along a jeep trail, trying to find a good way back to the main trail. Found a gate across one road locked. When you have to travel a road and you come to a fence with a cattle pass, there is usually a gate along one side through which people can lead horses. When the gate is locked, the only way to get across is to unwrap wires, or try to find a way around the fenced-in area, which we decided to do.

We got caught in an electrical storm between 1:00 and 2:30 p.m. In this range land, riders like us are good targets for lightning strikes. No flashes came close, though. I prayed that Mike and I not be hit. Four steel shoes on the ground are a good conductor of electricity. We finally stopped and made camp at 5 p.m.

For supper I made fried hamburger with sausage seasoning. I put in dried gravy mix and water, then a can of pork and beans. With mashed potatoes, it was good.

It's getting cold this evening. Tomorrow we'll try getting around this fenced-in area we're next to.

Thursday, July 21, 1983

I lost my glasses this morning. Rebelling against having a crupper under his tail, Bull started bucking–so hard that he fired my camera off the saddle and my glasses out of my chest pocket. His leather crupper strap–attached to the saddle to keep it from slipping forward–snapped. I got off to retrieve the camera, but could not find my glasses.

With Bull now happier without a crupper, we followed along the fence, and in about 1-1/4 miles we found a way around it. The trek was not easy. With steep hills to climb and two dead falls to cross over, it was rough going.

Clyde was in the lead, and at one point, as we were going up a steep incline, he lifted his front end to go over a log. Lace jerked back, pulling Clyde over backwards! He landed upside down near the log behind him. I have to believe the packs on his back are what cushioned his fall and saved him. He lay there, all four feet up in the air.

Quickly, Mike and I jumped off our horses, and while Mike held Clyde's head down, I uncoupled Lace from Clyde. Then we rolled him over, and after removing his pack (which was a struggle), we encouraged him to get up–which he did, none-the-worse for wear. I feel God is with us, protecting us. Clyde could have fallen on a rock or hit his head on the log behind him (which is what spooked Lace), or broken his neck. Some people call this luck or coincidence, but for some reason or other, I thank God often for the way things happen, and we survive.

We continued working south, still trying to find our way back to our trail. We tried different routes, but each petered out. I had noticed light filtering through in an area beyond dense woods, but for some reason kept ignoring it. I finally decided to check it out. I tied Clyde and Lace together, and asked Mike to watch and wait.

After riding a ways through the woods, I found, in the clearing, what turned out to be Slate Creek Trail. What a relief. That is what we had been looking for. I thanked the Lord because, when I go from hopeless to new insights and hope, God comes to mind and I am overjoyed.

GOVERNOR OF MINNESOTA? SURE, OLD TIMER, SURE.... AND I USED TO BE LADY DIANA, PRINCESS OF WALES!

(Reprinted with permission of the *Star Tribune*.)

And God showed me more than just the way to the trail–He taught me a lesson: how often do we travel along our own path, insistent we can find our way, resolved that we'll make it out of the darkness on our own. He seemed to be telling me, "Move into the Light and I'll show you the Way down from this mountain!"

I was overwhelmed. I wanted to just hang there and soak it in. I didn't want to go back through the woods–into the chaos of the dark. But I knew I needed to get back to the horses and Mike.

~ ~ ~

While I was gone, Lace had gotten her head caught by her lead rope. Mike got off his horse to help, and when he did, his horse ran off, dragging his mule along. Mike caught up to them down the trail a ways, but his stubborn horse turned rather than be caught, galloping back with the mule running behind–strewing his pack along the way. There definitely is chaos in the dark.

After packing up again, we moved through the woods to the light and followed Slate Creek Trail down off the mountain. We ended up at Kading Ranger Station and Campground. A perfect place: water out of a faucet, a corral with grass for Bull, and a fenced enclosure for the other animals. I made stew–with meat, carrots, and onions–and Mike made mashed potatoes. Unfortunately, black from the aluminum came off into the potatoes. We decided to put paper towels between the pans when we pack them in the future, so metal won't rub on metal.

It's dark and the moon is practically full.

Friday, July 22, 1983

In a chat with the ranger at the Kading Campground and Ranger Station this morning, I shared about the fellow we saw hiding in the woods a couple of days ago. "Poachers are real dangerous," he warned. "Catching one of them by surprise is like accidentally coming upon a still in Kentucky." He said elk antlers in the velvet are worth $1,500 a piece with the market in China.

We then left the campground and ranger station with its great facilities and headed south. It was a steady rise, but not difficult as we traveled up the Little Blackfoot River and made our way between Electric Mountain and Thunderbolt Mountain. The grade was terribly steep and extremely rocky. And the bugs were bad. The horses hurried us along, trying to get away from the bugs and their bites. That's one way to make better time without our urging the horses along.

We got down to the Whitehouse Campground a little after 4 o'clock and made camp about a mile east of there.

A family from Helena motored into our campground. Sure can tell we are close to civilization. The horses are an attraction for the children: four noisy girls. The parents use tough language with them. I helped them build a fire, and I pray the children will turn out well and get to know Christ.

Reflecting on the last three weeks of this trip, I realize that God has placed me right in the middle of His wonderful creation, and yet I really haven't taken the time to be with Him. I don't pray enough, I don't read the Bible enough. I expected when I was on this trip that I would have more time for this.

When I get up in the morning, my first concern is caring for the horses, cooking, making sure the packs are balanced, assessing the weather, reading maps, running through the to-do lists in my head. I do spend time on the trail in prayer. I have always been a praying man, but I have to admit I have never spent long hours in prayer. I do remember "praying without ceasing" when my dad lost his arm in a combine accident. Probably for fear of his death.

I wonder what happens when people pray. This has always been a troubling thing for me. I've asked many people this question, and I've never gotten a direct answer from anyone. It's upsetting.

Hopefully, we'll make Butte tomorrow. It looks to be about 18 miles, maybe 20.

CHAPTER FIVE

Crushed egos on the Razor Back

Saturday, July 23, 1983

As we left camp this morning, we headed east toward where the Thunderbolt creek enters the Boulder River. I could see by the map that the road ahead went quite a distance, crossed a bridge, went a couple miles or more and then looped back. I determined the loop could be eliminated if we took a shortcut down a steep stream bank. Mike and I had a little discussion about which way to go.

He decided to take the long way around. I decided on the short cut.

As Mike rode off, I brought Bull to the edge of the bank to survey the situation. It looked to be about five feet straight down, then there was a steep grade of eroded material to the stream bed. It truly was on the edge of being a dangerous jump. But the steep grade appeared to have enough sand and rubble for the horses to dig in when they landed, which would enable them to catch their footing.

Bull trusted me; I pressed him. He jumped, landing safely, with me still in the saddle. I had kept a hold on Lace's lead rope, and turned in time to see her peering over the edge, preparing to leap. Clyde (still connected to Lace) took a peak and began to run off to the side, just as Lace was ready to jump.

Anticipating a complete wreck with Lace jumping and Clyde running off, and I not being able to get back up the bank, I yelled at Lace–"Stop! Back!" Her front feet had already begun to rise for the jump, but her reaction was so fast, she was able to recoil, swing her body around, and come back down on the top of the bank–exactly what I wanted her to do. Still, I was amazed she was able to do it–especially since she'd already made the commitment to go over the edge. She knew what I was yelling, and she obeyed and stayed up on the bank.

Now I was faced with how to communicate with both Clyde and

Lace so Clyde would come behind Lace and both jump safely. I began to move along the bank as it got steeper. Clyde fell in behind Lace, apparently not knowing she was soon going to jump. I tugged her, gently calling her to go ahead and come on over. And she did. Clyde seemed surprised, but he had not braced himself, so all he could do was follow along. He jumped, too–and both were safe on the steep grade below the cliff.

This experience of relationship with my horses–being able to read them, their ability to read me, our understanding each other–gave me a strong sense of oneness with them.

I now had to wait for Mike. I wonder what possessed me to take this chance rather than follow Mike the long way around. My choice certainly saved me no time, since I'm now in "wait mode." It must have been the challenge.

~ ~ ~

As Mike and I turned south along Lowland Creek, we began to notice rubble along the banks of the stream, which seemed to get fresher and fresher as we moved along. Soon we met up with some gold miners. They were using heavy equipment to draw gold out of the stream, leaving piles of spoils in their wake. Sure ruined the beauty of the stream.

We traveled on gravel roads more than 20 miles today. Boring.

As we got closer to Butte, though, we went by a house close to the road. People out on their deck getting ready for a barbeque called to the two of us–Mike leading a pack mule and I leading two pack horses.

"How far have you ridden?" they called.

"Glacier," I responded.

They were astounded. "You've got to be kidding!"

"Nope."

"Where are you going?"

Without batting an eye, "Mexico."

They were speechless. I just smiled.

~ ~ ~

We arrived at Simon's Ranch about 5 o'clock, tired after six days of riding from Lincoln to Butte. We'll have a layover day tomorrow.

Sunday, July 24, 1983

Fred, Mindy, and I went to services at their church, Gold Hill Lutheran. I am thrilled that they have become such a part of this congregation. In the afternoon the three of us climbed to a lake on the edge of the Pintlar Wilderness. Mike got sick today. We may have to have more than one layover day.

Monday, July 25, 1983

Today was a day to do chores and run errands. Repaired the canvases which cover the packs (sharp branches and rocks had pierced them), did my laundry, and got medicine for Clyde's withers. I know now that sore withers–not stubbornness–is what caused his insurrection last week outside of Elliston.

Mike is still sick.

Tuesday, July 26, 1983

I drove to Whitehall and ordered pack saddle pads ($40 each) and to Twin Bridges to get a metal ring for repairing the crupper on my saddle. Got to watch some barrel racing while in town, then–back in Butte–I watched Fred's softball team get beat badly in the first game of a tournament. I also read a couple of novels, and after spending considerable time looking at maps in Mindy's bookstore, I decided it would be very difficult to ride from Butte to Yellowstone. I think it will be best to cover this section not following the Divide and going from Yellowstone to Butte, across the Gallatin Range. But I wonder how close I need to be to the actual Divide to feel fulfilled?

Clyde's withers are showing improvement. Mike is feeling better, too. We'll probably get out tomorrow.

Wednesday, July 27, 1983

Mike and I gassed up at the Husky station west of Butte on I-90 and drove to Squaw Creek Ranger Station on the Gallatin River where we left Mike's truck. We decided it would be easier to leave his rig on the west side of the Gallatin, and trailer the horses with my rig to Yellowstone. We drove to Big Creek to start this portion of our ride.

Before making camp, we went up to Gardiner to talk to the Yellowstone Park and Gallatin Forest officials who could help us check on the trail head location. Met a man in the Forest Service–Sonny Adkins-who worked with my son, Dan. Dan worked on trails for the Forest Service one summer in this area. Sonny told us we could stay at his place by the Rocky Mountain Campground and advised us to get a permit at Mammoth Hot Springs to ride in

Yellowstone Park later. He told us we'd also have to be going through some ranch land, and that I ought to get permission from the rancher beforehand. His name was John Ragsdale.

After getting directions, Mike and I drove to the Ragsdale Ranch. Mike waited in the pickup as I went up to the ranch house where a woman–probably in her 40s–came out on the porch. I introduced myself, told her I was looking for John Ragsdale, and asked permission for Mike and me to ride across their property. She said John was her husband, and that there would be no problem for us to ride on their property. She also told me where the trail head was. I thanked her and turned to leave.

Out of the blue, the name Guy (Pop) Karnes came to mind. I turned back and asked her if she recognized the name. "Pop" Karnes had been my high school chemistry teacher, track coach, Pony football coach and Hi-Y adviser. The last time I talked to him was at my 35th high school reunion about six years ago. When I was in high school, I heard him talk a lot about horses and ranching. I once remember his mentioning the name Ragsdale–a ranch where he'd been raised. For some reason, I had thought it was in Texas, but I soon found out it was right here in Montana!

The woman seemed puzzled at my question, but offered, "Guy was my husband's uncle. Why?"

I mosied back to the porch and told her that "Pop" had been one of my favorite teachers in high school. I told her about his reference to "Ragsdale," and then she turned, pointing in the distance to the "home place" on the ranch where Guy was born and said her husband's parents were still living there. I took advantage of this serendipitous occasion by going to the "home place" to visit her in-laws, Guy's sister and brother-in-law.

Guy's sister told me Guy had lived on the ranch until he was about 16, when their family moved to Illinois because of their mother's health. (I remember "Pop" having told me he went to college in Illinois.) As this woman continued talking, I learned that Guy's parents re-acquired the ranch when the person they'd previously sold it to couldn't make the payments. She said she had met a farm boy (by the name of Ragsdale) in college in Illinois, and after some time, they decided to move back to her parents' ranch–this "home place." They gave birth to a son, John, who was now running the ranch. She told me "Pop" died last year and that his ashes were spread on the mountain above us. "That was his request," she said, "to give some nourishment to the grass to feed the elk."

After admiring "Pop" so much, it was a thrill to hear these stories and be on the ranch where he was born. What a warm feeling it was to meet people who loved and were related to a person I loved, admired, and respected so much. Afterward, I went up to the hayfield and talked to John. I could tell he was an excellent, intelligent rancher.

Thursday, July 28, 1983

We stayed overnight in the ranger cabin at the Big Creek Ranger Station. I slept on the verandah, but would have chosen a different spot had I known I'd be sharing the space with several gutsy mice. They ran around me, over me, and even over my face. Shooing them away didn't seem to help. I didn't get much sleep last night.

Today we drove to the trail head to check it out. We met a young woman who worked for the former Ox Yoke Dude Ranch (now the Mountain Ranch). She was camping in a tent, and said she lived at the trail head so she wouldn't have to pay rent in town. I thought it was pretty brave of her to stay there all alone.

Friday, July 29, 1983

We headed out this morning. A sign about a mile along said, "Cooper Bench Trail," which, according to the map, was what we wanted to follow. But it took us onto a meadow–and then ran out. We thought it would show up again, so we continued on, and found, instead, what appeared to be an elk and hunters' trail. That led us higher up the mountain, but it, too, petered out. The terrain was nigh on to impossible to get through with all the dead fall. The trunks and arms of tree upon tree lay on one another as if in a tough wrestling match.

I told Mike to stay with the horses as I climbed on foot toward the top to see if I could get my direction and spot any trails. I went about a half mile. A gentle breeze moving from the top of the mountain cooled me as I trudged through the fallen timber. I finally reached a ridge that I followed around to the opposite side of the peak, and as I stepped to the other side, I found myself right in the middle of a herd of elk! I didn't know they were there, and they apparently hadn't known I was about to intrude on their solitude. I suppose the breeze coming down from the mountain carried my human smell away from them.

What a thrill to be among them. And what a horrendous noise as they almost immediately exploded in as many different directions as there were elk. Like animals that don't jump fences (they just force their way through), these elk rammed headlong through the jumble of the downed timber. What a racket! And then they were gone. It was totally quiet.

I stood looking down that side of the mountain–no trails for us here, either–only a steep drop into a basin.

I went back to where Mike was. With no identifiable trail to follow, we decided to retrace our steps. After being on the trail for six hours, we ended up about a mile from where we had camped last night. How discouraging.

But we kept on, following Cliff Creek. At 5:30, we rested a little. It was tempting to stay, considering the day we'd had. But the meadow was at an incline, so we decided to move on. I'm glad we did since we then came upon a flat meadow with several streams running from the snow in the basin. We made camp where someone else had previously been–they'd left a metal stove.

Before supper, I decided to go out and scout for trails. I stopped when I came upon a deer grazing; he stood still, just staring at me. I waited and watched. Then I noticed, through the trees, a pair of legs that seemed like those of a young horse. I knew it was an elk. I moved to get a better look, and at that moment, the deer bounded off through the elk herd.

That alerted the elk, but for some reason, they didn't move. From my vantage point, I could see an elk cow. And she saw me; I stood still; she watched; more elk came into view; I spied five of them. I knew others must be there, too, so I edged to the side for a better view. At my slightest move, one gave a big whistle and they vanished into the wilderness.

Saturday, July 30, 1983

My sleep last night was disturbed with the noise of rocks rolling into the basin. I reckon the elk were scampering to the top. We broke camp early and figured if the elk could climb their way out so could we. It was a tough climb without a trail to follow. But we made it to a ridge that we followed for about six miles.

Two of those six miles were quite exciting, though some people would probably describe this stretch on the Razor Back Trail as dangerous. The ridge was only about as wide as the horse tracks and dropped off 1,500 feet on one side and 2,000 feet on the other. One slip of the foot could have meant the end, so we got off and walked and led our horses. When I had talked to John Ragsdale back at his ranch, I had asked him if he had ever ridden the Razor Back. He said he hadn't, but that he would like to sometime. I'm not surprised. He seems to have the same sense of adventure as I.

We made it all the way to the top of Hylite Mountain–10,299 feet. We could see both the Yellowstone River on one side and the Gallatin on the west. We were elated that we made it all the way to the top. We were pretty proud of ourselves.

Our egos were soon crushed, however, when a smiling young woman came prancing along and full of joy that she'd hiked all the way to the top. She was wearing a t-shirt and shorts, and we were still cold with our jackets on. My macho self wants to explain that it is colder riding than it is when one hikes or walks.

The trail down the north side of the mountain was deep in snow, so we didn't follow it. Instead, we led our horses down about 1,000 feet to Hylite Lake on rocks and stones which had been swept clear of the snow and held back only by the angle of repose. It was so steep that when Mike's horse put his head down at a stream, the saddle slipped over his neck and front legs (the crupper had broken).

Then we climbed up to Hylite Bench where there was a sign that said 1.9 miles to Squaw Creek where Mike's rig was parked waiting for us. Or at least we thought the sign said 1.9 miles. Turns out we miss-read the sign and it was actually 19 miles.

I walked 10 of those miles to give my horse a break. It was getting late. Mike was pretty discouraged. I sensed his anger and anxiety as he wondered how something like this could have had happened. We are different that way. I, on the other hand, am stoic and just go plodding on, showing little emotion.

At about 8 p.m., when we were within five miles of our destination, a log truck came by. Mike decided to hitch a ride. I stayed on horseback.

Mike came back to get me with his pickup truck. We tied up the horses in a grove and drove all the way to Big Creek Ranger Station for my truck. Five miles of logging road, 22 miles to Bozeman, 25 miles to Livingston, 30 miles to Big Creek, and five rough miles to the ranger station. We got back to the horses at 2 a.m., fed them, and I'll now see what sleep I can get.

Tomorrow we'll drive to Butte. I get to see Gretchen and spend several days with her. I spend a lot of time thinking about Gretchen. I'm lonesome for her. I love the wild, the mountains, the trees, the flowers, the streams, the air, the nights, the weather (good and bad). But I love Gretchen even more.

Sunday, July 31, 1983

Anxious to see Gretchen, I arrived early at the airport in Butte this afternoon. When she and her mom, Ella Hansen, got off the plane, I started toward them, and Grandma Hansen walked right past me! I guess several weeks' beard growth and my dirty cowboy garb disguised the Al she knew.

We headed to Lincoln to visit Dan, Penny Jo, the children, and the Hoeffners. I took back roads so I could show Gretchen and her mom some of the places we'd been. Gretchen was a bit unhappy that I was taking gravel and then dirt mountain roads. At the top of one mountain, the road ended–this didn't bother me any–we just drove across a meadow where I found a descending trail on the other side!

Grandma was surely a good sport. She seemed to enjoy the experience, the danger, and my stories. I resonate with her.

We stopped south of Elliston and walked to the campsite where Mike and I stayed a couple of weeks ago. Would it be possible to find my glasses? I looked and looked to no avail. Then I figured I'd walk one more time over the area where they might be; on that last look, the sun glinted off one of the lenses, and there they were! What a wonder. I also found the crupper strap Bull had broken.

Finding these two things inspired me to stop at our first campsite out of Lincoln where I'd left my hatchet.

On the way, a big storm came on us. We raced ahead of it, out of the mountains and got onto Highway 279. We had to put all the luggage from the back of the pickup in front under Gretchen's and her mother's feet so it would not get wet in the rain storm. After the storm went by, I turned back into the mountains, and again drove over a mountain road–once again much to Gretchen's chagrin–to where I thought that first campsite was. I hiked to the spring where we had camped, and there was my hatchet just waiting for me!

Monday, August 1, 1983

We're having a great time visiting with our kids and grandkids.

Lincoln is remote–kind of wild and woolly, and very different from the big city.

Tuesday, August 2, 1983
We traveled to Butte today and are now with Fred and Mindy again. Fred and I tried our hand at panning for gold, and we were able to spend some time riding horseback in the country north of Butte.

Wednesday, August 3, 1983
Today I watched a sale at the stock yards; I bought a bay Quarter Horse, Dusty. Also saw a roping contest.

Thursday, August 4, 1983
We shared Gretchen's birthday today with Fred and Mindy.

Friday, August 5, 1983
Every time I am with Fred and Mindy, I learn more about them and have a new appreciation for who they are. Today, I learned that Fred is quite an historian. He gave us a tour of what he believed to be the "beautiful" part of Butte. To me, the area simply seemed run-down. But Fred, I discovered, can see beauty in parts of this broken down area of town that others will ignore simply because the neighborhood isn't new, bright, or in vogue.

Fred took us to a building that appeared quite dilapidated. Inside, however, he pointed out the lavish staircase and intricate leaded, stained glass windows. I could then see, as did Fred, that the builders had had an eye for beauty and must have wanted all who walked by to be moved by the results of their craftsmanship. Fred directed our attention to the banister, and I could see the rich wood beneath years of varnish and use. Some artist with a lathe and expert woodworking skills must have had great joy in seeing his finished product and great satisfaction each time he climbed that stair.

What stirrings have occurred in the souls of people because of seeing a window or climbing a stair in their mundane, day-to-day activity? Is anyone else affected by this beauty? Some, I'm sure. More, I'm quite certain, are too dead aesthetically to even be dented.

Surely, Fred's sensitivity enables his soul to be nourished. And those whom he leads to this beauty (like me) are affected more than if they blindly walk by.

But, just as the Holy Spirit keeps working on us without our awareness, perhaps even the dullest person may have something good happen to him as he might walk by...which wouldn't if the window was plain or the banister crude. Even an unbeliever must be unknowingly affected by God in a way that he would not be if there was no God or if God turned His back on him.

I also enjoyed the opportunity to browse through Mindy's bookstore again. "Butte Booksellers" is marvelous. Even though her store tends to have more books of an environmental nature and a feminist thrust, she has chosen excellent authors. I wish I could begin at one end and read right through the whole store beginning with Montana authors and poets. I'd be a better person-more aware of the world in a way I didn't know or notice before. Ivan Doig, a Montana author, is a fascinating writer; I read his novel, *English Creek.*

Another thing about Fred and Mindy is that I get introduced to ideas further to the left than I knew existed. But from visits to Watts and New York while in Congress, I knew there was something more to people who were part of the "underground" than what the regular press ever covered–something that isn't gross, mean, or violent.

During hearings in Watts–held when Congress established the Office of Economic Opportunity to fight poverty–a couple of "revolutionaries" came and talked to me.

"Why are you doing this?" one asked, knowing I was a Republican. "You know you are financing the revolution, don't you?"

They couldn't understand why "the establishment" would finance such revolutionary programming. And, indeed, I was interested in what lay behind their beliefs. Talking with these people, and with Fred and Mindy and their friends, I've learned you can engage in conversation with those who might be viewed as radical, and you can still hold to your principles; we can learn from one another.

~ ~ ~

It was good to take a break from riding this week–to rest and converse with my family. But I am ready to get back on the trail. I'm still undecided whether I'll do the big loop of the Continental Divide from Butte to the Idaho border, then south through the Bitterroot and finally east to Yellowstone. I will have to study maps and decide about going north to ride through Glacier before I make my decision about covering Wyoming south of Yellowstone Park.

After this far, though, I think I'll have a chance to make it to Mexico!

Chapter Six

Press coverage

Saturday, August 6, 1983

Dennis Cassano and Marlin Levison, a reporter and photographer from the Minneapolis *Star and Tribune*, will come today to spend a couple days with me. Al Severson, A.M. Lips, and Dean Cates—who, unlike the *Tribune* staffers, are experienced horsemen—are joining us as well. Dean owns and runs an Arabian horse farm near Faribault; Al grew up on a farm near Northfield like I did; A.M. is also from Faribault.

Gretchen got up at 5:30 this morning to see me off. I drove out to Simon Ranch north of Butte to meet Mike and get the horses. (Fred had arranged for us to leave them there while we had our layover.) On the way to Gardiner at the north entrance of Yellowstone Park (where were meeting the others), we stopped at Whitehall to pick up the saddle blankets Id ordered a week or so ago.

I drove into the Yellowstone Park Office to get a permit to ride through the Park. The process turned out to be a long hassle since they were not accustomed to setting up a horse trip through the Park. The biggest difficulty was finding a campsite for our second day out. Finally we agreed to do a longer second days ride that would land us at an acceptable campsite.

Sunday, August 7, 1983

Al and I headed for Lake Butte in Yellowstone at 7 a.m. to leave my truck and trailer so they'd be waiting for us after our ride in about a week and a half. Along the way, we saw buffalo swimming the Yellowstone River. The river where the buffalo crossed was not far from the road, and tourists were stopping their cars to watch. Some tourists got out of their cars to photograph the buffalo as the herd made its way out of the river and began crowding between the river and the road. I saw that a big bull was becoming uncomfortable with all these tourists preventing the herd from crossing the road; he began pawing the ground as bulls do when they are angry.

Just then a tourist, who apparently wanted a "good" picture, handed his camera to his wife and walked over to the bull so she could photograph her husband with the bull. Thankfully, a ranger came by at that moment, jumped out of his pickup truck and was so upset that he understandably chastised the man, using language unbecoming an officer.

The poor tourist (or should I say lucky tourist) learned a lesson without getting physically hurt. I bet he remembers his chewing out.

Later on our trip back, we had to stop for an elk calf running across the road; we saw antelope as well. Got back at noon. Long trip.

We finally got packed up at 2 p.m. and started on the trail. Arrived at first campsite a little after 6 p.m.

Monday, August 8, 1983

What a day! When horses get a mind of their own, they sure can cause problems.

We've rented horses for the *Tribune* reporter and photographer, Dennis and Marlin. All these horses are not accustomed to being with one another, and this morning we found the rented horses had wandered off. I caught and saddled Bull, and rode off to find them. I caught the rented horses just over a rise, and brought them back to camp. Then all the other loose horses ran off toward Gardiner, so then I went after them. About a mile and a half away, I stopped them and caught all but two. Deans horse, Jake, and Al's horse, Joe, kept going, so I sent Al, who had saddled Super, to go find them.

After eating breakfast, I worked around camp. By 9 o'clock Al still wasn't back. So Dean took one of my horses, Clyde, I took Bull, and off we went to see if we could help. After riding about five miles and seeing neither stray horses nor Al, I began to feel we were in a bit of trouble. I figured the horses had run back to Gardiner, and the process of retrieving them would slow us down so much we wouldn't be able to get to our next campsite on time.

I asked Dean to keep going to help Al, and I turned back, arriving back at camp a little before noon. I showed A.M. on the map how to get to the next camp–18 miles away–and left him there to wait for Dean and Al.

Marlin, Dennis, Mike, and I then headed out with our horses packed especially heavy since there were fewer horses to carry the load. We followed the Yellowstone River and crossed from the west side over a suspension bridge high above the water. Bull was a little spooked by the way it swayed up and down, but when he stumbled, the rhythm of the bridge stopped, and the horses settled down.

We got to the camp about 7 p.m., and another hour passed by the time we got everything set up. Water in camp is stagnant, so we strained it through my shirt and boiled it. I sent Mike to see if he could find a better water source.

Then, I saddled Bull, preparing to go see if I could find Al, A.M., and Dean. That's when Marlin and Dennis accused me of "testing the press" by leaving them alone in the wilderness.

"Sure, you send Mike off to find water, and now you're leaving us alone while you try to find the others!" they whined. It was all in fun, though.

I spotted our "lost people" about a mile from camp. They were tired and getting ready to set up their own camp. Al said he had ridden the entire 10 miles into Gardiner this morning looking for the stray horses. After searching all over town, someone told him he'd seen some horses following a girl into town and shed put them in her corral. Maybe they were the ones Al was looking for. Sure enough.

Since Al had only one lead rope, he used that to lead his Appaloosa, Joe (that had run away), and used a rein to tie Deans horse Jake to the Appaloosas tail. He'd gotten only a couple miles out of town when Jake jerked back, broke the rein, and headed back to town.

About that time, Dean was approaching, only to see Al taking off again to stop Jake! Together, they managed to catch him.

They then rode back with both horses in tow. That made it 36 miles for Dean, 38 miles for Al, and 32 for me–all in one day. We were bushed.

What a day. I apparently was over-confident after my experience with the horses we used from Glacier to Lincoln. And I realize, once again, the value in having Jeff Hoeffner as a wrangler. Also, I've learned I must be more careful with new horses that don't have experience in mountains or with strange horses.

Tuesday, August 9, 1983

Had to pack the horses differently today because Clyde's withers were puffed up on both sides from the extra heavy pack he carried yesterday. He looked terrible. I should not have piled so much on him. But I had no choice. The journalists carried stuff on their horses today, too.

Just as we started out, a big thunderstorm came on us, but the rain stopped as quickly as it began. We got drenched anyway. Quite an experience for Dennis and Marlin, but they didn't complain. Today was their last day with us. They will go back and write a story and print some pictures about our adventure. Having them along turned out not to be as much of a hassle as I thought it might. Even though they were inexperienced, they managed to do what they were told without much hand-holding.

~ ~ ~

Leading the pack, I struck out straight east to find the trail of Specimen Ridge. I found it a couple miles out. We traveled in spectacular scenery, climbing up to 8,700 feet on Amethyst Mountain and then down to the Lamar River, a steep decline for about two miles.

I gave Al the lead rope to my two pack horses and sent him, A.M., and Dean on their way to our next scheduled camp–about 13 more miles. Riding Bull and leading Clyde, I led Marlin and Dennis to Soda Butte where the Mileys (owners of the rented horses) were supposed to be waiting with a truck and trailer to transport them and the horses. I planned to leave Clyde, too, so he could have his withers doctored. We got there about 3:30 p.m. No truck.

We waited over an hour, and at about 5 o'clock we stopped an Interior Department truck and asked the employees to radio the tower so that someone there could call the Mileys. Turns out they had been there between 12 and 2 (when I had said we'd be arriving). They came again after work, but they hadn't gotten the message to bring a four-horse trailer, so they took the journalists horses and came back again for Clyde.

Marlin stayed with Clyde "so the coyotes wouldn't get him." I left a note asking the Mileys to give Clyde a shot of penicillin (if they had any), to take him to Tom Adkins pasture about 10 miles from Gardiner, and to call a vet to treat Clyde. I said I'd pay when I got back.

I took off, heading to camp and found the others trail where they hit the main trail at Chase Creek. On the way, I rode close by a cow moose standing in a swampy area.

I made it back to camp before 7 p.m. Horses were pooped. Its a nice evening. Tomorrow will be a much-needed day of rest.

Wednesday, August 10, 1983

Horses grazed at intervals today. Dean and I had good luck fishing on the Lamar. Nice sunshiny day. Saw big elk tracks (for a while I thought they might be buffalo).

A mounted trail crew camped at a ranger station just below us a mile or so. A woman was part of it. You seldom see women assigned to do manual labor, pick and shovel work. And it appears they were all living in one tent. About a year ago, I talked to a fellow who quit such a crew because he didn't want to be sleeping in a tent with a woman.

They had three good big horses and a mule. Looked like government stock–well-cared for and at ease in the wilderness.

I tried to take a nap this afternoon, but couldn't sleep. I don't seem to sleep much anymore.

Thursday, August 11, 1983

Broke camp and got out just after 9 a.m. I like to get started earlier than that, so we hit a good pace to make up the time.

Found a nice campsite to stop at for lunch. When we were packing up, I strained my back. The kink is bad and I'm in great pain.

We got to our camp for tonight–at Misty Creek Pass–about 3:30 this afternoon. Fishing is great here. Fish are small, but they hit hard and fast. We caught our limit for supper and breakfast and released many others. The grass was tall and bent toward the narrow stream; there was no more space to drop the fly than three feet between grass and the stream. We were all surprised with the abundance of fish.

Friday, August 12, 1983

I'm in so much pain that Dean had to put my socks and boots on me this morning.

Laces withers are sore now, so today was her last pack.

Mike skipped lunch today and rode right into Lake Butte so he could hitchhike to make a telephone call.

The rest of us went over Misty Creek Pass, along Pelican Creek, and out to the Pelican Valley Trailhead where we met a ranger sitting in his car. The others waited as he drove me into Lake Butte to get my truck and trailer. When I returned Mike was back from his trek to a telephone. He said it turned out that he had nine miles to go before finding a phone.

We all drove to Gardiner to pick up Goldie and Clyde and the other trucks and trailers from the Adkins–an hour and a half ride–with Dean and Mike sitting in back of the pickup on all the gear. We went to the Blue Haven Motel where we fond the Mileys, and I and paid them for hauling Clyde to Tom Adkins place earlier this week. Had chicken dinner at Cecil's Restaurant.

Gretchen was not home when I called.

No one was home at the Adkins when I went to pick up Goldie and Clyde after dinner, so I left a note and got in the truck to head back to camp. Nothing doing. I had a clogged gas line in my truck. Luckily, A.M. was able to fix it, and about 9:30 p.m., we started our 1.5 hour trip back to Lake Butte. When we arrived, I asked a ranger there if we could sleep in our trailer at the corral. She said no, since a bear was around and had just broken into someone's camper. So we loaded up all our horses, and just as we were going to leave, another ranger came by, wondering why we were preparing to leave. He said we could stay, and that he had planned to come down and visit us at our camp and bring us oats. Since we were all packed up, we drove to Eagle Trailhead anyway. Its now about 2 a.m.

Saturday, August 13, 1983

I did sleep in the trailer last night. Dean, Al, and A.M. slept in the suburban–Dean in the front seat and the other two in the back. Mike slept in his truck.

A young mountain man is at a camp nearby. We walked over to chat with him. Small world. His name is Keith and he worked for a Montana rancher both Dean and I knew–Jim Wempner.

We drove into Lake Butte for breakfast at the Shoshone Lodge, and then Mike left for home. He's been on the trail with me for seven weeks. He is ready to go home.

We took Clyde and Goldie to the Rimrock Ranch–a dude ranch owned by Gene and Alice Fales–where we could get some penicillin shots for the horses. We also rented a big packhorse from Gene for the rest of this trip.

In conversation with Gene, I asked if bears like horse feed. He said they like it better than human food. I will not sleep near horse feed anymore.

We ate lunch there, and when we got back to Eagle Trailhead, we had an afternoon of getting ready for tomorrow's ride while listening to the b.s. of Lewis, the farrier, and Keith, the mountain man. We ate at the Lodge again tonight. Lewis has a way with birds like sparrows. By twitching his fingers, he can get them to come to him and touch his hand.

Sunday, August 14, 1983

Just as it started to get light this morning, a grizzly came into the mountain mans camp and dragged off his horse pellets. Keith climbed about 30 feet up a tree, taking his rifle with him. He let off a couple shots, to scare the bear, which ran through the next camp dragging the sack of pellets and scaring the horses in that camp. They broke loose as the bear ran off. Keith was able to retrieve only some of his pellets, so we gave him some of ours. I realized Gene Fales was right.

We left camp on horseback at 9:30 this morning, and got to Eagle Meadows by 2 p.m. A.M. made homemade bread this afternoon. We had beef stroganoff and noodles, green beans, and raspberry cobbler for supper. Sometimes food on the trail can be pretty good.

I'm still in a lot of pain with my back. Doesn't seem to improve.

Monday, August 15, 1983

We went over Eagle Pass today at 9,600 feet. It was a spectacular view. From here we could see Eagle Mountain at 11,350 feet, Table Mountain off to our right at just over 11,000 feet, and Turret Mountain. I have seen so many sensational views now, that I may be a bit jaundiced. They are still impressive, and I appreciate their beauty; they just are not new anymore. Its a little like a second and subsequent dates being less exciting than the first.

The mountain man, Keith, caught up to us at Eagle Pass; someone had left two back packs on the trail, and he was wondering if they were ours. They weren't.

We went 10 miles from Eagle Corrals to the meadows, and 18 more miles to camp. Put up camp mostly in the rain. Mountain Man Keith is camping near us again.

Tuesday, August 16, 1983

It rained on and off all last night and most of today. Dean slept in the tent with Al and A.M., and I slept under my old orange tarp which leaked. Its hard to sleep when water keeps dripping on your face; I was really tired and hurting this morning. Ill have to spray this tarp with silicone when I get home.

But my sleeping bag has been great. Its warm whether wet, damp or dry.

We rode to the Yellowstone River and tried to fish, but the water was too muddy. We met Keith on the trail again today, and rode toward the south end of Yellowstone Park where the Thorofare River comes into Yellowstone Park, about a mile and a half from Bridger Lake.

Wednesday, August 17, 1983

I'm feeling somewhat better today. My back is improved, although I'm still in some pain.

As I sit here writing, the horses are grazing, and Al and A.M. are fixing breakfast. I'm ready to go home, even though this life certainly does appeal to me.

I love the majesty of the mountains, the stately trees, the streams roaring in the distance.

It is the life for a king. But my queen is not here, and I am anxious to get back to her.

~ ~ ~

We climbed up Eagle Pass and stopped for lunch just before we reached the top. I led Bull going down on the east side so I could save his shoulders. He is doing all right, but I feel he is getting pretty tired. Maybe its just my imagination, though, since I'm getting tired and my back hurts.

Coming back into Eagle Meadows, we could see there were no campers, but instead a big cow and bull moose. We decided to go on to the Corrals, which made it a 28-mile day–too long.

Three miles from the corrals, we came upon the place where the Crossed Sabres dude ranch group was camping. Each week, this group takes guests out for an overnight. There are 63 horses and 58 riders in this group–mostly pup tents and young people. Horses are tied to trees, and there is no feed. The horses eat before they leave and again when they get back. I cant imagine saddling 63 horses to get ready for a ride.

The last three miles today seemed long. Dusty was a little col-icky, so Al led him for the last couple miles. Bull finished strong.

The Corrals were full so we tied to the trailer. Al's wife, Doris, and A.M.'s wife, Lorraine, had been there and left a note saying they were staying eight miles east. Anxious to see their wives, Al and A.M. headed that way on horseback.

Dean and I ate at the Shoshone Lodge. We'll be heading home tomorrow. It's a good thing because my back continues to ache. The only place I am comfortable is sitting on a horse. The guys kidded me saying they would cut a hole in the roof of the horse trailer so I could sit on one of the horses on the way home. Like Chevy Chases aunt in the movie, *Vacation*.

Thursday, August 18, 1983

Drove to Cody, Wyoming, today and on to Buffalo. Spent about two hours at the Buffalo Bill Museum. Were staying at a lodge where the owners let us keep our horses in a little pasture nearby.

Friday, August 19, 1983

Got to Mitchell, S.D., at 10 o'clock tonight. The time change set us back an hour.

Saturday, August 20, 1983

Home again.

Monday, August 23, 1983

I have had difficulty sleeping indoors.

It's interesting that I got so lonesome for Gretchen while on the trail, but when people ask me why I quit the ride for the summer, I don't tell them the reason was because I wanted to get back to my wife. Instead, I say, "My pack horses' withers got sore." My inabili-ty to talk about my love for Gretchen must have something to do with my Norwegian-ness. That must change.

I learned so much this summer about horses, mountains, weath-er, nature, and people. Too bad Gretchen doesn't like this life and want to go along. It would be so wonderful if we could share the experience. I am thankful, however, that she has ridden with me a lot in the past. Before we were married, she rode with me, and when we were in Silver Spring, Maryland, she also rode. I must remind myself that she was along on three previous trips into Scapegoat, plus she went on a 38-mile ride from Dennison to Red Wing, Minnesota. So she certainly *has* allowed me to share this love with her.

I now know for sure that I like trekking through forests and wilderness areas more than going through parks. In state and national parks, one needs to pick campsites for the whole trip at the outset. And as we found out, there are so many unforeseen events that one may not make it to a specific camp. I also like the adventure of finding a campsite in unknown places where no one has camped before. But I always make sure there is no sign that we'd been there when we leave.

Next year, I think I'll follow the Continental Divide west of Butte, rather than be satisfied to cut across the big bend in the Divide. It will take longer, but it'll be more adventurous.

Here are the big questions I struggle with: Is it God's will that I make this trek from Canada to Mexico, or is it just my selfish desire? Did God give me this love of the mountains in order for me to stay away from them (because they are a temptation), or is it OK for me to go on these rides? Should I instead be spending the time helping people more directly? Are horses and mountains my temptation or gift?

1984

Montana/Idaho Border

Pintlar Wilderness
Bitterroot Range
Chief Joseph Pass
Sacagawea Campground
Lemhi Pass
Bannock Pass
Monida

CHAPTER SEVEN

'The horses will be back' -- and they were

Friday, July 20, 1984

We're staying at the fairgrounds in Buffalo, Wyo., tonight and have met several Minnesotans here for a National Saddle Club contest, plus Bill Johnson of Iowa. They were very helpful, letting us use one of their trucks so we didn't have to unhook ours to go have supper.

Saturday, July 21, 1984

Pulled out at 4:30 this morning after having gotten up at 3:30. We ate breakfast in Sheridan, then drove to Bozeman where we bought some fishing licenses, and on to Butte, arriving at about 3 p.m. After buying some horse feed and groceries, we drove to Sundance Lodge near Wisdom, arriving about 8 o'clock tonight. This will be our starting point for riding the Divide along the Idaho-Montana border this year.

With me are Lynn Street and Bill Manee. Tomorrow I will pick up Malcolm Marsh and Rick McIlhenny, and Doug Coe will join us on Monday.

I don't know Bill at all, other than he is from Boise, Idaho, and is a friend of Lynn. I know Lynn only a little from contact made while I was governor. I do know that Lynn–the principal of Scenic Heights Elementary School in Minnetonka, Minn.–is an experienced outdoorsman. He approached me a few months ago about going along on the ride this year. He'd read the *Star Tribune* article Dennis Cassano wrote last summer. Then he asked if his friend, Bill, who is good with horses, could come along. Lynn and Bill brought their wives; the four of them will go on a day ride tomorrow while I get supplies. Then just Lynn and Bill will be with us for about a week on the Divide.

I also do not know Malcolm other than the fact he is from Oregon. Doug wants him on the ride so he (Doug) could encourage him to give leadership to a prayer and fellowship group in Oregon. Some people call it the "fellowship." Doug worked with various youth organizations in Oregon before he came out to Washington, D.C., where he encouraged another group of lay people who believe in Jesus to meet, share, care for one another, and pray together. The "fellowship" has grown to have an international reach, but instead of an organization, it is simply a fellowship of people.

And then there is Rick, also coming along at Doug's request. I don't know him well, either. He was a strong Goldwater supporter in '76 when there was a battle in the Minnesota Republican Party. I do remember he has a great personality and tended to bridge the political lines. I liked his candor and integrity.

When Reagan was elected, he moved to Washington to work in the Department of Commerce. That's when he got to know Doug and became a follower of Christ. Doug wanted him along to give him a chance to be with a couple of guys who had known each other in Christ for a long time.

I'll get to know Malcolm and Rick a little more when I pick them up in Butte tomorrow.

Sunday, July 22, 1984

Rick's plane came into Butte around noon, and I picked up Malcolm around 7:30 p.m. tonight. In between, Rick and I went to Mindy's bookstore and got the frozen meat she was storing for us. We also took a look at the Berkeley Pit, the giant open-pit copper mine in Butte that is filling with water; we visited a local museum, and we watched some jackpot roping.

During the trip back to Sundance Lodge, I learned that Malcolm had gone on rides like this before. He apparently is an excellent fisherman and, from what I can tell, is a wonderful person who loves his fellow man.

Rick is totally inexperienced about horses and camping in the mountains. He will be no hand with the horses but seems eager to pitch in and help where he can. He is a joy in his new close relationship to Christ. When he shared his story with me, I was reminded of the joy in the hearts of Jesus' disciples after Pentecost.

When we got back to camp, the Streets and Manees hadn't returned from their day-long ride. I was worried. It was close to 9 p.m. I felt responsible. What if they had gotten lost?

Les Davis, owner of Sundance Lodge, calmed my anxiety, reminding me, "There is no way they could get lost or in trouble, even if they stayed out all night. When the weather is nice, the horses can find their way back." He was right.

Soon, the four rode into camp, absolutely bushed from a 26-mile ride that had taken them on a climb that was better than 2,000 feet.

Monday, July 23, 1984

I wanted to get an early start this morning, so I got up at 5, fed the horses in the dark and started packing things. A misty rain started and continued for the next few hours; I was sweaty and wet when we finally moved out.

Bull was shivering. I don't like that. When a horse's muscles are shivering, you can be sure he is going to be feisty as can be. When we started out, I asked him to side-pass to keep his mind off bucking.

The trip up the mountain was uneventful. The views do not seem to be as spectacular as last year. Of course, it rained most of the day, so we couldn't see much scenery. The last two miles were a steep, steep climb, and the grass was poor. At 8,200 feet, I guess spring is just arriving–even though it is mid-July.

After camp was set up, I left (about 5:30) and rode back to meet Doug. I'd arranged for someone to pick him up at the airport around noon and drive him to Sundance Lodge where people there would help him get saddled and on his way–probably by 3:30. Doug knew little about horses before riding with me last year, and I knew he'd need help.

I had given clear instructions to him regarding the trail to take to meet us, and I calculated he and I would meet around 6:30. Spotting movement ahead, I turned into the woods to watch. Sure enough, it was Doug on the trail.

Like a child wondering where his mother is, he had a forlorn look in his eyes. When out in the mountains, I sometimes wonder about the anxiety in a person's countenance. I figured I should let him know I was there, so I moved back out onto the trail. When he saw me, his face lit up like the sun coming out from behind a cloud.

He looked great on Dusty (the Quarter Horse I'd bought for Gretchen last year and for Doug to use on these rides). He was mounted on his brand new, hand-tooled Fallis saddle that he'd ordered and had shipped to me; I'd left it at Sundance Lodge so it would be there waiting for him. This saddle has a forward-riding seat that makes it easy to balance. With his new bridle and this beautiful saddle with matching saddle bags, he sits the saddle well.

Doug and I had a good talk on the way back to camp, and we had a good laugh about some comments that Bob Flaten had made to me recently. Bob (formerly of Northfield), was a State Department employee who owned a home by the Cedars (a place where people meet around the person of Jesus Christ) in Alexandria, Va.

"Al," Bob had said, "I think there are some people involved in a cult down the street from my house." Interested, I asked for more information. "There are always people coming and going, and sometimes people seem to live there for short periods."

On further questioning, I discovered the "cult house" Bob was concerned about was none other than the home where Doug and his sons lived, and the "cult" was the "fellowship"–people learning to live as Christ taught.

I told Bob the home was no different than those Paul wrote about spending time at in New Testament times. Some people did live at Doug's home for a while, as kind of a live-in period of growth for their walk with Christ. Others would come and go for prayer and Bible study.

~ ~ ~

We are all finally together. The camp was quiet before Doug got here. None of the rest of us are big talkers. The place really comes alive with Doug around. He is interested in everyone and has a way of drawing people out. Everything about him exudes acceptance–especially his body language. Doug has a way that attracts more people to Jesus–just by his behavior–than anyone I know.

Tuesday, July 24, 1984

We traveled only 12 miles today. I'm realizing we won't be able to make 15 sections on the map each day. The switch backs are adding too much effort and distance.

From Warren Lake we went down 2,000 feet, and then took a sharp right, climbing back up about five miles to Rainbow Lake.

Crossed the Continental Divide, making this the first time this summer I've seen the Pacific side. It is a most magnificent view looking down on Martin Lake and Johnson Lake where we made camp.

We turned the horses loose[9], but later saw a sign that horses were not to graze here–they were to be taken to a nearby meadow.

We'll take them there tomorrow on our layover day.

Wednesday, July 25, 1984

More camaraderie developed today. Bill, Lynn, and I share a common love for horses, the mountains, and the outdoors. Malcolm is a pretty good hand for a non-horse owner; Rick surely does help out, bringing in great quantities of wood, washing dishes, and assisting however we ask.

We all went fishing. I caught the most–10 keepers.

For breakfast each day, we've been having two eggs a piece with canned bacon (which keeps really well) and pancakes. Each evening we're having steak, mashed potatoes and a vegetable. I fried onions and cooked carrots last night. Peaches for dessert were great.

I wonder if our food will hold out since I forgot the emergency freeze-dried meat at home. I also worry that our syrup won't hold out–nor our margarine.

Thursday, July 26, 1984

Traveled along the Continental Divide today to Mystic Lake.

As we were climbing a steep grade today, Lynn's pack horse (Chub) bolted–she panicked when her pack started slipping to the side, and then she went down, landing in a clump of brush with the pack partially split open.

Normally in a situation like this, I'll tie Bull up to one tree and my lead pack horse to another, leaving the other two pack horses tied to the lead horse. But for some reason, all my horses were pawing and acting nervous. I couldn't imagine what the problem was. Maybe they were upset because this other strange horse was down. So I tied each one of them to their own tree while I helped Lynn.

We unloaded Chub's pack and noticed that she also had some sores. So Lynn decided to ride Chub and pack his other horse, Roudy. I had to re-pack the stove and all the utensils.

When we started out again a Grizzly bear caught our attention. He'd been off to our right just sitting, watching us. That's when I realized it was the Grizzly that'd had my horses upset. They knew all along he was there.

I wonder if the bear could sense an animal in distress (Chub) and was waiting for a meal. He ran off as we approached.

We're at Mystic Lake Ranger Cabin tonight; we couldn't camp close to where our horses graze. They are a half mile away. Not a big deal, but it does slow down the breaking of camp.

Friday, July 27, 1984

We followed the mainline trail today, but it is so faint at times–especially across the meadows–that it was hard to stay on it. We stopped at Surprise Lake, but it was a cramped camp spot–no fish seemed to be in the lake anyway. So we went over to Violet Lake. This is a larger camp and there is good grazing.

Lynn tied his saddle horse to an old dead tree. Lynn! The experienced one! I tell all the greenhorns, "Don't ever tie to anything dead." But Lynn is an old horseman. I figured he'd know better. No sooner had he tied up, than his packhorse tried to go between the tree and his saddle horse, breaking the tree and dragging a log between them. They looked like they might run into my pack string, so I had to dash over to head them off.

After supper, Lynn and Bill went to a meadow to look for elk, and Malcolm, Rich, Doug, and I climbed a mountain and looked at all the other peaks level with us for 360 degrees. I took out my pocket Bible and read from Psalm 66.

"Shout with joy to God, all the earth! Sing the glory of His name; make His praise glorious. All the earth bows down to You; they sing praise to You. They sing praise to Your name. Come and see what God has done, how awesome His works in man's behalf!"

Then I shouted, "Praise the Lord!"

The mountains must have agreed, because I heard them echo back to me–three times!

Saturday, July 28, 1984

On this, our layover day, it rained from about noon to 3 p.m., so we just sat under the tent and told stories. Malcolm led us in a study of Philippians, and Doug told us about Democratic Congressman Roland Libonaty again. He was the attorney for Al Capone and represented the Chicago area in Congress. Doug seemed to enjoy people who had come from an unsavory past. He definitely practiced Jesus' teaching to accept everyone–not what they stood for, but the person. It was at Doug's invitation that Libonaty became involved in our Thursday morning prayer breakfasts in Washington.

Sunday, July 29, 1984

Packing is getting routine for Doug, Rich, and Malcolm, and they are becoming more and more helpful.

We climbed out of the Violet Lake area, ascending high to get good views. It was a fascinating day. We saw elk, lost the trail, and then looked for blaze marks on trees until they pointed us to the trails again. I thought I was getting good at this trailblazing, but finding our trail after having lost it this time took longer than ever before.

We'd hit an overland trail after thinking we were on one spot shown on the map–then found out we were on another! The splendid views made up for our frustration and lost time, though.

Sometimes the trees that are down are so thick we can't pass. To get through to our campsite, we were forced to chop trees to clear a trail.

As the rest of us began to set up camp, Lynn and Bill kept on going, expecting to meet their wives where a gravel road crossed Elk Creek Trail. They were to be there waiting with a trailer. I gave Bill a letter to mail to Gretchen.

Monday, July 30, 1984

I got up at 5 a.m. today and turned out the horses after tying up Bull and putting the Sundance horse in hobbles. Doug was up shortly thereafter. We ate bacon and pancakes made by Malcolm and got onto the trail by nine. Pretty good time.

It was not much over a mile to the gravel road where Lynn and Bill were to meet their wives last night. After riding along it about a half mile or so, we saw a sign shoved into the gravel road: "Lois and Jean." About a mile further we saw evidence that a trailer had turned around, and a mile further, just before reaching the asphalt road, another sign: "Lois and Jean." I could also see the hoof prints of Lynn's and Bill's horses.

It was apparent they hadn't met up with their wives immediately. At the first sign there was evidence they turned and went back a ways, wondering if their wives were in that direction. Then they turned to go ahead, and where the trailer had turned around, they once again looked back. By looking at the tracks, I sensed the anxiety they must have experienced, knowing their wives had been there, wondering where they now were, thinking they might have missed them.

~ ~ ~

We rode a couple of miles down the asphalt road to May Creek Camp, planning to cut across on a trail that led down to Ruby Creek where we were going to meet Les Davis, who was to bring our trailers from Sundance. However, the caretaker of the May Creek Campground refused to let us go through. He was real difficult. The rules said there should be no horses in the campground. He would not even let us pass through, even though I informed him the people I had spoken to in the Forest Service had told me I could. There was no gate to get through–only a cattle guard on the roadway–and he had no suggestions how we could reach the trail, which he claimed was only for hiking anyway.

We tied up to some trees, and I surveyed the fence. I walked about a mile and found no gate, but I found a spot where we could knock down the fence enough to get the horses to step over.

I went back to tell the others, and Malcolm–an attorney–said we'd be in trouble if caught. So we talked to the caretaker again–to no avail.

We decided that one of us would have to hitchhike to the Big Hole Battlefield where we could call Sundance and let Les Davis know where we were. We sent Malcolm since he had shaved a couple of times along the way and didn't look as ugly as the rest of us. He'd most likely be able to thumb a ride.

~ ~ ~

When Les got there with the trailers, we loaded the horses and drove around to Ruby Creek where we're making camp tonight and where we met up with Darrell Cade, a friend of Rob Linner, my son Joel's brother-in-law. Rob will be joining us tomorrow. Darrell is from Rapid City, South Dakota, and Rob is from a Minneapolis suburb. Both are in the food business, supplying convenience stores and truck stops.

We had to boil water at this camp, since cows had been grazing in the area.

I struck up a conversation with an old miner working nearby on his Caterpillar tractor. Norman–a Dutchman, he said, from Ogden, Utah–will be 80 years old in a couple months, and he still works 20 claims on 5,000 acres. He was surprised I could just let my horses out to graze without hobbles or picket, confident they would come back to me.

As we watched the horses graze their way further from camp, he said, "You will never see those horses again."

I said, "They will be back in three hours."

Two hours and 50 minutes later, there was no sign of them. I was worried.

But ten minutes later I heard them coming. Was I ever relieved, and was Norman ever amazed! These are all experienced horses who know each other.

Soon after, Fred arrived from Butte, and Doug, Rich and Malcolm took his car and drove back to Butte, and Darrell went to Wisdom to wait for Rob, leaving Fred and me by ourselves. I cherish the times I can be alone with my son–so different from me in so many ways. But the differences make our relationship interesting and challenging at all times, and I learn so much. I love him.

~ ~ ~

Last week I was wondering if the food would hold out. No need to have worried. Tomorrow I'll be able to go into Wisdom and stock up again for the next leg of the ride.

CHAPTER EIGHT

Exploring the Dark Horse Mine

Tuesday, July 31, 1984

We grazed the horses until 8 o'clock this morning and then drove in to Wisdom, Mont. to pick up groceries, then to Miner Lake Campground where we left our rigs. We packed up and then Darrell, Rob, son Fred, and I started out about 1 o'clock.

We had some tough climbing–about 1,000 feet in a mile.

We made it to Berry Meadows where we met a couple of hikers who were nice enough to take a card from me to mail to Gretchen. I hope it gets there in time for her birthday on August fourth.

We're camping by an old log cabin tonight.

Wednesday, August 1, 1984

Today was a miserable day. First of all, I don't like traveling on gravel roads and jeep trails. And then it was raining most of the day.

We got up to Dark Horse Lake–just below the Divide–in time to get our tent and tarp up before it began to pour.

The tarp is great to have–even though a part ripped in the wind, and a hole was burned in it when the wind blew the stove pipe against it.

Thursday, August 2, 1984

A great layover day. Did some hiking (found a waterfalls source that comes right out of the ground) and snooped around an old, deserted mining town. I was fascinated by what I observed as I walked among the buildings–tin cans, old bed springs. I imagined what the miners ate and envisioned lumpy beds they probably slept in. I pretended to be an amateur archaeologist, digging around for clues as to how these people lived and mined.

While poking around, Fred and I found an old raft and some boards that we could use for paddles. We took the raft and paddles out on Dark Horse Lake and found the raft to be very seaworthy but hard to navigate. We'd paddle; then the breeze would drift us back.

Again, Fred and I were alone part of the day. Our conversation is always different when it's just the two of us–comfortable, intimate, and confrontive at times, which I enjoy.

This afternoon I had time for a nap; took a bath (used a T-shirt for a wash cloth and, boy, did it get dirty from my face); then washed some socks, under shorts, and the T-shirt. Refreshing in the 4 o'clock sun.

At supper tonight, we spotted elk on the mountainside where we'd be climbing tomorrow morning. Soon, we heard rocks sliding, and I knew if the rocks were rolling under the elk hooves, that it was going to be a difficult climb for us tomorrow. I'm anxious about it, but I won't let on to the others.

When I turned out the horses for their evening graze, they took off. I expected they went up to the mine. By 8:30, I was beginning to wonder where they were, but thought they'd be back by nine. Sure enough, they came back at 9 on the button. We battened everything down, and everyone was in bed by 9:30.

Fred, Rob and Darrell surely enjoyed the day, the rest, the Dark Horse Mine, and the opportunity to explore the area. They are good partners.

Friday, August 3, 1984

I slept until 5:30 this morning. That's late for me. I'm usually up at 5 or before. I rode Bull out to watch the other horses graze. They like grass on dry areas more than in the boggy areas. At 7:30 I headed back to camp, and all the horses followed me.

The others in camp had eaten breakfast and were beginning to break camp. Even so, it took until 10 o'clock to get started. Turned out, the climb up the rock slide was easier than I thought it would be. It was a steep, treacherous trail, but we let all the horses loose to pick their own way, and that made the difference.

We had about 12 miles to go today, and this mountain was tough to navigate. Once again, finding the trail quickly was a difficult task. At one place, it was obvious that a fire had gone through some time ago, and the dead falls were thick. When we finally broke out of the trees, the view was beautiful.

We finally went about 1-1/2 miles down the mountain to Eunice Creek Trail to get good grass for grazing. We ate kielbasa sausages that Fred had brought, mashed potatoes, bread, and corn. Water was running on both sides of the camp. Plenty of logs to build a make-shift table.

I spent a lot of time silently praising God and feeling love for Him tonight after climbing up the mountain a ways. I love this country and this life. Did Jesus go to the mountain, a "solitary place," to both be alone with the Father and, at times, to be with people? I find a great yearning in my soul for this during the year, and a great satisfaction and awe while I'm here.

Saturday, August 4, 1984

Today was the last full day with Fred, Rob, and Darrell.

Our morning routine usually involves letting all the horses graze except Bull, and then letting Bull graze while I pack the others. This morning I got careless, I guess. For some reason I was feeling sorry for Lace, and I let her be with Bull.

When we'd packed all the horses but one, I looked around and neither Lace nor Bull were anywhere to be seen. Apparently they'd had enough and, with each others' company, decided to leave. Never again will I let that brother-sister duo graze loose together. I sent Fred on Clyde to find them. He located them grazing only a couple miles away on the backtrail we traveled yesterday.

~ ~ ~

It was 10 o'clock by the time we climbed out of Eunice Creek and followed a road all the way to Horseshoe Bend Creek where we're camping tonight. When we arrived, we found a tent that looked like it had been set up for some time, a dog, and a couple of cats, but no people. And no one showed.

This is a good site because there is a great spring, but we're camped on a slight incline. I'll probably have a difficult time sleeping tonight on the side of a hill with my cot sideways!

(After sleeping on the ground in previous years, I decided to buy a lightweight cot that would collapse into a small package and that would be easy to pack. I found one at the Eddie Bauer store on the first floor of the Foshay Tower in Minneapolis. I can sleep better on canvas suspended four inches above ground than on the ground where stones and grass tufts poke through.)

After supper, the young men and I climbed to the top of the mountains east of us and saw great vistas of mostly grassy hills. With binoculars, we could also see Selway Range, Lemhi Pass, and snowy peaks.

Before heading back to camp, we read Romans 9, a bewildering chapter in many ways. Why does God choose some and not others? If God determines whose heart is hardened and whose is not, how can God blame anyone for having a hardened heart? I don't know. I do know I am chosen by God; I have a trusting heart; I have confidence in my salvation.

It is enjoyable to discuss these issues with others who have biblical knowledge. It is good to be challenged.

Sunday, August 5, 1984

I woke up at 5, let the horses loose, and lay down on the cot outside for a while, remembering that yesterday was Gretchen's birthday. Then, at 6, I walked up again to the top of the mountain to watch the sun rise and hung out there until after 7. While there, I saw a couple of horse trailers at the pass several miles below. I wondered if they are the trailers of the guys from Minnesota who are on their way to meet me for the next leg of the ride–Mert Schwarz, Bob Cashin, Al Severson, A.M. Lips and Norm Madson.

We took our time getting ready today because we didn't have very far to go. Fred, Rob, and Darrell seemed eager to get going, but I knew they wouldn't be able to leave until the new guys all came.

When we got all packed up, a rainstorm came over, so we waited under the trees until it passed. Out here it's safe to wait out an electric storm under trees because there are so many of them. But you want to be sure you don't get near a tall one. It is likely to draw lightning.

We took off a little after 10 with Fred in the lead. After about three miles we reached Lemhi Pass where the map said we'd find Sacagawea Campground (recognizable, I found, by only a single picnic table). This is where I told Mert, Bob, Al, A.M., and Norm to meet us. Mert's truck and trailer were there, but only Bob's trailer and four horses. These were the trailers I had seen with my binoculars early this morning. No people, nor any sign of Severson, Lips, or Madson.

Rob, Darrell, Fred, and I took the packs off our horses, tied up the pack animals, and rode down the hill looking for our friends. Turned out that Severson's Suburban hadn't had enough power going up the mountain to Lemhi Pass and he had turned around. He also thought Sacagawea campground must be further to the east, and he had missed it. In fact, it was right near the pass, but the locals he'd asked didn't seem to know it was there. I guess one picnic table doesn't make much of an impact.

When we were all back in camp, we removed supplies from the vehicles and started packing up the horses. I took one look at what Bob Cashin had brought–two duffel bags weighing about 40 pounds each–and I began questioning him.

"What have you got in there?"

"Stuff I need to bring along."

"What can you leave behind?"

"Nothing."

"Well, you're not taking all that with you unless it is all on your own pack horse!"

I've always told people they can bring no more than 30 pounds worth of belongings–including sleeping bag and clothes.

I started going through his stuff and pulled out extra changes of underwear, shoes and clothes. I got his stuff down to about 1.25 duffel bags, and said he could finish the job. He was not happy with me.

I found out later that he slipped a couple things back in when I wasn't looking!

~ ~ ~

Bob, a builder in Faribault, Minn., is a horseman and friend of Al Severson. I invited Mert on the ride at the suggestion of former Speaker of the Minnesota House, Rod Searle, from Waseca. Rod told me about this "good horseman"–a retired sheriff of Waseca County–that I'd enjoy having along.

And Norm I know from St. Olaf. He is an architect and is also head of all the grounds at the college. His wife passed away a few years ago, and each summer since, he has gone on an adventure–maybe as an escape. The first year he flew a light airplane around the United States; last year he rode a motorcycle around the U.S.; and this year, rode the cycle from Northfield to Butte. Now he's adding horseback riding along the Divide to his list of adventures.

He's an inexperienced rider, but because of his motorcycle travels, he at least knows how to pack light.

~ ~ ~

Darrell loaded his horses into Cashin's trailer, and Fred and Rob each took Mert's and Al's rigs to Butte. They then will need to get Darrell and my trucks and trailers before they can head for home. The rest of us got packed up and headed out at about 5 p.m. toward the only place on the map where it showed possible water–an intermittent stream along the mountain side about 3-1/2 miles up.

When we got there, we found no water, so Al rode off to find water. It took him a long time to get back to tell us we'd have to have a dry camp right here. The horses will be thirsty by tomorrow.

CHAPTER NINE

Riding in circles?

Monday, August 6, 1984

Not only were the horses thirsty last night, they were also restless. I walked a long way down the mountain this morning to the intermittent stream for water. But it was such a steep, long climb, that I took only about a half-pail. That was a lot of effort for just a half-pail, but I knew I wouldn't be able to carry more than that.

We spent all day looking for Black Canyon Trail–one that would lead us down from this mountain. We never found it in the 10 miles we rode, so we're camping on top again. We're melting snow for drinking water. We tried filtering water from puddles we found here and there, but the mud plugged our filters. The horses have been drinking from puddles, though.

Tuesday, August 7, 1984

When we left camp today, I reached down to take a look at the small ball compass pinned to my jacket. It was gone. It must have come loose and fallen. None of the other fellows had a compass, either, so I tried to read direction by the sun today.

As the day wore on, I couldn't find any of the sites we were passing on my map. I was a little disoriented, but thought, "As long as I continue going southeast, I'll make it all right."

What I failed to remember was that the angle of the sun is different in various parts of a time zone. And I also totally forgot about daylight savings time.

Eventually, we came to a road, and Bob Cashin said, "I've been here before."

Figuring he'd been hunting in the area some years before, I asked, "Oh? When was this?"

"When I drove in two days ago."

"When you drove in here???" I repeated in shock.

It was then I realized I'd been canting to the left all day as I was trying to read the sun! We were on our way to completing a circle!

I, the supposed leader, was mortified. The others took it pretty much in stride. Al joked, "Well, let's just make another circle this week, and then we can go home!"

We still had about 10 miles to go before we reached Bannock Pass, and it was now past noon. All we could do was push our horses in a fast walk to make up for lost time and distance.

There is good grass where we're camping tonight, and while it's quite a walk to a spring, the water is good.

I'm still unhappy with myself.

Wednesday, August 8, 1984

This was supposed to be a layover day, but the campsite we were at last night didn't have enough water and grass for us to spend an entire day.

We rode eight miles, turned left at Cruckshand Creek and then right at Big Bear Creek. We climbed until we ran out of blaze marks, and then cut across high open country to get to Reservoir Creek. We came out below the body of water shown on the map, so we traveled downstream to Howley Creek and stopped at what seemed to be a public camp spot with a picnic table. We had misgivings, but will stay here tonight. The grass is short, so, again, we will not layover.

Thursday, August 9, 1984

We left early today, heading out by jeep trail. We found a spot with lush grass and stopped for 20 minutes for the horses to graze, then pushed on. We traveled about 15 miles to a spring two miles above Morrison Lake on the Montana side of the Divide. It looks like sheep have been in the area. This will be a good spot for a layover day tomorrow. It was cause for great laughter when one of the guys thought the sheep droppings were a sign that elk had been here.

Friday, August 10, 1984

Clyde got sick last night. It always troubles me when a horse gets sick. When I was a kid we had a beautiful horse that died from colic, and when I was in Congress, I had a Quarter Horse mare that died on our front lawn from the same thing. In that instance, all the veterinarians in Maryland were at a convention, so I couldn't get one to come and help. Since there are no vets out here in the mountains, I got worried. I didn't want the same thing to happen to Clyde. So I stayed up and walked Clyde until he relaxed, his digestive juices started flowing again, and his stomach began to rumble. Healthy horses' stomachs make a noise. And walking keeps a horse from lying down and trying to roll, which can cause a horse to twist a gut. Clyde was OK this morning.

~ ~ ~

We climbed down to Morrison Lake to go fishing this afternoon (caught none), and the strenuous climb back was tough on Norm. We're a little worried about him. He doesn't seem to be able to take the physical exertion. Or maybe the altitude. At the end of the day, he is very exhausted. When I ask him if he will open the packs (thinking this is one of the less strenuous tasks that need to be done to set up camp), he will lie down on the ground next to the packs, rather than lean over them, to untie them. We will keep an eye on him. His personality, though, is a mixed blessing—while his humor keeps our spirits up, it also makes us forget about his exhaustion. I'm thinking we don't watch out for him enough.

~ ~ ~

We had a good time watching a sheepherder today. I am fascinated by how he controls the sheep, how they seem to know his voice—all two or three thousand of them. His relationship with them, I guess, is not unlike mine with horses—he just studies them. He does, however, have a lot more animals.

He put up an interesting tent; it had one pole in the center for a pyramid look. Bob went over to talk with him and found out he spends all summer in the mountains. Once a week the sheep's owner finds him and brings supplies.

Saturday, August 11, 1984

It was so light by the full moon last night that I woke up about 1 o'clock, thinking it was morning. I heard Mert's horse pawing, so I got up and moved the horses. I walked around in the glow of the night for a while, enjoying the beauty. I heard the sheep moving north, which seemed strange for the middle of the night. I also sensed rain was coming in.

This morning the herder came by and asked if we had seen his sheep–they had wandered away in the night, and he'd slept through it! Though I didn't know where they were, I could tell him what I'd heard last night. The rain has obliterated the tracks; he'll have a hard time finding them.

~ ~ ~

We followed jeep trails all day. Passed Deadman Creek, and we're making camp in a few trees around Pine Creek. The horses are tired. So am I.

Sunday, August 12, 1984

If anyone along on these rides seems to have an interest in helping put together a worship service, I let them. But I'm usually the one who does it. Typically I pick a Bible passage, read it, share the meaning the Holy Spirit has revealed to me, and then ask questions to engage the others. Each person then prays as the Spirit moves. And we end standing together, praying the Lord's Prayer. When Al Severson is along, we have music. He's the only one so far with a good voice.

Today we used the last chapter of the book of John in our Sunday service. Jesus' question of Peter, "Do you love me?" is a good lead-in to ask the group, "How do you know you love God?" Many people don't think about that, and wonder instead how they can be sure God loves them. The question left them blank at first but gave us all something to mull over in our minds.

~ ~ ~

We rode over Medicine Lodge Pass today and right away were on the Divide. We came upon a travertine rock mine, and there–sitting as though it had fallen off a huge truck and people had no means to re-load it–was an 8-cubic-yard block of travertine marble.

We didn't make great time today, but that's OK. Some days this bothers me since I want to get as far as possible. Some days it doesn't bother me since it is so enjoyable to be having this marvelous experience. We saw three antelope; found our way with maps to Garfield Mountain and Little Sheep Creek.

We'll have another layover day tomorrow.

Monday, August 13, 1984

We fished this morning with no luck, so we went back to camp and took morning naps. We went fishing again this afternoon and this time caught 16 trout but threw many back. After supper, we went out and looked for elk; saw four deer–one with big antlers. We also saw a coyote today. This is beautiful country.

Tuesday, August 14, 1984

It was raining as we took off this morning; I let Norm wear one of my yellow slickers for this trip. He is much shorter than I, so it dragged on the ground a little as he walked, but riding with it was fine.

As noon arrived, we came upon a large corral, evidently used for roundup and shipping cattle that range over this land. We tied our horses to the logs of the corral and walked over a little ways so we could eat lunch and lean back against the corral. That is, all of us but Norm. I noticed he was still standing where he had tied Clyde, eating his lunch.

"Norm! Why don't you come over here and eat with us?"

There was a slight pause; then, "I can't. Clyde is standing on my coat!"

~ ~ ~

'Lace jerked back, pulling Clyde over backward!' July 21, 1983. (Chapter 4)

Each person's personality and interests lend a special dimension to the dynamics of our group. Norm has a dry sense of humor and is a great companion. Al's stories can get us laughing better than anyone's. A.M. relives his elk hunting experiences, and he is capable of doing anything and fixing anything. Mert is very careful of his horses; he is stable and happy. He is a straight arrow in every way.

Bob seems to be enjoying the trip–even though I didn't let him bring all his gear! He shares about his horse and his occupation, which is home building. He is the youngest and calls the rest of us "the old fogies."

~ ~ ~

We traveled through ranch land this afternoon, and we found, on top of a butte–practically on the Divide–a big cow tank filling with water. It seemed strange that water would be pumped this far up the mountain. After riding a little further, a truck came up and stopped by us. We asked the driver, who turned out to be a ranch hand, about the water, and he said it traveled from a mountain spring about 4-1/2

miles away. Imagine! Having pipes running that far up to a water tank.

After the truck left, I could tell the other guys were a little uneasy. Al asked if ranchers would be unhappy that we were on their land; in Minnesota, a farmer would not like "trespassers." Another wondered if the guy in the truck had a 30.06.

~ ~ ~

We made camp about 5 o'clock, a little down the mountain where the timothy grass was lush and green. A small spring came into a pond, but it was covered with moths at the surface, so we dipped our canteens under the surface to get clean water.

There were no dead trees to use for firewood; thankfully, we have A.M.'s gas burner. We had freeze-dried beef stroganoff, corn, green beans, and blueberry cobbler for supper.

Mert put up his little tent for himself and Bob; the rest of us are using tarps for sleeping tonight.

At sunset tonight, the horizon looked as though an artist had used broad strokes to paint rich, rainbow colors across his blue canvas background. I think I'll stay up a while and enjoy the night sky.

Wednesday, August 15, 1984

Last night the moon and stars were brilliant; the sage hens noisy, and the horses contented. Sometimes I wonder what it would be like to stay up all night and just look at the stars. They are so enormous out here. There have been nights when I have gotten up to walk and pray and look at the stars. Last night I did it before I went to bed.

~ ~ ~

I had wanted to go all the way to the Yellowstone Park boundary this year, but we've had so many hard days that have been tough on the horses and the men that we're not going to make it. Maps of this area don't show much good riding country from Monida to Machs Inn, anyway. We'll go into Monida tomorrow and call Fred and each of our wives; we'll be done Friday.

I'm wondering how Gretchen is, whether she is angry with me for going on these trips. Will she be glad to hear from me? How is her painting going? Is she fed up with our home at Marsh Hills over-looking Lake Ella? Does she like being alone? Does she want me to quit my out-of-doors living? Might she want to go (ugh!) into the city to live so she can have people closer to her?

I get angry at the thought of people having to live close to other people just for safety. As I travel in the West, the only species that gives me anxiety is the human species. All other animals are predictable.

Thursday, August 16, 1984

As we left camp, we used field glasses to look ahead and saw what appeared to be a viaduct we'd have to go under. Turned out, about an hour later, we reached a railroad underpass. We followed the tracks, and made it the rest of the way to Monida, where we found no public phone and no one home in either of the two houses that appeared to have telephone wires going into them. The third home–a trailer inhabited by a prospector named Clay–had no phone.

Monida once had a hotel and bar, grocery, garage, and livery. Now, according to Clay, there was only a mail carrier, an elderly weather station watcher, and himself living there.

Since there was no phone, I hitched a ride with a Highway Department water truck to Lima and called Gretchen and then Fred, asking him to meet us in Monida tomorrow.

Fred said he couldn't haul the trailers down, so he would send someone else to bring four of us back as drivers. The water truck then brought me on a slow trip back to Monida. About a half mile away, the driver stopped to wash a bridge, so I thanked him for the lift and walked the rest of the way.

~ ~ ~

Clay had given us directions to the West Fork of the Corral Creek, where we're camping tonight. On the way, we saw some groups of antelope, four elk, and a Sandhill crane.

As soon as camp was set up I took Bull to explore. I told the guys to go ahead and make supper, and if I didn't get back, not to be concerned. I said if I didn't come back until after dark, don't worry about me. I just wanted to get alone and ride out there by myself.

I climbed up the mountain and made a big swing, across two ridges, riding south, east and then north around the camp. I saw two spotted fawns with their mom, but she never saw me until I was 50 feet from her; then the three of them bolted. Also, a big buck with huge antlers, but few points, jumped up.

I checked the East Fork for coming back into camp. It was too steep so I came down via the Middle Fork. It was in a different spot than I expected so I came out further north than planned, running into a fence. I followed it south, and I came out high above the West Fork. I walked and led Bull down the rest of the way.

When I got back, Al, Bob, and Mert were saddling Super, Dusty and Goldie–the only horses left in camp. The other five horses had heard Bull whinny once, and they had dashed out of camp chasing after the sound of Bull. The horses never caught up to us, though, so these guys were going out to find them.

Al and Mert went all the way around the top above camp, as I had, but Bob figured right–he went searching along the backtrail, and that is where he found them. It looks like it will rain tonight.

Friday, August 17, 1984

It rained hard last night; the spray came under the tarp and hit my face. I put a mantie on top of me. Most of the thunder was only 7 seconds after the lightning, but there was one lightning strike that was very close with a terrible thunder explosion immediately following. I got up to see if anyone or anything in camp had been hit, or if any of the horses were knocked down. No one was hurt, but Mert and Bob got pretty wet in their tent.

All but I were eager to pack up and leave this morning. So I went fishing while they packed, riding Clyde to the spring. He pulled over the first tree I tied him to, so I tied him to a bigger tree. Did he ever have a fit! He is always eager to go back to his friends. Fishing was great. I caught 12 in about an hour and then rode back. Clyde is certainly hyper in such a situation.

We left camp about 9 o'clock. I told the others they knew the way back to Monida and let them go without me so I could take a different way back. I wanted to ride alone again. Spanish Bull and Lace (whom I packed) really moved now. I got back to Monida well before the others, and on the way saw a cow moose and some Sandhill cranes. The cranes are practically like ventriloquists in their ability to throw me off regarding their location. Something I've never read about in bird books.

Arriving at Monida about 3:30, Clay told us that some old rancher had come into Monida, planning to call the sheriff because we had ridden across his ranch land. Clay said we ought not to worry about it–he was a miserable old character, anyway, usually upset with something.

We made calls at the mail carrier's house and then made a fire to cook the fish. Clay brought coffee and rolls for us. He is real nice. An interesting guy, but he wouldn't let me take his picture.

A car came by at 6 o'clock, but the driver (a woman) didn't stop. We wondered whether it was the transportation Fred was sending.

After a while, I got Clay to drive me east, and we met the same vehicle coming back. Turns out it was our ride. Fred had been busy, so he sent Joan Combie to get us. Norm and I stayed back while the others went to Butte to get the rigs.

Norm was puttering around after he changed into his clean clothes, dragging some tree branches into a nearby barn. I wondered what he was up to. He put some sticks in the legs of his jeans, so they would stand up by themselves. He took pictures and said the caption will be, "This is what jeans look like after riding a couple of weeks in them!"

~ ~ ~

I'm disappointed we didn't make it all the way to Yellowstone, but it is not possible to get there by riding on public land (because there isn't any in this stretch), and I don't like riding along roads. I wonder if I will ever ride the stretch from Monida to Yellowstone.

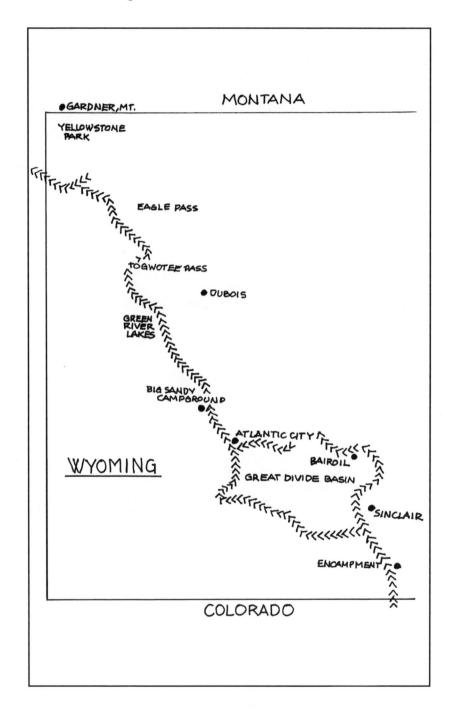

1985

Wyoming

Bridger Teton
Thorofare River
Togwotee Pass
Wind River Range
Big Sandy

CHAPTER TEN

In a helpless instant: three cracked vertebrae

Monday, July 15, 1985

During the last several days, Gretchen did not seem fully happy with my going to the Divide this year, but this morning, as we pulled out about 5 a.m., she seemed OK with it. Maybe it's because her mother is with her for a while, and her company will take away some of the loneliness that comes with my being gone.

Now that I think about it, I guess Gretchen has never been happy with my going on these trips. But she supports me in it. I always tell her she could go with me if she felt strongly enough about wanting to be with me! But these adventures don't appeal to her. Pain is not something she enjoys.

Gretchen brings so much more to my life, though, than I could ever experience on these rides. If I had not met and married her, I would never have an appreciation for art–or for opera. She's helped me enjoy food I would otherwise not even have tried. I remember, when we were dating, how struck I was by this person who could talk about philosophy. I, on the other hand, was more of an exact-science, clear-answers kind of guy. Philosophy, to me, had a lot of fuzz to it. Gretchen helped me in blending the two areas of thought. She's the mother of our children; she has firm moral values; she has simply made me a fuller person.

~ ~ ~

It seems I've spent more time planning the trip this year than I have in the past. I built a box out of thin plywood–including shelves for kitchen supplies–so that it will be easy to find things once we get set up in camp each night. I also built some boxes out of white pine for carrying the horse's feed. In the past, we've put the feed in duffel bags and mantied the feed packs. Boxes will stay more balanced on the pack horses.

And then there's the harness I made for the boxes with snaps that I can hook into D-rings–it'll make hauling the meat cooler much easier.

I rode my horses quite a bit this year–but only twice for longer than 1.5 hours, and only in the last two weeks did I have rides that were over an hour. I wonder whether the horses will be in condition.

We plan to start the ride where we left off in 1983–at the Thorofare River near the south edge of Yellowstone Park. A.M. Lips and I will ride into the Bridger Wilderness to the Thorofare River, across from where we finished that year, then we will follow the Divide to Togwotee Pass where the others will join us.

A.M. and I are staying in a motel tonight in Harrison, Neb. We left the horses in the rodeo arena at the fairgrounds. Members of the local Volunteer Fire Department who were meeting there found a policeman who gave us permission.

As A.M. and I were travelling today, I gained entirely new insights into this man. He shared about his experiences putting in the utility poles throughout this whole region of the U.S.A. He also talked bout his role as a ship builder in California during World War II. No wonder he can fix anything and is so confident in what he does.

Tuesday, July 16, 1985

Up early and out again at 5 this morning. We drove to Casper, Wyoming, then to Riverton where we bought our fishing licenses and some horse feed. On to Pavilion and the Wyoming Horse Ranch owned by Lonnie Mantle. He has 40 head of horses, and I picked four to rent for Frank Rawlins and Jerry Franz who will be joining us in a few days.

I met Jerry at a National Prayer Breakfast in Washington, D.C., a year or so ago. He talked to me then about going along on one of these rides. He has a small appliance store in Billings and is active in the Prayer Fellowship movement in Montana. I had heard Jerry was a great trout fisherman and thought it would be good to have someone like that along.

He then said, "If you want someone who is really a good trout fisherman, you want Frank Rawlins. May I bring him along?" So that's how Frank ended up on the ride. Frank, a chemist, is active in evangelism in Idaho. I understand he has feed plants in Idaho, and a ranch in Nevada where he has 12,000 head of cattle.

Lonnie will trailer the horses to Togwotee Pass for us on Sunday.

We gassed up at Dubois and then went on to Togwotee Pass, and then to Turpin Meadow Lodge at Moran Junction, where we are staying tonight.

Wednesday, July 17, 1985

It took A.M. and me some time to get our pack loads down to 110 and 122 pounds; we had to leave some of our stuff in the truck, which we are leaving at the lodge. It started raining just as we were mounting up a little before 10 a.m. Wouldn't you know, we had packed our overshoes away–not a smart thing to do–so wet feet were in order. It was a real soaker–the middle of the afternoon before it let up.

The water was high when we got to the Yellowstone River, so we scouted around to find the best way across. I found what I thought was a good spot. A.M. said he'd found a better way, but it looked to me like we would have the benefit of more sandbars if we went across my way. I suggested, "How about if I go first and you watch."

My horses were not afraid; I nudged them down the bank and into the river. The water–shoulder-high on the horses–poured over the top of the panniers[10] on the upstream side, and my saddle blankets got soaked. Water came into my boots–I couldn't get my feet high enough. But I made it across.

After seeing how deep the water was, A.M. decided it would be better to cross a little further down at the place where he'd chosen. That was a mistake. I caught a glimpse of his horse and pack horse frantically swimming as the water swirled around them, carrying them further downstream. It looked as though A.M. was desperately clinging to his horse's neck.

The trees along the river bank were thick. From my position, there was no way I could help. I prayed. A.M. and his horses drifted further away. I prayed some more.

Peering through the trees and the rain, I saw his horses go lower in the water. This could be good. Maybe they were getting their footing on the sandbars.

It was true. Soon A.M. and his horses were climbing up the muddy banks of the river. Praise God.

When I reached A.M., he said he thought it might have been the end for him and his horses.

By 5:30, the rain clouds were coming at us again. Shivering in our cold, wet clothes, we hurried to make camp, built a fire, and changed into some dry duds. I don't want to take any chances with hypothermia.

We packed 20 miles today. Tonight we're in the shelter of some trees near Hawk's Nest.

Thursday, July 18, 1985

For some reason, Bull and A.M.'s pack horse, Joe, decided they were going off on their own this morning. I jumped on Goldie to head them off, but it wasn't as easy a job as I thought it would be. Just as I approached them, I saw the lead rope coming loose from Joe's pack saddle. He jumped forward, Bull got spooked, and then they both took off again. Goldie and I continued after them, though, and this time when we approached, Bull and Joe let us get near, and they followed us back to camp.

We packed 24 miles today, going into Yellowstone Park so I could connect with the spot where I stopped in '83, and then we went back out again. We fished in the Thorofare River today where it enters the Park–caught nothing. Then we followed the Yellowstone to Woodward Canyon where we are camping tonight.

Friday, July 19, 1985

The trail out of the Canyon this morning was steep and rugged. We headed for the Buffalo Fork River, had a little trouble finding the trail, and lost about a half hour. But we made good time after that, packing about 24 miles to where Cub Creek enters the Buffalo Fork.

The horses seemed very hungry, so we let them all graze as we set up camp. After a while, I glanced up, and the horses were nowhere in sight. I went after them on foot, thinking I'd find them in the next clearing–nope. I yelled for A.M. to come and help, and that's when I heard splashing. I saw the horses crossing the river below me. And Goldie had hobbles on!

I ran down the bank, and about the only thing I could do by then was to go across on foot and try to catch them on the other side. The river water was up to my hips. When I got to the other side, I took off after the horses, but soon discovered it was too hard to run with 16-inch high boots full of water.

So I lay down on my back, put my feet up, and let the water drain out. Water ran from my boots into my jeans, and when I got up, my jeans were so wet that some of the water went back into my boots!

I ran through downed timber, trying to get around the horses to head them off. But I finally had to simply get on the trail following them. I called and called their names.

Bull let me catch up to him, but the others kept going, with Joe now in the lead. I tied Bull up and got him to whinny, which, I thought, would draw the other horses' attention. Pretty soon Dusty started coming back. Then Goldie. Finally Joe.

Saturday, July 20, 1985

We broke camp in record time this morning, leaving at 7:25.

We passed Upper Buffalo Lake and Birch Lake on our way to Togwotee Pass, 17 miles away, where Pastor Paul Nelson, Al Severson, and Mert Schwarz would be meeting us today, and where Frank and Jerry will be meeting us tomorrow. We made it by 2:30, tied up and dropped the packs. A.M. stayed there as I scouted for a campsite. Found a good one about 1-1/2 miles away toward the west.

Pastor Paul and Al arrived about 4:30, and got in about 5:30 this afternoon. A.M. and I drove in Al's rig back to Turpin Meadows to get my truck and trailer. When we got there, I decided it would be a good time to take a shower, too. The owner of the lodge wasn't happy about it, but she let us shower for $5 a piece. I think she was reluctant, because she didn't want the hassle of cleaning the showers and washing our towels.

We drove back to Togwotee Pass and unloaded the gear and groceries brought by Paul and Al. With everything strewn around, it looks like there will be no way we'll be able to pack it all. We'll deal with it tomorrow.

Sunday, July 21, 1985

We held a worship service after having a breakfast of eggs and pancakes. Pastor Paul read from the Psalms, and then we talked and prayed. Paul is pastor at Bethel Lutheran Church in Northfield, Minnesota, where Al and I are members. He had been a pastor in North Dakota for a while and has had some experience with horses; he owns the two he has with him.

It took us a while to sort out all the stuff in camp, and about noon we had decided on what we could take and what we would have to leave.

We waited–impatiently–for Frank and Jerry. When they hadn't arrived by 3 o'clock, I rode down to Togwotee Lodge about nine miles away and tried calling their homes to find out if they were on their way. Lonnie Mantle's semi was there with the rental horses for Jerry and Frank, who finally arrived at 5:30. I made Jerry reduce his gear to one duffel bag.

I advise everyone who rides with me to pay attention to what they don't use while on the trail, so that if they ever go along with me again, they'll know themselves what to leave behind.

Jerry and Frank helped me pack horse feed into camp, and I then went back and packed in their gear, arriving in camp as it got dark.

Al, A.M., and I drove our three trucks and trailers to Big Sandy Camp Ground–a five-hour drive each way–so there will be transportation for us when we arrive on horseback in a few days. At 11 o'clock tonight I rode out to wait for them. Nearly three hours later, at 1:45 a.m., I was shaking with cold when they finally got back. They left my trailer at Big Sandy and drove my truck back. We left it at Togwotee Pass and rode the horses I had led out with me into camp in pitch dark. It amazes me how horses can see their way in the blackness of night.

Monday, July 22, 1985

Even though I had only a couple hours' sleep last night, I still got up early. Seems I can't sleep late, no matter what, when I'm out here.

Nearly as soon as we started down the trail–about 10 a.m.–a man and his wife and son rode up telling us there were some dynamiters ahead conducting seismic testing. They offered to show us a way around the workers.

Once pointed out, we could see the dynamiters in the distance. They had trucks they'd used to bring in their dynamite, and we saw a helicopter, too. I was thankful to have help in finding a way around their testing site. The noise would certainly have spooked the horses.

Along the way I could tell Frank was having trouble with his horse which seemed excited and was prancing around, maybe because the flies and mosquitoes were bad. I traded pack horses with him, thinking that might help.

We went on our way, until I heard a sudden commotion behind me. I whipped around just in time to see Frank getting bucked off his horse. He was still hanging onto his pack horse's lead rope, which had gotten caught under his horse's tail. The pack horse lurched back to pull the rope out from under the bucking horse's tail, and in the process, jerked Frank backwards while his horse was bucking him off.

In a helpless instant, I watched the lead rope pull Frank through the air, and the bucking horse's back hooves went high as the sky. In mid-air, Frank got smacked solidly in the stomach by one hoof, which continued on up to his chin. Frank's head jerked back–and then his body dropped to the ground. We didn't know if he was dead or alive.

We jumped off our horses and dashed to where Frank lay. Mert had the most first aid experience, so he took charge. Al Severson went to get help from the seismic crew, who were now about a quarter mile away. He was going to ask them if they would use their helicopter to lift Frank out of here and to a hospital.

We heard Frank moan as he regained consciousness. Thank God he was alive. I asked if he could wiggle his toes. He moved his feet, but we still treated him as though his back might be broken.

As I went to take a canvass off one of the packs, I couldn't help but think about how often I tell guys, "If it looks like you're going to have a wreck, drop the lead rope. Your life is more important than any of these horses." But I hadn't told Frank.

Al came back with help from the seismic testing crew, one of whom said he had had experience on an ambulance crew and he therefore knew how to handle the situation. We worked the canvass I'd removed from one of the packs to get it underneath Frank, and then we rolled its sides. There were enough of us to stand side-by-side on each side of the canvas, and we were able to keep it stiff as a board as we picked him up.

Unfortunately, the helicopter was too small to carry Frank out, but one of the workers had driven a panel truck over, so we moved Frank, lying prone, into the back. They then headed for the hospital in Jackson where, the dynamiters said, the doctors have a lot of experience with broken legs and backs because of skiing and rock climbing accidents. Jerry rode along with his friend.

The rest of us turned around, heading back to last night's camp–we'd only gotten about 2-1/2 miles out–but our troubles were not over. I was leading Jerry's and Frank's pack horses; others were leading their riding horses. On the way, Jerry's long fishing poles on his pack horse began poking Bull.

I had tried to talk Jerry and Frank into bringing collapsible fishing poles, but they insisted on their regular fly rods. Since they were the "professionals," I gave in.

But Bull was not happy. The poles would ram him; he'd kick. So I tried to get Jerry's pack horse to move to my other side. I swung Bull around and that's when the pack horses exploded. I let go, and Jerry's pack horse broke loose from Frank's; stampeding into Mert's pack horse. That shook everything up, but there was no damage. Then Frank's pack horse jerked back and went over backwards, ending up on his back, upside down, with one pannier on each side, not able to move. Just like Clyde in 1983.

To get him up, I took his lead rope, made two wraps around the saddle horn and Bull pulled him up; he surely made a mess of the panniers.

After we were back in camp, we separated out Jerry's and Frank's gear and re-packed everything. Al and I rode over to Togwotee Pass, leading the rented horses and carrying Jerry's and Frank's gear.

We telephoned the hospital in Jackson; found out that Frank had a torn ligament and had cracked his last three vertebrae. He was told that if he'd moved his head on his own, he might have broken his spinal cord. They are planning to fly him to Boise by ambulance plane tomorrow.

Jerry told me on the phone that he is dropping out of the ride–maybe he'll join me in another year.

I arranged for Lonnie Mantle to come back to Togwotee Pass to get the rented horses, and we stashed Jerry's and Frank's things at the Lodge for Jerry to pick up later.

I see the hand of God in helping us through this accident. The dynamiters so close. The experienced ambulance crew member. The availability of the panel truck. The doctors and hospital in nearby Jackson. The fact that Frank wasn't paralyzed.

I know there are some people who would question me: "The hand of God? How can you say the hand of God is in this? Why do some people die in accidents like this and others live?"

These people also wonder if I would still be praising God if Frank had broken his spinal cord, or even died. I think I would, not for the serious injury or death, but because of the feeling of God's presence through the experience. In this case, I was not praising God just because Frank stayed alive. Praise comes because of what happens to people through the event. God allows things to happen for His purpose. An event can make us better, nobler, or more compassionate and just. Or we can respond to an event entirely in the opposite–I expect our reactions depend on our relationship with God.

I thank God when an event causes me and others to draw nearer to Him. Coming closer to being one with God is what I praise God about–in all circumstances.

I don't understand why the Lord allows some people to suffer more than others when they fall from a horse. Even die. I don't understand, but I trust God. And I believe His hand is in everything. It is great to be in God's presence, seeing His hand working in the way He did today.

~ ~ ~

Al and I rode back into camp in the dark again. And in my mind, I continue to have the clear image of the moment I turned around and saw Frank being bucked off. What I see is like a still, snapshot of Frank in mid-air, his saddle horse's hoof between his belt buckle and chin. It is so vivid. Too vivid.

CHAPTER ELEVEN

A fresh start with 'The Press'

Tuesday, July 23, 1985

We got out at 9:30 this morning. Rain followed us all day. We found our way through rough terrain to the North Fork of Fish Creek as we headed for Beauty Park Creek where we met two Forest Service employees and asked them the way. That was a mistake; their advice led us in the wrong direction. Consequently, we're making camp high in the mountains tonight. Thankfully, there is water, and the view of forested and rocky peaks all around us is beautiful.

Wednesday, July 24, 1985

We got going early again today, and found our way over steep precipices to Purdy Basin. Coming down from the mountain, we ended up in a low area–grassy and soggy with a stream to cross. The others hung to the side as I explored and found a good place to get to the other side. Bull acted thirsty, so I rode him part way into the stream, thinking he could take a drink before crossing.

As is his custom when drinking from a stream, he turned parallel to the banks. Only this time, for some reason, he turned not upstream but downstream–maybe because the water was milky-looking from glacial runoff. You couldn't see down into it. And as he put his head down to take a drink, he stepped forward-and right into a deep hole, but not much wider than his body. His head went under; I threw myself to the side onto the bank to get off and rolled away from him. Still hanging onto the reins, I was able to pull Bull's head up so he would not drown. The water was practically up to the saddle horn, and his front feet seemed stuck, while his hind feet were still on the firm stream bed above and behind him.

I yelled for Mert to bring me a rope, but before he got there, Bull reared back and was able to thrust his whole body up and out of the water-filled hole. This horse has amazing strength and agility.

You would think Bull would not have had anything to do with me after that. After all, he trusted me; and, by his way of thinking, I led him right up to that hole. But instead, he just stood there by me–soaking wet and shaking–waiting for his next instruction from me.

Mert told me later that this was the first time he ever saw me excited. "You're such a calm guy," he said. "But when I heard you yelling for that rope, I knew something was wrong!"

We let Bull rest as we ate lunch, and then we rode uneventfully to South Fork Fish Creek where we camped for the night. This is a beautiful site with wavy meadows, a babbling stream nearby, and snow-covered peaks in the distance.

Thursday, July 25, 1985

Got out in good time this morning. To me, "good time" means getting out of camp by 8:30. It's up at 5 for me and let the horses graze. We fix breakfast, wash up, pack up, saddle up. Others sleep later, but I don't need much sleep out here. From 6 a.m., though, everyone is hustling and pitching in.

We rode up the South Fork of Fish Creek today where the riding was treacherous. There were granite remnants from a previous rockslide slipping beneath the horses' hooves, and the faint trail made it difficult to find our way. We finally came upon a large open area where cattle were grazing. After lunch, we found a jeep track and followed it to a road which led us to a house trailer. A lady there–whose husband was a logger–offered us water and told us how to find the road to Pinion Ridge.

We followed that for miles, but when it turned north, we decided we might not be going in the right direction again, so we moved off onto a jeep track that led us in a southeasterly direction. Finally we saw a log fence, and as we went through the gate of this drift fence, we found ourselves on the precipice of a sharp drop to the valley. We peered over the edge and could see the Green River running 200 feet below; further down was Lower Green River Lake and across the valley, high on the other side, was Square Top Mountain. What a spectacular and awesome sight. But, it was too steep to bring horses down this rocky place.

We carefully moved back from the overhang and headed east through scattered aspen trees and good grass toward Gunsight Pass. The steep drop on the trail (with no switchbacks) was so severe that we dismounted and led our horses down. Gravity forced one of the pack duffels on Dusty to shift forward, so we had to stop and re-pack

Once the trail leveled off, we found ourselves in the midst of thick aspen. Beautiful but extremely difficult to navigate. I got frustrated that it was taking so long to get through the trees. Maybe my frustration stemmed from the fact that Paul–instead of me–was in the lead. I find that I'm more patient when I'm in charge. Anyway, I couldn't take it anymore, so I left the others and headed down the mountain without a trail to follow. I knew where we were going to end up, and I met the others when they reached the bottom.

It's been cold all day today. We're camping at a great site on Roaring Fork.

Friday, July 26, 1985

Six riders approached us this morning as we were packing up. They were a rancher and friends doing a count on their cattle. They asked if we'd seen any of their stock grazing. I was able to tell them about the cattle we'd seen yesterday near the South Fork of Fish Creek.

They showed us the easiest way down to the valley floor. We traveled by the Green River Lake, and from there we were able to look up and see the precipice we'd been on yesterday.

We traveled past an abandoned, run-down ranch, past Square Top Mountain and Granite Mountain to Beaver Park, just past Pixley Creek. What an awesome majestic experience. I could not help remembering the stories I'd read of mountain men and their annual rendezvous at Green River Lake. Those were rugged men, seeking their fortunes in beaver pelts because of the English hat trade. They were heavy drinkers, according to the novels, and partook in hard fighting. Are we ever a bunch of pansies in comparison.

Later today, A.M. spotted a large animal off the in the distance, and wondered out loud if someone's horse was loose.

Paul immediately agreed that that must be the case. I looked and saw that it did appear to be a horse–it was the right size, the right color. But we couldn't see its head. Just then the animal moved and we discovered it was a moose! This is the closest we've ever come to one and all laughed at our mistake.

We're camping at Beaver Park tonight. A.M. and I each caught a fish, so we'll have them for breakfast.

Saturday, July 27, 1985

Pastor Paul's pack horse Coco is a fidgety one–a stubborn, bully-type that does not want to be dealt with. Every day it's a struggle to pack her, so I've been running my jacket through her halter to blindfold her. When we pull the jacket off, she sees everything that's been packed, she makes a few jumps, and we're on our way.

I finally got disgusted with that whole process, and today told Paul, "We've got to teach this horse to be packed." He gave me permission.

I first tied up one of the mare's hind legs so she would be standing on three legs and couldn't buck or even shy away. Some horses don't rebel at all at this; then, again, there are others that do. And then there are some–like this one–that really rebel and throw themselves around. Coco obviously had never had her feet taken away and been made to behave. So I just let her work her way through it.

She finally settled down some, and I began to pack with one hind leg tied up with a rope from around her neck. She watched. And fidgeted. But she came out all right, quieting down in the end.

That's when, in this learning process, one needs to be kind to the horse and rub her all over. That comfort encourages her to take the easier way of standing still next time.

A farrier once told me this is a lot like our relationship with the Lord. Some people just naturally belong with God. Some resist a little bit, and then realize it doesn't make any sense to rebel. And they let go. Still others really rebel and throw themselves around like the world is coming to an end. Finally, when they hit bottom, they say, "OK, I guess I'll obey."

As with Pastor Paul's pack horse, peace can only come when we yield.

~ ~ ~

We headed for Jean Lake and Elbow Lake this morning–both are high up. When we got to Summit Lake, we met a young packer and asked if he knew whether there was good camping at Elbow or Jean Lakes. He said there were no trees, so we're camping at Pass and Twin Lakes instead. There isn't much feed here, either. Tomorrow is a layover day, so maybe I'll ride up to Elbow Lake alone and check it out.

Sunday, July 28, 1985
It was cold and stormy today. We put a tarp up and put a canvas behind it to block the driving, wet wind. We dressed ourselves in everything we owned, wrapped mantee tarps around us, and huddled behind the tarp to get out of the wind.

It was mid-afternoon when the wind and rain started to let up, so A.M. and I decided to go fishing. We saddled up and headed up to Elbow Lake. The trail was terrible. It reminded me of the time I climbed the Capitol steps in St. Paul on horseback with each step on a ledge three feet above the one you're on. When we reached the top, I wondered how we were going to get back down without hurting the horses, but we made it. We caught no fish, which was disappointing.

I was filled with anticipation, however, to be able to tell the others about the fearsome trail, and, after regaling them, to announce that tomorrow all of us would need to ride up over those rocks.

Monday, July 29, 1985
It continued raining through the night and stormed all day today.

The rough weather, combined with the rocky trail we were on, made for treacherous travel. I looked ahead and saw large rocks on the trail jutting up from the ground in all directions. As we worked our way through them, we hoped our horses' hooves would not slip into any of the crevices.

Bull's did.

His right hind foot got caught in a crevice between two parallel flat rocks in a steep descent. He lost his balance, as those two rocks seemed to grab hold of his hind hoof and refused to let him go. I immediately jumped off, and was horrified to see my horse nearly hanging on the slope with all his weight pulling against that one leg with its hoof jammed between the rocks. I was powerless to help him.

But Bull is a terribly strong horse. He looked at me, and then I watched him brace himself. He grunted, and with pure determination, forced his hoof right out from between those rocks. I was amazed because he could not compress his hoof enough to free it. But when he jerked his hoof out, the rocks unyieldingly hung on to his horseshoe. I leaned over to examine his hoof; there were gouges from the rocks on both sides.

Mert, an experienced farrier, had equipment along and was able to re-shoe Bull as soon as the trail leveled off. He's a great guy in every way.

Tuesday, July 30, 1985
Rough riding again today. We followed the Horseshoe Trail, heading to Christian Lake west of Fremont Trail, and then on to North Fork Lake.

We had onions, carrots, and potatoes with meat in a dutch oven tonight.

The horses are pooped. We'll layover tomorrow.

Wednesday, July 31, 1985
I walked all around the big North Fork Lake and found where the fish were. Al, A.M., Mert, and I went on horseback and tied up; Dusty and Super followed. I caught no fish; Mert caught his first two.

We read the entire book of Galatians tonight. I read Psalm 146 also.

Tomorrow is our last day. We'll ride to Big Sandy Campground where everyone's rigs are (except my pickup, which is still up at Togwotee Pass). Mert's daughter and son-in-law will meet us at Big Sandy.

It will be an interesting encounter, since Mert's son-in-law is Nick Coleman, a writer for the Minneapolis *Star and Tribune*. While I was governor, he wrote several columns chastising me for holding the annual Al Quie Trail Ride in Houston County, Minnesota. The ride went through the Beaver Creek Valley State Park where horses normally are not allowed. But my trail ride committee asked the Minnesota Department of Natural Resources for permission to ride there, and they got it.

It seemed to me that the Minneapolis paper was always on the lookout for any time a politician appeared to have an advantage over other citizens. And the DNR's granting us permission to ride through the park was, I guess–in the *Star and Tribune*'s mind, anyway–one of those times. My committee and I didn't think of this as an advantage for me; rather, it was a beautiful experience for 550 people to ride through a gorgeous scenic area on trails that people, and, in some cases, DNR vehicles, already traveled. And the locations we chose for crossing the stream that went through the park were, in every case, those used by DNR trucks in planting and/or maintaining trout.

Trout fishermen were disturbed that we would cross the stream, apparently thinking that doing so in two or three places would in some way ruin their fishing.

Well, Nick had a reputation for writing critical articles, and he did one on me. I was angry at the time, and I have to admit I harbored that anger for a while.

Nick showed up on the Beaver Creek Valley State Park ride, and he talked to me when our paths crossed. I soon found out that I could not sweet talk him into writing what to me would be a more balanced and sympathetic article. I remember his saying that he was not a member of the Republican Party or the Democratic Party, but the Cynical Party. When he said that, I knew there was no hope.

He then told me a little about his father-in-law Mert Schwarz (whom I didn't know yet), and Mert's horses. I offered to let Nick ride my horse, Spanish Bull, back to camp, and I'd walk back. He refused. He was too smart for that.

Now that I think about it, I probably had two motivations for offering him a ride on Bull. First of all, if I were nice to him, he might be nicer to me in whatever article he was about to write. Secondly, my devious nature (doesn't everyone have one harboring somewhere within?) had an ulterior motive. I'm the only one who has ever ridden Bull, and whenever I had previously let anyone else just get on, Bull would hump his back and act like he might buck them off. So I'd have the new rider dismount immediately. I wonder if I was thinking that if Nick had gotten on Bull (and his admission was that he was not a good rider), maybe Bull would buck him off on his head. (I guess I should not admit that such thoughts as this pass through my mind!)

After the Beaver Creek Valley ride, I got a letter from Trout Unlimited. The letter indicated that their organization had monitored us, and they admitted that our ride through the stream was not as bad as they had expected. But the letter also said three things did happen as a result of our being in the park.

First, we caused some turbidity in the water from a crossing that lasted for about an hour. Second, we had dislocated some insects. Third, we had caused some trauma among the trout. The offer of the olive branch was made, hoping we could work together in the future.

In response, I dictated a letter to them saying that I, too, had noticed the turbidity in the water, but because there was crushed rock at our crossings, I suggested there probably was less turbidity than when DNR trucks crossed before the rock was laid. (The DNR had laid the rock to protect the streams and to make it easier for trucks to cross in the future.)

Also, in my letter, I agreed that we had obviously disturbed some insects because a mosquito had gotten on my arm as I crossed the stream; he stayed there sucking blood for about a half mile before he got off. "Sadly," I cynically wrote, "I don't know if he found his way back home." And lastly, in the letter, I asked members of the organization–the next time they caught a trout–to please apologize to the fish for the trauma we had caused.

My secretary, Esther Allen, would not type the letter. She said she thought it better for me to leave these issues alone. I took her good advice and was later able to accept an offer for cooperation from the organization, which was a far better choice. But it sure was fun dictating the letter.

I did send a letter to Charles Bailey, editor of the Star and Tribune, the next year when we were planning a ride at Camp Ripley (a Minnesota National Guard training area). I asked the paper for permission to ride there, since they seemed to be the keeper of Minnesota purity. I wondered whether the paper would be worried that we might possibly mess up some tank tracks. (I think I still need the forgive-and-forget talent...)

Chuck wrote back saying he could see I got enjoyment in writing the letter. (A soft answer turneth away wrath...)

Well, that all happened over five years ago. Maybe I can get a fresh start with Nick tomorrow.

Thursday, August 1, 1985

As expected, Nick was waiting when we reached Big Sandy Camp Ground. After a little discussion, it was decided that Nick would be the one to drive me back to Togwotee Pass to get my pickup. It was a five-hour trip, one way.

On the way, I found out Nick is a very decent person. He has a keen interest in Native Americans. At his suggestion, I plan to read "Crazy Horse." He also recommended "Fool's Crow" and "The Lance and The Shield" by Utley, which I had read.

After he dropped me off, we each had the five-hour trip back to Big Sandy in each of our vehicles. It gave me a lot of time to mull over my good experience with Nick.

Our time together proves that, if a person will listen and be aware that each human being is created in the image of God and that there is good in everyone, we can respect each other even though the other may approach an issue in a different way. (It's also great to look at a person whose columns one reads or whom one sees on TV with a kinder perspective, as I now do with Nick.)

~ ~ ~

The road out of the Big Sandy was so rough that it took me more than an hour to go the first 10 miles with the trailer load of horses behind. And the country was so remote that I didn't find a phone to call Gretchen for 120 miles.

The stretch for next year's ride is the rest of the way through the Wind River Range and then across the Red Desert in Wyoming. I'm worried about the desert. It's a long way. Will I find water? Does one need a backup supply? Is there any grass? You can't pack enough feed for a 200-mile trip.

I haven't ridden Glacier yet, either. I want to go back and do that. Maybe next year I should go back to Montana and ride Glacier. That would give me time to find out more about the Red Desert before I cross it.

1986

Northwestern Montana

Glacier National Park
Ptarmigan Tunnel
Bob Marshall Wilderness
Benchmark
Chinese Wall
Danaher Meadows

CHAPTER TWELVE

'And what does Jesus say to you, Mother Theresa?'

Thursday, July 17, 1986

Dean Cates and A.M. Lips met me at 6:30 this morning at my home in Minnetonka. Gretchen and I moved to Minnetonka because of her loneliness in the country due to of my frequent absences as a result of my work as Area Director of Prison Fellowship of Minnesota/North Dakota with offices in the Billy Graham Evangelistic Association in Minneapolis. I hope she gets along well in this new home.

Dean, A.M. and I loaded the horses and gear and headed out for Medora about 7:30. I'm using Balou (a black Arabian belonging to Dean) as my pack horse this year, and, of course, Spanish Bull, for riding. A.M. is packing Dusty (I purchased him at the Butte stock-yards in 1983 for Doug Coe) and will ride his horse Goldie, which I have packed when A.M. is not along. Dean brought Jake and Catez, both Arabians.

I decided to go north and do Glacier this summer for two reasons. First of all, I am still leery of going through the Red Desert in Wyoming. Traveling without water fills me with anxiety. I haven't been able to find any books about rides through the area. If I could read about someone else's experience, that would help. I have stud-ied the maps in detail, but I just don't have the confidence yet.

Secondly, there are a number of people who have indicated they want to ride with me. So I want to take them somewhere where I feel certain. On the third leg of this year's trip, an eclectic group will be with me in the Scapegoat Wilderness, located south of the Bob Marshall Wilderness. It will be especially gratifying for me to ride in this area since, when I was in Congress, I was privileged to be co-author of the bill that established it as a wilderness area.

Many of the people joining us on the last leg of this trip, which will be in about three weeks, have one thing in common: we all have an active, informal connection in Jesus Christ, which some call the "fellowship."

Jerry Franz, who had to leave the ride last year to help the injured Frank Rawlins, will be joining us after I finish riding Glacier Park; Doug Coe will be back, and Martin Bostetter, a judge from Washington, D.C., who also was active in the "fellowship," also will be on the ride this year. And then there will be Jerry Potter, a friend from Minnesota who is a Bible study leader in prisons; Tom Pritchard, whose dad bought and sold horses in Northfield and from whom I'd bought a pony for Gretchen and my children while we were farming in the 1950s; and Tom's son Scott. The second leg will be in the Bob Marshall Wilderness with Mert Schwarz (who was on part of the 1984 ride); regulars Al Severson and Bob Cashin; and Claire Erickson, with his daughter Suzy.

Claire is a mule man from Grantsburg, Wisconsin. He has heart problems and wants to bring his daughter Suzy–a nurse–in case he has some problems on the trail. I've never had a woman along before and do not think kindly about the idea. But I agreed to it. I am concerned about modesty, safety, her ability and the impact on male interaction.

Right now, I just have Dean and A.M. with me. A few weeks ago, it looked like I might have only A.M. at the start of this ride. Al Severson couldn't promise to go because he thought workers in his company might go on strike. I figured I needed a third person, so I asked Dean if he could come. He'd been on the ride in '83, and we got along great.

However, his wife, Florence, had some medical problems, and she was leery of having Dean gone in case something would happen to her. So I went over to their home near Faribault to talk with them. Dean wasn't home when I arrived, but Florence invited me in, any-way.

After chatting a while, I told her I could understand why she didn't want Dean gone for two whole weeks. And then I added, "It probably wouldn't be so bad if he were gone for only one week." She agreed!

I had always planned to do Glacier in one week, so it might have been a little devious of me to first talk about how awful it would be to have Dean gone for two weeks–then suggest that one week might not be so bad.

When Dean came home, I said, "Hey! Florence said you could go to Glacier with me!"

"She did?!" he asked incredulously.

I didn't tell him how I had been schmoozing with her to get her to say yes. That is something I think wives usually do with their husbands, and here I was being the mischievous one!

~ ~ ~

A.M. rode with me today; he brought his C.B. along so we could talk with Dean along the way. We didn't use it enough to make it worth my buying one, though.

We got to Medora about 8:30 tonight, and after eating downtown, we put our horses in the rodeo corrals, and parked alongside. Lips and I are sleeping in the head of the trailer, and Dean is sleeping behind in his pickup.

Friday, July 18, 1986

A.M. snored so much last night that I had a hard time sleeping. I finally hit the side of the trailer to make enough noise to wake him. Then he'd quit. So each time he woke me with his snoring, I hit the side and he'd quit. Not a very restful night. Plus, at about 1:30 in the morning, a man who drove tourist buggy rides in Medora came by drunk. I heard him stamping around, and peeked out in time to see the shocked look on his face when Cates sat up and started talking to him.

Then–about 2 a.m.–there was thunder, lightning, and pouring rain. Woke up about 5 to see the stream bed near us (which was dry last night and which we drove across to get to the rodeo corrals) running with 4 feet of water. It receded some–enough for us to drive back across before we left.

We drove to Choteau, Montana, today on the east side of the Bob Marshall Wilderness area. Dean's pickup was giving us a lot of trouble. We think he must have picked up some bad gas. He and A.M. cleaned the gas line.

Dean said he knew a veterinarian–a Dr. Johnson–who would

probably show us where we could put our horses up for the night. She was an acquaintance of Dean in the Arabian horse business.

Dr. Johnson did give us a place to stay the night.

Saturday, July 19, 1986

Got up at 5 again, loaded our horses and were out by 5:30 for an early start for East Glacier. Just past Browning, we had more truck problems. Mine overheated and Dean's simply stopped. We took the carburetor out of Dean's truck and waited a while for my truck to cool down. Then we went back to Browning to get the carburetor fixed. The mechanics found a piece of plastic inside, removed it, and charged only $2.40 for parts and labor! We were amazed. People in mountain country are great.

But a shop owner seemed derogatory toward Indians. I noticed a three-pronged hook lying in the corner. "Where do you fish with this?" I asked as I picked it up to examine it.

"Nowhere," came his blunt answer. "It's illegal. Only the Indians are allowed to fish with that." I sensed resentment in his tone. We are in Blackfeet country here.

An awful lot of white people–even those who live among Indians–don't understand that Indians have all of our rights, plus extra ones because of treaty arrangements and certain sovereignties that apply to their nation alone.

Because of my Indian Education work in Congress, I developed sensitivity to the rights of Indians. But, then, I've always been interested in trying to understand Indians and their culture.

~ ~ ~

We finally got to East Glacier–much later than planned–and that's when the real hassles began.

I had talked to the superintendent and the assistant superintendent to get permission to ride in Glacier Park. But neither was around today, and no one who was there could give us permission to ride in the Park. So we drove on to the Cut Bank Ranger Station where we planned to drop 100 pounds of horse feed. We'll pick it up on the last leg of our Glacier ride. (We have to carry feed with us this year because the Park Service will not let horses graze in the Park. I brought pelleted all-in-one ration that I'd purchased from the Grain Terminal Association in Faribault. On this five-day ride, with six horses eating 12 pounds of feed a day, we need over 300 pounds of feed.)

Ranger Lamon Baker at Cut Bank was very helpful. He was willing to give us a permit to go all the way through the Park, but, he explained, there is a rule that requires a new permit every time you cross a highway. That would have meant going another day's ride to get that permit.

Lamon said he would check with other Rangers to see if they would agree to one permit, but the last supervisor–in the south end of the park–said, "No, we need to go by the rules." (In government bureaucracy there always seem to be people who are proud of their power and want to use it to the letter.)

We were, however, able to get all the permits we needed at Many Glacier office on our way north to the Canadian border. We also made another feed drop at Many Glacier.

We arrived at the Chief Mountain Customs Station on the border at about 8:30 p.m. We took everything we needed for the trip out of our rigs (left some kitchen gear behind) and packed our horses–Dusty and Catez carried panniers and Balou had my mantied pack boxes with groceries. We left our trailers and trucks in a parking lot in front of the station, and at 10 p.m. took off for Three-Mile Camp.

On the way, I'd realized I'd left my Maytag washer lid frying pan back in the truck. Rats. I've discovered that that lid makes the ideal fry pan. The size is perfect for a group of campers, and because it is made out of cast aluminum, it's lightweight and conducts the heat evenly.

I like these lids so much that I keep my eye out for them–especially when I'm in small towns that have Maytag dealers. When I find the washing machines, I buy the covers and give them to my camping friends.

Once when I was campaigning for Congress, I stopped in a Maytag store in West Concord, Minnesota. At first, the owner was pretty impressed that "the Congressman" would stop by. He was a little taken aback, however, when I asked whether he had any old washing machines sitting around–the kind with aluminum lids (you don't want the enamel ones!). He took me to the back of the store where five machines sat waiting for the junk pile. What a find! I ran my hand across each of the lids to make sure they were smooth and not pitted. I bought all five at $5 a piece!

That small business owner, I'm sure, thought that was the nuttiest sale he'd ever made: "Here the Congressman is in my store, and what does he do? He buys five washing machine covers!"[11]

~ ~ ~

We reached camp about 10:45 p.m., set up and started cooking before it got so dark we'd need flashlights. (This far north, it stays light a lot longer than in southern Minnesota!) We ate steak (prepared over an open fire), Cates' bread, and coffee and Tang.

Dean lost his camera on the trail from Chief Mountain Customs Station. We noticed it too late for us to go back and look for it. It's now 1 a.m., it is dark outside, and I'm going to bed. It's been a long day.

Sunday, July 20, 1986

We were back up at 5 a.m. For breakfast, we had pancakes, omelets and bacon, and then we packed up and were ready to hit the trail along the Belly River, heading south towards Ptarmigan Tunnel.

I looked up at a trail angling up the sheer side of a cliff that looked to be about 500 feet tall. The slight indentation on the rock face of the mountain seemed no wider than a line on a graph. I exclaimed, "That can't be our trail!" But it was.

I suspect it had been well maintained in earlier days when pack trains would travel to the chalets, but most chalets are no more, and weather had taken its toll. As we began our trek upward, I could see, in many places, where freezing and thawing over the years had caused parts of the outer edge to crumble and fall away. In some places, a small wall about a foot high had been laid on the outer edge to make it safer.

About three-fourths of the way up, we came upon a place where the trail had eroded so much that the outer part had fallen away, and, on the inside of the trail–which was a vertical rock wall–a large rock jutted straight out from the mountain. It appeared we could not get Balou past because his packs stuck out farther than the panniers on the other pack horses, and they rode higher. The trail was also too narrow for us to be able to turn around. Any slip would mean a fall to the death.

And, it was too narrow for me to dismount and take the packs off Balou. What to do?

I reminded Lips and Cates that they were more important than their horses, and that their saddle horses were more important than their pack horses.

Then I decided to move ahead. If perchance the pack on Balou would move back (as mantied loads can do, and panniers cannot) and then slide forward again, we would be all right.

I looked back at Balou. The ride so far had reduced some of his energy, and he looked quite calm. We proceeded. I looked back again to see Balou walking on the very edge of the trail, and the rock jutting out from the side of the mountain pushing his left pack over onto the top of his back. I held my breath, prepared to let go of the lead rope at any moment. The wrong move by Balou, and the left pack would slip over to the right side, throw him off balance, and to a likely plummet to his death.

I prayed. The pack slid back to its original position, and Balou was safe. I heaved a big sigh of relief, began breathing again, and silently thanked the Lord.

Then I watched as Dean and A.M. passed the same spot with their pack horses. All was well since their packs did not protrude as far out to the side.

The enormity of the risk, however, continues in my mind.

On another trail this afternoon, Dean had to get off his horse to adjust the pack on Catez. We noticed the tops of some small pine trees right alongside the trail, and as Dean got off his horse, he stepped back onto the pine tree tops–which turned out to be tall pines that had disguised themselves, growing up from the bottom of a drop off! As he dropped, there was no hesitation on Dean's part; he managed to grab his stirrup, and he pulled himself to safety.

~ ~ ~

We went through Ptarmigan Tunnel, which is about 150 feet long. A high wall of rock made it easier for the Park Service to cut a tunnel for passage through the mountain, rather than making a trail around or over the top. Huge steel doors are on each end. I wonder how they got that heavy steel up here.

Many mountain sheep were waiting for us when we left the tunnel on the south side. One of the men wondered out loud, "I'm curious to know if the Park Service planted them here for the benefit of tourists."

I told him, "Not likely." Except for a few hardy hikers, no one comes this high in the mountains. These were wild Bighorn Sheep, but since they are never hunted, they seem to have little fear of humans.

~ ~ ~

We must have climbed 2,000 feet from camp and then come down the same. We got over to the horse concession station near Many Glacier about 6 p.m. tonight. Yesterday, when we were in Many Glacier, we had asked the concession operator if we could keep our horses there overnight tonight, and hadn't gotten an answer. Today, the answer was "No." From what I could tell, it seemed the concession operator had gotten into an argument with his boss and was taking his anger out on us.

The park ranger tried to get a place for us to keep our horses, but again, his boss (the "all-by-the-rules" guy), said, "No. If the commercial horse concession said 'no,' then we say 'no,' also."

We did talk the concession owner into letting us use his car. We drove up to Chief Mountain Custom Station to get our rigs.

While there, Dean went into the station to inquire whether anyone had turned in his camera. We figured it would be a long shot if anyone found it, and if they did, that they would turn it in. But sure enough, a hiker had found his camera and left it at the station. We were amazed, and Dean, of course, was delighted.

We brought our trucks and trailers back to Many Glacier, went to the Lodge for dinner, left our horses in the trailers for overnight, and are spending the night ourselves in an old tourist attraction, Many Glacier Lodge–to the tune of $77 each (a single room for each of us).

Monday, July 21, 1986
We left the Lodge and went to get our horses, then rode back to the Lodge for breakfast. We were quite the sight for tourists as we tied our three saddle horses and three pack horses to the old hitch rails that probably hadn't been used for some 60 years.

The dude riders from the concession had trouble getting their horses to go past ours. They apparently were bothered by different horses and odd-shaped ones (because of the packs).

~ ~ ~

We put bells on our horses today when we came to huckleberry bushes–so we would not surprise any Grizzlies. One of the bells was a goat bell that I bought in Switzerland. It is cast brass and has a most melodic tone.

In the latter part of the '60s, when I was a delegate to the International Labor Organization meeting in Geneva, I had the opportunity to do some climbing in the Swiss Alps. Some of the same flowers (like Dog Tooth Violets, sometimes called Glacier Lily) that I saw in the mountains of Switzerland I am now seeing here in Montana. What a joy!

One thing (of many) that these rides are teaching me is to appreciate the flowers. For the first time in my life, I'm learning their names. I used to know only a geranium. Now the flowers are becoming friends of mine because they have names and I remember them.

I am becoming knowledgeable about them, too, and can share this information with others. When I do, I always use their names. It's sort of like introducing people to my friends.

When I go past a low, swampy area and see Elephant Head flowers, I'm thinking, "What a beauty you are; what a unique thing you are; you bear the symbol of the Republican Party!" In jest, I wonder if any party members know there is a symbol of them in this glorious spot!

But do I talk to the flowers? No. I am just with them.

It's a little like how I view my communication with Gretchen. She likes to have me with her and paying attention to her and communicating with her. I, on the other hand, feel like I am with Gretchen whenever I'm anywhere in the vicinity.

I guess I have more of an Indian way about me. It's like the story of an Indian in pioneer times who said to a settler, "Had a great visit with you."

"When were you over?" asked the settler.

"Last Monday."

"Where were you?"

"We just sat against the wall of your house and communed with you from there."

"I didn't even know you were there."

"Oh, we never said a word. We were just in your presence."

That's the way I am with the flowers. I don't talk to them. I am just among them.

For the same reason, I found myself resonating with the response Mother Theresa gave during an interview with Dan Rather. "What do you say to God when you pray?" Rather asked. Her simple answer was, "I don't say anything; I just listen."

After Rather cleared his throat, he asked, "Well, what does Jesus say to you?" And Mother Theresa answered, "Oh, He doesn't say anything, either. He just listens."

Communication without words.

CHAPTER THIRTEEN

The need for a horse whisperer

We tried again to feed pellets to the horses when we stopped for lunch at Piegan Pass. They still don't want much to eat. We're carrying enough for them to eat about 12 pounds a day; instead, they go through about 9. That means we're needlessly carrying a lot of extra weight.

The view of the jutting mountain peaks and the valleys dropping below is breathtaking. Today we saw more Bighorn sheep that don't seem to be bothered by us–they simply look up, stare a while, and then go back to grazing. And there is still a lot of snow at the high elevations. I washed my hands in it today.

After lunch, we traveled down a grade that dropped about 2,000 feet, and then it went straight up again. We crossed "Going to the Sun" Highway, passed Deadwood Falls (saw lots of swirl holes in the rocks), and passed Gunsight Lake–all on our way to our designated campsite, which, we were told, would be "right after the river takes a loop to the right." We came upon the loop, but never saw a campsite, so we continued.

Eventually, we decided to backtrack to the loop. I realized then that the campsite was on the *other* side of the river.

Lips refused to cross since the river looked deep. He evidently remembered last year's experience at Yellowstone when he was in danger of being swept downstream. I thought Lips would maybe cross if he didn't have a pack horse to think about. So I took his pack horse, Dusty, with me, knowing Dusty would follow Bull.

The bank was more than three feet high and the water was rushing, but Bull was not afraid. With the lead rope from Lips' pack horse in my hand, I nudged Bull; he jumped off the bank into the water and Dusty followed, just as I figured. I had to hold my feet up to keep from getting wet in the river. On the other side, I tied up Dusty and went back with Bull to help the others.

Balou, who hates water, was running back and forth along the bank in a panic and obviously scared to jump in.

Cates, riding Catez, tried to go down the bank into the river, but his pack horse, Jake, wouldn't budge. So I let Cates ride Bull, and I climbed on Catez. He went over the bank and into the water with no problem, and Jake followed.

Now, seeing it was entirely possible to cross the river without incident, Lips allowed his horse Goldie to jump in the river and come across to the campsite.

That left Balou. I rode back to the other side on Bull and tried to get Balou to follow me without leading. I thought he would not want to be the only one left. I did get him to stand behind Bull and me without a problem; I nudged Bull, who leapt over the bank into the river. But Balou got excited, and took off down the trail at a gallop. I was concerned that he might throw his pack to one side and have a wreck, but thankfully everything stayed in place as I watched him race back and forth.

Since I was already in the river, I proceeded to the camp side. When I got there, I could see that Balou was back at the opposite river bank, still pacing. Maybe he would come across, I thought, if he didn't have a pack on. So I quickly removed the pack from Dusty and led him back through the water. Then I transferred Balou's pack to Dusty and led Dusty back across the river, thinking Balou would now follow. Still no luck. Enough of this. I left him all alone on the opposite side as we got things ready for camp and supper.

The tarp filled the only space of sand there was. There is little grass, but we aren't supposed to graze in Glacier, anyway. The rest of the campsite consists of stones.

Our supper was ham patties, mashed potatoes, corn, and canned peaches.

After supper, I decided I'd try once more to get Balou to cross the river. I rode Bull back through the water to where he was still standing on the bank. After feeding him some pellets, I stacked two piles of logs on either side of where we were standing on the river bank, hoping these would keep him from running back and forth. I put a lead rope on Balou, positioned him close to Bull's right hip, and inched toward the river bank. When Bull jumped off the bank and Balou began to brace himself, I spurred Bull on and jerked Balou into the water. Success!

Arabian horses are notorious for not wanting to go across water. Cates once told me about a time that Balou refused to go across a creek for him. So he got off, tied a long rope to Balou, and waded through the creek himself. Then he pulled on the rope to get Balou to come across. Balou was conflicted. He'd been taught to lead, and wanted to obey Dean's tug on the rope, yet he didn't want to cross that water. What was he to do? In resolution, he just tucked right up and leaped across the creek–so high that he wouldn't have to touch the water–and he landed nearly on top of Dean.

Some people might think, "What a mean horse!" But from the horse's perspective, going through the water was a dangerous proposition; he saw a safe place on the other side; he saw his owner standing there safely; he just thought, "I'm going *there*."

Dean told me about another time when Balou kicked him in the head; and another, when he started bucking and bucked right through a board fence. Dean had wanted to sell Balou then (a black Arabian gelding like Balou is especially rare and valuable), but Dean knew he'd never be able to sell him in this lack-of-control condition.

It was then that I offered to take Balou for a while. I like horses that are a challenge to me. I told Dean I'd take Balou on one of my Divide trips and make a gentleman out of him. And here we are.

But before bringing him on this ride, I knew I first needed to break him of a bad habit: refusing to let me catch him. Can't have that in the mountains.

So one day I took off about 2 o'clock, telling Gretchen I might not be back for supper. I picked up Balou from Dean and took him out to my pasture. When I let him loose, he ran off to the other end of the pasture. I started walking toward him, making the mistake of stretching my hand out in a gesture of friendliness. As I approached this independent thinker, he snorted and took off in the opposite direction–going as fast as he could, as far as he could.

I walked to the middle of the pasture, sat down in the grass and waited. It was a good thing I told Gretchen not to hold supper for me.

~ ~ ~

Balou stared at me for a while. He paced back and forth along the fence-still as far away from me as he could get.

An hour passed. I waited. The sun beat down.

Balou grazed with one eye on me and one in the distance.

I waited some more. Then Balou started walking around the perimeter of the pasture, perhaps to get a look at me from the back side. I didn't move.

Cautiously, he started to edge a little closer to me, but then he stopped. Thinking better, he bolted once again to the farthest corner of the pasture.

I picked a piece of grass and played with it in my fingers as I waited.

Balou paced along the fence. Then he calmed down and started to graze, still keeping an eye on me.

I waited.

Occasionally Balou would paw at the ground and snort, letting me know he was determined to be the victor in this match.

More time passed. The heat of the day began to let up as the sun approached the horizon. I waited.

With his eyes intent on me, Balou inched away from the fence. He grazed some more, paced a little, then grazed and inched closer—all the time keeping one eye on me. I waited.

The sun set. And I waited.

At 10 o'clock, our battle ended. I remained quiet and still as Balou approached. He paused, then came closer, all the while looking at me with both eyes. When he got next to me, I didn't move; I let him sniff me. When he seemed done, I reached up to pet his nose. Gently I rubbed his head, and eventually reached up to his halter. I got up slowly and rubbed him all over. Then I led him home. From then on, he was easy to catch.

And there was one other thing I needed to teach Balou before bringing him on this ride: how to hobble. Usually, I do this by taking the horse out to pasture, and when he is grazing, I will hobble his feet. The horse generally will wiggle around some, but because he is thinking about eating, he won't pay much attention, and he soon becomes accustomed to the hobbles.

The day after teaching him to be caught, I took Balou back out to pasture, and, as he ate, I hobbled him. All of a sudden he realized he couldn't move. He jumped up and exploded in the air. Then he took off out of the pasture, over the hill and off into the distance. Full-bore with his hobbles holding his front hooves less than a foot apart!

I ran to the top of the hill and watched him rush down the road. He tore past an empty farmstead and disappeared behind it. Then he circled it, and headed back, coming through a soybean field. Finally, he gave up and just stood there. I walked down to him, petted him all over, lifted up his feet, took off his hobbles and led him home. Ever since, I've had no problem hobbling him.

~ ~ ~

There are no trees at this campsite for tying up the horses. I always teach people to tie their horses at eye level or above, but we weren't able to do that here. We tied the horses to some logs we had dragged ashore from a sandbar, where they had lodged. The horses are spending the night standing on stones. Our tents are taking up the only soft space where horses could comfortably stand. I don't like it if my horses can't rest comfortably, but they can sleep standing up; we humans need to lie down for sleep.

Tuesday, July 22, 1986

Lips didn't snore last night. Well, maybe he did and I just didn't hear it. I was wearing earplugs.

To get back to the trail this morning, we had to cross the deep river again, and jump up the bank. Thankfully, the horses cooperated, and we managed without incident.

The climb this morning was spectacular, but the trail was not good. Alders were growing haphazardly, reaching into and growing up in the trail's path. Below, we could see Lake St. Mary where an excursion boat slowed when the passengers saw us traveling the mountainside. I wonder what the people on board were thinking.

We tried to make Red Eagle Lake by noon but didn't, so we stopped and ate by a stream. We had cheese and sausage sandwiches, apples, and Snicker bars.

Coming off Triple Divide Pass, our narrow trail had a sheer wall rising on our right and a sheer drop on the left. I took many pictures as the others went ahead.

~ ~ ~

We reached our camp at Atlantic Creek at 8:30 tonight. The camp is small. Two young women were already here when we arrived. The tent area is on one side of the trail, and we have to do our cooking on the other.

The Forest Service had built a scaffold for campers to tie up food so the bears wouldn't get at it. I threw a rope over the bar and went to get the second pannier. On the way back, I saw Dean and A.M. pull the first pack up and begin to wrap the rope around a tree. I didn't know if he knew which knot would hold, so I walked over to where he was working the rope, took it from him and tied a knot to bind it.

I wished I hadn't.

I could tell by Dean's body language, as he walked away, that he was miffed. Usually I let the guys try, and then I help if they need it. Learn by experience, I always say. Usually. For some reason, I quit the teaching mode and just went and did it myself this time. Sometimes I can be so insensitive. I've got to let people do things and make their own mistakes–if they are going to make them at all. Many times they are only doing it differently, and sometimes even better.

We fixed supper in the dark tonight. In the valley, the dark comes quicker.

Friday, July 23, 1986

Balou had a bit of a sore back when I checked him this morning. When I take the saddles off at night and when I curry the horses in the morning I run my fingers along their withers and along their backs, and I press on their loins to see if there is any soreness or tenderness. We put the sawbuck on Balou today-it should be a little more comfortable as it rides a little farther back than the decker saddle[12].

Another way I give the pack horses a break is to ride them and pack our riding horses. I taught Bull to carry a pack a long time ago in case I ever needed him for that.

We had originally planned to go into Cut Bank Ranger Station today to get more horse feed, but we missed the turn. Instead, we went up Pitamakan Pass. It didn't matter because, since the horses aren't eating like we thought, we have plenty of feed.

We made the final climb to the top at Cut Bank Pass–8,296 feet. I wanted to make this climb because I knew if I didn't, I'd always wonder what was on the other side. It was breathtaking. Going down was the steepest descent we've had, and, necessarily so–there were many switchbacks. At the bottom, two trees were across the trail. Bull and Balou went over them like troopers. The others followed.

I went up Pitamakan Mountain myself, since the others seemed anxious to get to move on. Again, spectacular! I saw deer, Bighorn sheep, and mountain goats. The trail down was steep and treacherous. No place for the easily frightened!

~ ~ ~

We're spending the afternoon in Oldman's Camp. There is a hitch rail for eight head of horses, a cook area, and a tenting area. We're sharing the cook area with two pairs of other campers. One set is from St. Paul; the other, Wisconsin.

People who exert themselves to hike in the Glacier area are wonderful. They seem to have a lot of environmental knowledge, care about their surroundings, and are careful to follow the instructions of the Park Service.

This is a great place for resting and writing in my journal while someone else (Cates) does the fishing and makes sure the stock are all right. Continuous riding covers ground, but the relaxed time together is great.

A.M. Lips amazes me. He's 67 years old, and this isn't the first time he's spent his birthday out here rather than being home with his wife, Lorraine. (It bothers me some, that Gretchen has to celebrate her birthday alone, too–every August 4.) A.M. also has a weak left hand, but rides and handles chores like the rest. There could be no better partner.

I braided some rope this afternoon, visited with A.M., and took in the fantastic sight–the 1,500-foot mountain wall that we came down early this afternoon. It stretches 180 degrees from left to right in front of us.

These mountains surely bring out the beauty, majesty, and challenge of God's creation. They make me want to live with more respect for nature.

Aunt Caroline would have been impressed. What joy it would be to tell her about this. She passed away in 1979.

And God is creator of it all. There are skeptics who, when I point out this beauty, will quickly note the existence of evil in this world, as well. Sure, God allows the bad, but I don't believe He causes it. I believe all things–good and bad–work together for the good of those who are called according to God's purpose.

We so often forget God and don't appreciate Him. We ignore the fact that we are created in His image and therefore have Him in us. We only have to believe in His son Jesus Christ, whom He sent as a substitute for our sins–the sins of all of us. He wants us back again and wants us to believe that He is God, that Jesus the Christ is His

Son, and that His Holy Spirit is in those who believe. The Kingdom of God is in us. Beauty and blessing is outside of us; His holiness, inside us. What a blessing! Why do some people enjoy this so much and others ignore it?

~ ~ ~

For supper tonight, we had corned beef, tomatoes, mashed potatoes, blueberry cobbler, and soup.

Food has been hung up to keep away from the bears, and all have gone to bed–the day has been strenuous, and the mountain air invigorating. It's also raining–that leads to sleep, too.

I've taken cover under a plastic tarp, which is not as good for listening to rain as is a tin roof, but it's close.

Unfortunately, the mosquitoes also have taken cover under this tarp and are trying to get their supper. Some, however, are in the process of meeting their deaths. My theory is to let them eat a little so they become less suspecting. Then I nail 'em.

A beautiful Beargrass flower is looking right at me. We are at the elevation where they are in full bloom.

Gretchen is in the middle of her week at Holden Village near Chalen, Washington. It's an old mining camp, now owned and operated by the Lutheran Church, high in the mountains. You have to take a 45-mile boat ride to get there. There are few lakes deeper than Lake Chalen, especially at such a high elevation.

Gretchen is there with an artist friend, Dorothy Divers. They will also spend time at the Grunewald Guild (another art camp) in Leavenworth, Wash., before visiting Fred and Mindy in Butte.

Saturday, July 24, 1986

Lips was snoring again last night. I woke him, and 10 seconds later he was snoring again. He turned on his side, but that didn't help. I woke him again, and he sat up and said, "I guess I'll just have to stay awake."

Fifteen seconds later he was snoring again.

On a recent night when he was snoring loudly, I called out three times to Cates (who was sleeping next to him) to wake him. Not able to rouse Cates, I wondered if there was something wrong. I turned on the flashlight and found Cates sleeping with both ear plugs lodged in his ears and his fingers holding the plugs tight. I tried it, and it works. I'm going to get my own set of earplugs.

~ ~ ~

Lips and Cates took down the tent this morning while I cooked breakfast. The dried eggs were terrible. I spit them out. The pancakes weren't very good, either. Maybe it was the water.

We left camp at 8:30 and rode down Dry Fork to Two Medicine Camp Ground where we got directions to East Glacier via Mt. Henry.

The directions took us up a very rugged trail with sharp switch-backs and at times a steep stair-like climb over rocks. This would be a terrifying climb if alone. I wondered for a few moments, as the climb got more difficult, if it really was a horse trail, or if it was intended only for backpackers and climbers on foot. The wind blew so hard that we had to hold our hats in one hand.

We made it to the top and lunched with a spectacular view of East Glacier and the Two Medicine River, where we started in 1983.

The decline was steep but not as rough as our ascent.

When we got to the horse concession in East Glacier, we tied up, removed the packs, and left Lips to watch the horses while Dean and I went to the motel to get three rooms (at $25 each) and located corrals for the horses. We talked the bell captain into giving us a ride up to Many Glacier to pick up our rigs. We left at 4 p.m. and returned at 7:15, had dinner, and then went to our rooms.

I have great satisfaction in completing the ride through Glacier National Park. And we did it in less than a week—just as I promised Dean's wife, Florence. He'll be leaving us tomorrow, and A.M. and I will drive down to Augusta to meet those who will be joining us on the next leg of the trip: Mert Schwarz, Al Severson, Bob Cashin, Claire Erickson and Suzy Erickson.

CHAPTER FOURTEEN

A woman on the ride

Sunday, July 25, 1986

I'm usually the early riser, but A.M. woke me up this morning! We went to the corrals of the horse concession, put feed in buckets in the trailer, put saddles and hay in the back of the pickup, hooked up the trailer, and left about 6:30 to go down to Augusta.

We had a big breakfast in Choteau, and then we parted company with Dean, who is making a stop to visit Jim Wempner at his ranch in Big Timber before driving back to Minnesota.

Jim and I became friends when I was in Washington. He represented western state bankers, and while I wasn't on the Banking Committee, we nonetheless discovered each other through mutual friends. We hit it off because of our similar interest: love of the West.

A.M. and I swung through Fairfield to pick up the pad and cinch that I'd ordered from Blue Star Canvas in Missoula and requested to have shipped to the Fairfield Post Office. Now, while I don't want to make a statement about the competency of postal workers in general, I will say that the three who work in the Fairfield office leave a little to be desired. They first said my package had not arrived; then they changed their story to say it had arrived, but they sent it back. They claimed it "had the wrong address," even though the package had a note that said, "Please hold for pick up." I'll just have to figure out another way to get the pad and cinch.

My pickup was heating up badly, so when we got to Augusta, we parked the trailer under shade and drove over to Great Falls for a fan clutch. After much trouble, we finally found one (plus a couple of wrenches needed for proper installation). A.M., the mechanic and former auto parts store owner, installed it.

Back in Augusta, we hooked up the trailer about 4 p.m.) and drove up to Benchmark Trailhead where we met Mert, who'd gotten there about noon.

After supper in Augusta, A.M. and I drove to Lincoln where I'm staying the night with son Dan, his wife, Penny Jo, and daughters, Brooke and Kari. A.M. is over at the Sportsman's Motel.

Monday, July 26, 1986

Up at 6 a.m. Worked out the menus for the next several days. Looks like there won't be quite enough Bisquick, but plenty of frozen meat which I'd purchased at the grocery store in Lincoln. We headed for Augusta about 11 o'clock, and then on to the Benchmark Trailhead to meet the others who'd all arrived–Claire Erickson and his daughter, Suzy, Bob Cashin, and A.M. Lips. Al Severson, I learned, couldn't come because of the potential strike at his company.

We had steak, potatoes, carrots, onions, lettuce, blue cheese dressing, and graham crackers for dinner, and then got everything in order to take off tomorrow morning.

Tuesday, July 27, 1986

I got up at 5 because I was having trouble sleeping. Even though A.M. was in the tent and I was outside under a tarp, his snoring still kept me awake.

We set out at 9:30, and soon noticed Balou's lash rope loosening. I stopped to tighten the cinch, but it broke. So I told the others to go on ahead while I rode the mile back to the trailer to get a couple cinches off another saddle. Then I had to ride fast to catch up to everyone.

We covered 15 miles today and reached Glenn Creek Camp on the Sun River by 4 p.m. Mert's horse is fast, and the mules move fast, too.

Claire, I'm learning, is an excellent mule man. Suzy, his daughter, is 28 and getting married in about two months. While not an experienced rider in the mountains, she does very well. I had wondered what it would be like to have a woman along on the ride, thinking she wouldn't be able to keep up. I was wrong.

Mert, Cashin, and A.M. are all good horsemen. Cashin brings a lot of humor to the ride. I am concerned about A.M. getting his food on time–important for a diabetic.

We saw many horses along the trail today–packers with strings of mules, and dudes and fishermen. And I saw a most beautiful white tail buck with a big rack.

Weather was a bit warm, but otherwise it was a terrific day. We have a grand view across the Sun River with beautiful trees to the west.

We ate steak, potatoes, corn, and sauce made from dried fruit for supper.

Wednesday, July 28, 1986

Things went together well this morning. We got out of camp around 8:30 with all packs staying in place. We went up the North Fork of the Sun River until we reached Moose Creek. We decided to ride along it instead of following the Sun River to Gates Park and then up to Spotted Bear Pass and Larch Hill.

When we came from Two Medicine north of here and just south of Glacier in 1983, we camped at a site east of the falls. A deer came into our camp just as in '83.

As I write, I hear the others near the campfire tonight telling stories about seeing big game.

Thursday, July 29, 1986

Got up at 5:30, let the horses out and waited a little before making breakfast–bacon, eggs, pancakes. Sometimes I feel like I'm a short-order cook. Cashin, Lips, and Suzy want only one egg, and they all like them broken and hard. Claire likes his unbroken and hard since he gives his yolks away. Mert is now a two-egger. He and I are the over-easy guys.

Bull is lame today–probably because I have been tethering him at night. He does not tether well. Since today was a layover day, I let him rest, and I rode Dusty instead.

We rode out at 8:30 to follow the Chinese Wall. On the way, we saw a large herd of elk, just like three years ago. No one had binoculars, so Claire went back to get his. As we moved over the hill, closer to the Wall, we saw a goat on top. Later we saw three more, and on the way back, we saw another lower down; so 45 elk and five or six goats made it a grand day.

My horses do well and behave themselves; other horses do a lot of chasing around. Claire's four mules do well, also. For supper we ate four pounds of hamburger, three onions, a third of a head of cabbage, and salad seasoning all mixed together.

We again sat around the campfire tonight, sharing stories and ideas.

At the beginning of this year I became Area Director for Prison Fellowship Ministries in Minnesota and North Dakota, and since Schwarz is a former sheriff, some of the talk turned to jails, inmates, and criminal justice. There are some along on this ride who wonder whether criminals ought not to be put in jail and kept out of the way. Aren't they second class citizens? Are they redeemable?

Mert also told us about a lay pastor in Waseca, Minnesota, who used to visit the prisoners in his jail. "There was a time," he said, "when a couple of these prisoners came to know Jesus as a result of this pastor's ministry, and these prisoners wanted to be baptized."

Since this pastor was of the theology that baptism must be by immersion, Mert said he went and got a horse tank, put it in the back of his pickup truck, brought it to the jail, filled it with water, and the pastor immersed the guys right there.

We also exchanged our beliefs about horses and mules, trying to convince one another that "our way of thinking" is the better way. Horsemen like horses; mule men (like Claire) like mules. Each talks with pride about the characteristics of the animals we've owned–mules, Appaloosas, Arabians, Quarter Horses. All of us have special relationships with our animals and communicate with them in different ways.

I say that when you're on your horse, you're always communicating with him. Mostly when you aren't talking. Sometimes you do a lousy job, and sometimes you do well.

It's the same way with our lives. We are always witnessing. Sometimes for Christ and sometimes against Him, whether we are talking or not. It's easier for me to witness with my actions than my words. I have to work really hard at talking about my relationship with Christ. I read the Bible and try to associate with people who are good at expressing their faith. That helps. I feel sorry for us Norwegians. We don't articulate very well about our faith.

We had a lot of fun around the campfire teasing Suzy, too. With a name like Erickson, why would she want to become a Johnson?

The sky is clear, the air is crisp–a sign it will be cold tonight.

Friday, July 30, 1986

The water in our buckets was frozen when we got up at 5:30 this morning. The layer of ice melted, though, as soon as the sun was up.

We took off at 9:30, and saw a man and woman backpacking near the Chinese Wall. Sometimes I wish I'd taken time to climb the Chinese Wall yesterday. But when you've got many days' ride ahead of you, you don't want to wear yourself out.

We also saw the elk herd again. It's always a great thrill every time we see these majestic elk.

A new trail has replaced much of what we used in '83. We climbed to Cliff Mountain, then down 2,000 feet to Pine Creek, then up and down to Indian Point Ranger Station. The meadow was posted for renovation so we went on three to four more miles and camped where there was some grass at least for grazing.

'Mike caught up to them...but his horse galloped back with the mule in tow, strewing the pack along the way.' July 21, 1983. (Chapter 4)

Saturday, July 31, 1986

As I made breakfast this morning, I kept my eye on Bull, since all the horses had been turned out overnight. The horses ate all the grass last evening, so there was slim pickin's for them this morning.

We had just started the pancakes when Claire noticed his mules were missing. He ate his pancakes and then left on Goldie–via the backtrail–to see if he could find his mules. Mert's and Cashin's horses were gone, too.

As soon as I ate my four pancakes, three eggs, and three slices of bacon, I saddled Bull and checked the two trails going south just in case the horses had gone that way. Then I headed for the backtrail, too. About a quarter mile out, I met Cashin's horses who were on the way back to camp. I found out later that Claire had met them and two of his mules about one and a half miles beyond that. He'd tied up his mules and had sent Cashin's horses back to camp, as he rode on in search of Mert's horses.

When I caught up to Claire, we rode together to Indian Point Ranger Station, where we found Schwarz' horses. We took them with us and went back and untied the rest of the mules and returned to camp with all the animals.

I find it very interesting how horses will follow their tracks from previous travel to arrive back at a destination, even if it means they have to travel much farther. When I tracked Mert's horses out of a meadow and up to the ranger cabin corrals, I saw that his horses had followed their tracks perfectly from the day before.

Yesterday, when we were in the same area, we missed the trail as it turned right in the meadow. Instead, we rode straight across the meadow to a stream. We traveled along the stream for a ways, realized we still weren't where we wanted to be, and turned into the meadow again, but traveling a different route. We probably had gone 50 yards along the stream when we turned and found the trail we'd missed about a quarter mile back at the edge of the meadow.

Today, instead of cutting right across those 50 yards, Schwarz' horses made the same half-mile loop across the meadow to the stream and then back into the meadow until they got back to the trail.

Horses aren't hound dogs, but they have a fantastic memory for stuff around them.

We got a late start (10 a.m.) because of having to search for the horses this morning. We got to the Basin Ranger Station at 4 p.m. and

A woman on the ride

decided to camp at a spot where the Blackfeet Indians and Flatheads had a memorable battle in the last century.

Sunday, August 1, 1986

We got out of camp this morning at 9:30 and arrived at Danaher Meadows at noon. I'd been looking forward to coming back to this camp since going past it on the '83 ride. The camp site I wanted was already taken, so we made camp just down from the guard station.

Three years ago, we came into the camp from the north. Back then, Doug Coe and I were riding close to each other; and Bill Starr, Jon Coe, my son, Ben, and our wrangler, Jeff Hoeffner, were further back. It was about noon. As our eyes took in the view, I remember thinking it was one of the most beautiful sights I have ever seen. Doug seemed to share the feeling.

The sun was shining warm on our faces, a warm breeze blew across the rich, green meadow grasses, and big trout were swimming in the stream. I knew it would have been a great place to camp, but since it was noon, we had to press on. We could not stop in the middle of the day.

And so, for three years, I have reminisced about this spot, remembering it to be as close as one gets to heaven. At the time, Doug and I both talked of bringing Jan and Gretchen here to share this beautiful heaven-like experience. I realize that was fantasy.

Today, as we approached the same spot, I looked out over the meadow–and the feeling was different. Why was this? Maybe because this time we came two weeks later in the year. It was a bit cloudy, the grass was brownish due to lack of rain. We could see no fish in the stream.

It might be that the topic of Doug's and my conversation three years ago was what made the difference. Sharing with a brother in Christ about the working of the Lord gives one a different perspective, and that may be what made this place look so beautiful back then.

Who knows?

I am reminded of the time our family first returned to the farm in 1959 after having moved all of our belongings to our new home in Silver Spring, Maryland, the Christmas before. The farmhouse sunroom had benches that stretched beneath the windows, and the benches themselves had lids that disguised the storage area inside. As soon as the farmhouse door was opened, our three-year-old Joel raced with excitement to those benches where his toys had been kept.

Nothing was there. And I'll never forget the sheer look of disappointment and bafflement on his face as he looked at me beseechingly. It's that same disappointment I felt today.

~ ~ ~

The stream next to the Danaher Meadow was small coming out of the mountain, so we drank right from it this afternoon. And then, this evening, when Bob went to get water from the stream, he came back empty-handed, saying, "You won't believe this, but there is no water in the stream!"

We didn't believe it, so we all went to look. He was right–there was no water. We then went about three-fourths of a mile upstream, where we found the water was still running. Strange.

I am reminded of Aunt Caroline's description of the rushing water falls she experienced one afternoon, and, upon returning to the same spot the next morning, found no water cascading down the rocks. In her experience, however, I'm guessing the cause was related to cold temperatures and freezing water upstream. In our situation, I wonder if the stream is dry because the water evaporates before it gets down stream.

Monday, August 2, 1986

To our surprise, we found water running again in the stream by our camp this morning. For breakfast today we had pork chops with pancakes.

On this layover day, I took a long walk in the morning as the others slept, and then we all explored the abandoned ranch site, imagining the Danaher brothers horse ranching here. I found where the house must have been located and also the bunkhouse. Parts of horse mowers and dump rakes were found. The location of one group of mower parts indicated it must have been smashed by a runaway team. I understand these brothers raised oats as well to feed the horses. Everything had to be packed over the mountains to make this ranching operation work.

In the afternoon we goofed off, I slept some and then went for a ride on our pack animals. I rode Balou. He was no pleasure. His stride is too short, he has a rough trot, he kept shying from objects, he wouldn't step out in the lead, and he wouldn't cross the stream unless following another horse. Thank goodness I have Bull.

Tuesday, August 3, 1986

I heard Balou (who was tied) whinnying in the middle of the night last night. When I got up this morning I knew why. He had been watching Dusty and some of the other horses leave camp. So I saddled Balou and went after them. Thankfully, they were only a hundred yards away, obscured by some trees.

It was cloudy and warmer this morning with a little red in the sky, which told me we'd likely have bad weather today. We made sure we had our raincoats out when we rode off.

There were thunder showers around all day, but none hit us hard.

We went up Dry Fork Pass, and then turned left on Dry Fork Trail. It was very narrow with trees on both sides, evidently not intended for a pack string. Our pack animals at first tried to miss the trees, but after a while, they just gave up and kept banging their packs against the trees.

This trail brought us near and just under Flint Mountain, which we skirted. The ascent was terribly steep, and we took quite a while getting through it. Near the top of our climb, with Flint Mountain virtually hanging over us, I (in the lead) came upon a huge, sliver-tipped Grizzly bear on the trail about 200 feet ahead.

The wind was fairly strong in our direction, so he apparently had not caught our scent. If he did hear us, he probably thought the sound came from elk. So there he stood. Staring at us. But not for long. He turned and ran off with speedy, lumbering strides.

None of the others had seen him, but when we arrived at the spot where he had been, we found the biggest pile of bear scat I had ever seen. Either we came upon him at the moment he was doing his "morning's morning," or else seeing us scared it out of him!

~ ~ ~

When we finally arrived at the top of our climb, I felt like we were on top of the world. We stopped to let everybody rest. Mert was pooped and worried about his horses after that strenuous climb.

During this break, Bob and A.M. seemed to be really enjoying themselves, talking together. Claire and Suzy seem to fit in well with this mountain travel. She is a joy to have along. I guess this life doesn't need to be restricted to just men after all.

After a bit, we went on to Cabin Creek. We're making camp on the side of the mountain tonight.

CHAPTER FIFTEEN

Dissension in the ranks

Wednesday, August 4, 1986

Woke without a good night's rest this morning, after side-hill sleeping all night. Sometimes it is impossible to find a flat place to camp. I also noticed the air seemed warmer than usual (which simply means the water in our buckets wasn't frozen).

We left Cabin Creek at 9 a.m. By noon we'd gone over the top of the Divide by Scapegoat Mountain. It's a terrific view; we saw many elk on this ridge. After lunch, while the others rested, I tried to climb higher on foot, but could not make it–too steep and the rocks were crumbly. In fact, descending was more difficult than climbing up. When I returned, the others–refreshed from their rest–expressed worry about my climbing.

We mounted, and took a steep decline to the Debrota River.

Over Labor Day weekend in 1970, I had come off Scapegoat in this vicinity when son, Fred, and I rode with Cecil Garland. Today, I looked for the trail we'd been on back then but couldn't find it. I guess, after 16 years, I should figure it would be difficult to find. I remember, though, that it was a trail that had a lot of trees in the way. In fact, I had to cut a tree down in order to get Cecil's pack string through.

We continued on, and about three miles farther, I saw a small tree lying across the trail. It was then I realized we were on the same trail. This was the same tree I'd cut those 16 years before! It had weathered over the years, but I knew it was the same tree because of the way I'd cut it, the angle of the ax marks that were on it, the way it fell.

This was not like finding evidence of pre-historic man, but was nonetheless thought-provoking for me.

When I come upon a felled tree and can count its more than 400 rings, I think of the events that occurred during its life. Likewise, when I am at an abandoned mine or cabin or campsite, I try to imagine what the person or persons were like who left the things I am able to observe.

Seeing this tree across the trail was like witnessing an old site, and the experience of 1970 came back to me as I recalled what Fred, Cecil and I had done.

~ ~ ~

We turned on the Tobacco Valley Trail going east and then followed the White Tail Trail to the Dearborn River. About a mile beyond the river, we found a good campsite. I rode on to make sure that we were where we were supposed to be. Some signs I found confirmed we were, and I also found an old outfitter's camp.

This evening the sun was bright but the air cool. As the sun went down, dew came on the grass for the first time in days.

Thursday, August 5, 1986

We rode back to the Dearborn River this morning. I showed the others the outfitter's camp; then we crossed the river, turned left and proceeded to Welcome Creek Guard Station. Others were surprised by the huge spikes sticking out from the planking on the station's front door–to discourage the Grizzlies, according to Cecil Garland who had told me this back in 1970.

As we approached the station, we met a ranger who took my name and our destination; he warned us about a Grizzly on Cave Trail. We thanked him and kept going a few more miles. After making camp farther along–near the Dearborn River again–we all left our pack horses behind and rode up Cave Trail. It was a nice trail, and sure enough, on the way, Cashin and Lips did see the Grizzly the ranger had told us about across the ravine.

I was disappointed, however, because we could not get up to the caves. Instead, when we got to Lost Cabin Trail, we turned hard right on a trail that was not on the map. It took us around to a point where we could see the wall of Scapegoat, and the view from there was spectacular. We saw a goat on a narrow ledge, just nonchalantly strolling along as though it was nothing for him to keep his balance.

There also was a waterfall on the wall. The water was coming out of a large hole with such force that it extended straight out like a water spout. We were quite a distance away but could still hear the roar of the falls. I wondered what it would be like to explore a cave that led to a waterfall. What if I slipped inside the cave, fell into the water, and came out the spout!

For supper tonight we had macaroni and cheese with tuna, onions, and carrots added, and pudding for dessert.

Friday, August 6, 1986

I'm writing from the top of Scapegoat Mountain. The others have left me and returned to camp. More about that later.

Bull tried to walk out at 6 o'clock this morning with three horses following him: Goldie, Balou, and Dusty. I don't know what got into him. Luckily, he was easy to catch.

We had a scenic ride this morning as we left the main trail and turned right to go to Half Moon Park. We didn't see any game, though.

We went past Green Fork Guard Station and set up camp at 11 a.m. near Cigarette Creek. After lunch, we rode our saddle horses, leaving pack horses behind. I had changed to the pack horse, Dusty, and went up Cigarette Trail, which was long and steep. We stopped near the top, about a mile past the pass.

Mert, Claire, and A.M. decided to stay in the shade by the trail and rest while Bob, Suzy, and I climbed to the top of Cigarette Mountain; I particularly wanted to see Cigarette Rock. I saw it for the first time when I was on that ride with Fred and Cecil about 16 years ago. We looked from various vantage points but could not spot it. I figured we'd maybe gone too far to the right of the peak.

We began our trek down, and as we wound our way through the trees, I finally spotted the rock below us. Wow. I'd forgotten how commanding was this piece of God's creation. A natural obelisk about 50 to 75 feet high and about 10 feet across, it pushes majestically up and out of the mountain, demanding that we take note of it in its position of grandeur.

We continued down the trail, winding through the trees, looking for Mert, A.M., and Claire. Eventually, it became apparent that we'd gone past where they were waiting for us. We called out to them as loudly as we could but got no answer. I wondered how we could have missed them so completely.

Then Suzy assessed the situation: "They're probably close by and simply can't hear us," she said. "A.M. uses hearing aids, my dad has a copper wire in his ears, and the other guy is always responding with '*What*?' whenever you talk to him." She didn't mean for her comment to be funny, but the thought of those three relaxing in oblivion while we were calling out to them was hilarious.

So we continued down the mountain, found our original trail, and followed it back up to them. Then we all rode over to Cigarette Rock, so everyone could see this spectacular sight. From there, I tried to find my way across Scapegoat Mountain, with the others following.

On one bit of steep, loose rock, Goldie stumbled and threw A.M. off. He was all right, but the others got pretty worried.

It was the beginning of dissension in the ranks.

When I led the others to a precipice, they did not want to get off their horses to view the spectacular sights over the ledge.

I then started riding up the mountain on shale that was nearly on the angle of repose. The others started following me, but then they decided not to.

I didn't want to turn back, and since the others wouldn't follow, I suggested they go back to camp and I would continue on by myself. I told them how to get back, and Cashin said he would take the lead. Rather than use landmarks, however, he said he wanted to retrace their tracks.

"Just like a horse would do," I thought to myself.

So here I am, on the top of Scapegoat Mountain alone and hoping they make it back to camp all right.

Marvelous view–higher than any mountain around except Red Mountain in the distance at 9,400 feet. I took pictures 360 degrees around me and then sat down to write and meditate–mostly because I could not find a way off this peak, except by the way I came up.

I think continuously about the five who went back. I pray to God for their safety, thankful to God that I can be up here, and thankful I have a steady, careful, and sure-footed horse. I rode Dusty today. Flies are biting him, and as he shakes his head, he slaps me on the back with his reins. I'm sitting on a precipice looking a thousand feet below. If Dusty wanted to get rid of me, all he would have to do is give me a little nudge with his nose! Dusty is slow but a no-nonsense steady horse. Coming up, other faster, more nervous horses had to stop and rest often. Dusty would catch up as they rested. By the top, he was way ahead of the others.

~ ~ ~

Gretchen is visiting son Fred and his wife, Mindy; son Dan, and his wife Penny Jo, and their daughters, Brooke and Kari, in Butte and

Lincoln right now. I hope she has been having as grand a time as I have. She loves having these members of our family all to herself.

Out here, I don't worry or think about my work, or problems in Minnesota or in the world. I just thoroughly enjoy God's great earth and my riding friends. Doug told me once that when he is out here riding he not only puts his worries aside, he can't even remember what they were!

And, once again, I was out in the mountains riding on Gretchen's birthday, which was two days ago. She is a wonderful person to let me go like this. I am glad she is so happy in our new house in Minnetonka. Also, I hope all is well with it, so when she gets back to it tomorrow, she won't have any problems.

I just noticed that it is 5:15. I'd better get back. I worry about the others, but they might be worrying about me, too, so I'll stop writing now and head out.

~ ~ ~

Coming down off the mountain, I let Dusty have his head, and he did pretty well at finding his way. Once, though, we stayed a little too high on the trail, and it got steeper and more rocky than I felt was safe, so I had to rein him to the left to get a little lower. When we tried going around the end of the butte that had the steep hole that scared the others, we still hit it too high; I had to go back and approach it lower. I ended up walking off the butte instead of riding.

When I went to the left of the small pond (as I had told Cashin to do, and he instead wanted to use the back trail), I worked my way around logs; the contour took me out exactly on the pass. Going down from there, I tied Dusty's reins to the saddle horn and walked ahead, swinging both arms. It made walking easier. Dusty didn't crowd until we came to a meadow; then he tried to pass me. I grabbed him, and after that he stayed in place. Just at the end of the meadow, a cow elk came right up toward us. It stood and looked and then, apparently in boredom, walked off.

I walked all the way down except for about 50 feet. When I got to Cigarette Creek, to my amazement, the creek, which at noon had been flowing at a good clip, had stopped. I was reminded, once again, of Aunt Caroline's story of the falls she encountered. And then more Aunt Caroline stories flooded back to me–especially the story of her mule hanging his head over the precipice on the Grand Canyon. She would have loved this ride with me.

I got back to camp about 7 o'clock, and the others were happy to have me back. They mentioned about the dry creek, as well, and said the horses even seemed to be amazed. Balou still hates to get his feet wet, so he must have appreciated it.

Thinking back to earlier today, it is surprising to me that a former sheriff would be so concerned for safety. But, since Goldie had slipped and A.M. bailed off, I guess I can see why he would be. I was happy they would nicely leave and let me go on alone. I spoke my appreciation. Cashin said they were worried that I'd be angry that they'd left me. I didn't tell them it had perturbed me at first; then I told them I like being alone and was happy to have the chance, which was true.

Little do they know that they are along partly for my safety and for Gretchen's peace of mind. In truth, I would like the challenge of doing these rides all by myself. I imagine most people would think my friends used more sense than I did today.

Saturday, August 7, 1986

I overslept this morning, not getting up until 5:30. But we managed to get out by 8:30 and headed straight for Benchmark Trailhead, arriving at noon. We loaded everything into our trucks and trailers and then drove to Augusta.

After a root beer float, I said good-bye to A.M., Mert, Bob, Claire, and Suzy. Claire would like to come on another trip; Suzy said she wants to come again and bring her new husband. I figure their whole family can go by themselves now that they have had this experience.

I wonder if Mert will go again, but A.M. will go at the drop of a hat, and Severson and Cashin will, too. That makes four of us.

On my way to my son Dan's outside of Lincoln, my engine overheated and the radiator boiled over. I limped into Lincoln and had a big hassle trying to get a new fan clutch at Lincoln Auto Parts. But the problem, I discovered later tonight, was not the fan clutch at all. My problem was that the radiator was too small for my truck; it wasn't capable of cooling the water as the engine works to pull big loads in these mountains.

The Ford dealer who sold me this truck back in Minnesota was wrong. He'd said a regular size radiator would be big enough. Not if you climb mountains pulling a rig like mine and there is a tail wind. Never again will I buy a truck without an oversize radiator.

CHAPTER SIXTEEN

Much too young to die

Sunday, August 8, 1986

A day of relaxation. I got in touch with my secretary, Cheryl Carlson, back in Minnesota to find out when my friends from Washington, D.C., would arrive. She said Doug Coe, Jerry Franz, and Martin Bostetter would meet me at 10 o'clock Monday in Augusta, as will Dick Whitmore, who is coming from Michigan, trailering his own horse. Jerry Potter is flying a plane in from Minnesota tomorrow with Tom and Scott Pritchard. He'll land on the mile-long airstrip at Benchmark Trailhead that was built for bringing fire fighters in as needed for forest fires. It is a narrow strip right on the edge of the wilderness, leaving no room for error during landing.

I'm really looking forward to spending some time with Doug. His youngest son Jonathan, who was with us on the ride in 1983, died of cancer a year and a half ago. He couldn't have been more than 23 years old. This will be the first opportunity since Jonathan's death that Doug and I will have had for deep sharing.

Monday, August 9, 1986

I got up late this morning, packed up, loaded horses and went into Lincoln for breakfast. Started grocery shopping for the next leg of this year's trip and bought some canteens for the guys who are joining me. I forgot to tell them to bring them along.

Then on to Augusta by 11. There was no sign of Doug Coe, nor of Jerry Franz and Martin Bostetter. I must have had a miscommunication with my secretary.

I did find Dick Whitmore, who, I learned, had arrived yesterday. Another miscommunication. Dick is a believer. A mutual friend from the "fellowship" recommended that I invite him along and disciple him a little.

Dick and I drove up to Benchmark, thinking Coe, Franz, and Bostetter might have arrived at 10 (as my secretary had indicated) and gone on to meet us there. We arrived about the same time Jerry Potter was touching down with his plane–about 12:30.

The five of us went to set up camp. Doug, Jerry, and Martin finally showed up at camp at 4:30. Martin had too much gear, so we went through it all, with my telling him what he could take and what he had to leave behind. It is tough to follow my packing instructions. At least Martin wasn't as upset about my cutting his gear back as some others have been in previous years.

I found out that these three guys (Doug, Jerry and Martin) had had a "conference" in Lincoln on Thursday, Friday, and this morning. Here, I'd been in the same town and didn't even know about it! Yet another miscommunication between me and my secretary. I guess I'm going to have to listen more closely.

About suppertime, the wrangler Kenny and Mary Faith Hoeffner had hired showed up with the horses I rented for everyone but Dick and me. I could tell by the smell of his breath that he had been drinking. I wish Hoeffners had sent their son, Jeff, who'd been our wrangler back in '83, but he was busy on another trip.

After the horses were settled in the corral, the wrangler went to another campsite to party.

Tuesday, August 10, 1986

I got up at 5 this morning; the others woke up at various times. Among them, Dick Whitmore got up first, perhaps because he has his own horse along and wanted to tend to her. There was no sign of our wrangler. I went up to the camp where I'd seen him go to party last night. Found him hung over and still asleep by some bushes. This behavior doesn't set well with me. We didn't get out until 10:30.

We will do another loop trip, beginning at the Benchmark Trailhead and ending there. After the Glacier Park leg, I now have the opportunity to share beautiful country in the Bob Marshall and Scapegoat Wilderness areas with friends. Doug Coe is the only one who has been here before as he rode with me in 1983.

We first went down the South Fork of the Sun River a little, then crossed over and went south to Hoadley Creek and followed it northwest to Stadler Pass, Stadler Creek, and southwest to Basin Creek, where we are camping.

Doug led devotions by the campfire tonight. He told about his trip to Mongolia, where he had opportunities to talk to non-believers. The people there, he said, are willing to hear about Jesus Christ (not about Christianity, but about Christ because they do not associate Him with any special religion). Doug always makes the distinction between Christians and Christ because Christians have done bad things to other people, but Christ came for all people.

Our wrangler does not want to have anything to do with our evening devotions. Even though Doug invited him, he hung around the horses while the rest of us gathered 'round the campfire. Doug has a lot more patience with him than I do.

Wednesday, August 11, 1986

Heard coyotes last night. I slept outside under the fly, even though there was a light rain.

This morning we got out of camp at 9:30—better than yesterday, but still not as early as I'd like. We rode over to the Danaher Meadows, arriving about noon, which is about the same time we arrived the other two times we've been here. Arriving at mid-day usually makes it possible to pick our campsite. No other campers were here when we arrived today, so we took what I deemed as the "good" campsite. It has more room than the site we had two weeks ago—ample room for 18 head of stock, and the water in the stream is deep enough for us to dip with a bucket rather than a pan.

I noticed a couple of tethered horses off in the distance on the flats. Strange. One was black with what appeared to be a white "belt" around its middle. Made me think of the coloration of a Dutch belted cow. I rode over to take a look and saw that the white was, in fact, a bandage around the horse's stomach. Very curious.

Some of the men went fishing tonight. I stayed in camp to organize things and put everything under cover. My work was impeded, however, when a big wind came up, blew the 8-man tent down, and broke the pole. Stiff winds are hard on tents. Next year I'll use two-man tents only. (Besides, with everyone in a large, single tent, the snorers keep the others awake.)

I've noticed the men get very tired on the trip, but they won't admit it. I think we'll take a layover day tomorrow, even though we've only been riding for two days.

I decided to follow Doug's lead and invite our wrangler to devotions tonight; he declined.

I wonder what I should bring to Gretchen as a belated birthday gift.

Thursday, August 12, 1998

Doug and I slept outside under the tarp last night; all the others were inside the tent. We lay there for a while listening to the sounds of night–a coyote howling in the distance, the hoot of an owl, then just the still of the night. The peace seemed to give Doug permission to talk about his son Jonathan.

All six of Doug's and Jan's children are outstanding, beautiful, caring people of strong character, but Jonathan was the most similar to Doug. He enjoyed life and people, had high energy like all the children in the family, and he truly had a heart for Christ.

Doug believed he would be the successor to his work–a minister to political leaders all over the world.

Doug and I reminisced about the vacations our families had taken together. About the times he and I would take just our sons on trips. About how Doug always turned everything into a competition: who can climb the tree the fastest? Who can throw the stone the farthest?

I was reminded of the time in 1977 when Jonathan, his parents, and Gretchen, Ben, and I went on a week's vacation to Maine. I had decided to take that vacation because I needed time away to decide whether to run for governor of Minnesota. I remember what a delightful kid Jonathan was and how much I enjoyed having him around.

The last time I saw him was at the National Prayer Breakfast two years ago in February. He approached me with sparkling eyes, face shining with excitement as he asked me to speak to a group of college students he'd been discipling. I accepted immediately. How could I say no to this enthusiastic young man?

A couple of months later, he went to see a doctor about a pain he'd been having in his throat. The cancer spread quickly, and there seemed to be nothing that could be done to stop it. It wasn't long before Jonathan had difficulty breathing. Mere months passed, Doug said. And finally, standing next to his wife Jan, who was holding Jonathan in her arms, Jonathan died.

Enormous anguish came over him, expressed in uncontrollable sobs. I witnessed a grief that must have been tearing him apart each day since Jonathan's death; but out here in the loneliness of the night in the mountains, it was as if this unbearable grief could be unleashed. What could I say? What could I do?

Nothing. Just be there. I wanted to do more. It's tough not to be able to do anything for a friend, except be a friend.

Because of my love for Doug, I grieved for him. My heart ached. But there was nothing I could do but listen.

Doug kept begging for an answer: "Why?" "Why?" "WHY?"

There is no way to know. Job, who suffered great losses, asked the same question. Did Job ever get an answer? No. He got a question, "Where were you when I laid the foundations of the Earth?" And that question was followed by more questions we cannot understand.

Doug told me how people had come to him in the same way Job's friends had. They suggested that God brought about Jonathan's death as a means for punishing Doug for something he had done. They asked whether he had problems with God that he needed to straighten out, and they questioned his faith.

I got so angry when Doug told me this! "These people are nuts! You can't believe that!" But my anger wasn't helpful. Doug just stared at me.

So I calmed down and simply encouraged him to trust in Jesus. I reminded Doug it isn't our level of faith that determines whether we suffer in life or whether we receive blessing. Just as people of great faith have been blessed immeasurably, so have people of great faith met unspeakable suffering. The determining factor in whether we are blessed or whether we suffer is not whether we have faith or how much faith we have–God is the determining factor.

It is simply up to us to trust that God is better than anything good that can happen to us, and that He is better than anything bad that can happen to us. Just trust God.

Of course, Doug already knows all of this. But I hope it is good for him to hear it again.

Things quieted down, then; Doug's sobs subsided. Emotionally exhausted, he fell asleep. I lay awake for a time longer, continuing to ponder, feel inadequate and love this friend. And like a good Father, there came from God, "Just Trust Me."

CHAPTER SEVENTEEN

A young wrangler reforms

Doug woke this morning after I'd been up, turned the horses loose, started the fire, poured water into the coffee pots, and washed the kettles. I guess all my racket woke him. Jerry Franz heard us talking, so he got up next, then Jerry Potter and the rest. The wrangler got up last. (He should be the first up, and should be the one taking care of the horses.)

Breakfast was bacon and french toast (not very good, at that).

Some of the men went fishing at 9:30. Dick and I sat around and chatted, waiting for our horses to return.

While getting ready to go fishing, Martin fell over twice while trying to get on his horse. He can't handle his horse too well. I think I'll have him and Scott Pritchard exchange horses tomorrow.

I watch these things carefully (I would even if we had a good wrangler), cognizant of which horse is which, making sure that these inexperienced riders are on the horses that suit them the best.

Most of the time I watch and let people learn by experience, but if they really need my help, I'll step in.

But then there is the problem I have when an experienced rider needs help. Today I had to tell Tom, who's been riding Goldie, that I was going to pack Goldie, and that he could ride Balou instead. His response was that he liked Goldie, and wanted to keep riding him.

Then I was faced with having to tell the truth. I told him Goldie had sore withers and needed a day of rest.

"I haven't noticed that," Tom said. So I had to show him. I put my hand on the right side of Goldie's withers and pressed in. He jumped.

"How did you know?" Tom asked.

Because of his experience with horses, I didn't want to tell him how I knew, but now I had to. "I've noticed that when you get on, you don't always "right" the saddle, which makes you ride off to the left side a little. This puts constant pressure on Goldie's right side, which finally made him sore. You've gotta bring the saddle over so it balances properly."

Next to me, Tom knew more about horses than anyone else on this ride. He was embarrassed. I didn't want to hurt his feelings.

~ ~ ~

I am at peace here in the mountains. Life is so simple and beauty abounds. There is solitude, quiet (except for the birds), slender pines, rugged mountains that conjure memories of mountain men and their stories. There are horse and weather in rhythm, elusive nocturnal animals (one of which had built a nest on my saddle blanket!), water gurgling down a stream, red and tan rocks in the bottom of the stream, beavers struggling to get food and make homes amongst the alders.

~ ~ ~

I went for a walk late this afternoon, first going south on the trail past the broken hay machinery, then I saw a sign indicating the Danaher Cabin had been nearby. After a bit, I walked to the east to explore higher up on the side of the mountain. Then I angled north and came upon a ravine coming down the mountain. To my surprise, over the brink, I did see a cabin roof. Exploring further, I discovered the cabin well-hidden among some trees and mostly built into the side hill.

Soon, a boy about 15 appeared. I wasn't too surprised that there would be people here, since I'd seen the horses tethered on the flats yesterday (though I didn't see them today).

The boy said his uncle was inside and that his father had gone out for supplies. He told me his parents owned a grocery store in Great Falls, Montana, and his mother would run it until they returned. He said they planned to stay in the cabin until elk season. I quickly calculated this would be about a month to six weeks, and wondered how the boy could skip that much high school.

I asked the boy about the bandage I'd seen on the horse yesterday. All he would say is that the animal had been injured, and that was the way they had doctored it.

I could see they had insulated the cabin with fiberglass batting, with the aluminum side exposed.

When I went back to camp, I told the others about the boy and the cabin, and Dick and Doug said they wanted to see it. So the three of us took off after supper, re-tracing my steps from this afternoon. The cabin is so well hidden we almost couldn't find it.[13]

~ ~ ~

For supper tonight, we had pork chops, potato buds, green peas, onions, carrots, and pudding for dessert.

The ever-competitive Doug Coe challenged everyone to knife games tonight. One game was mumblety-peg and the other throwing a knife into a stump. (I won't let him throw into a live tree.) We also competed at lassoing the stump.

Tom led devotions around the campfire. He pointed out that mountains are mentioned 564 times in the Bible. Our wrangler continued to keep his distance, but when I glanced toward him during sharing time, I could tell he was listening. Maybe he is softening. Maybe I am, too.

Friday, August 13, 1986

We left Danaher and rode toward the Carmichel Cabin area. We went down the Dry Fork Creek, and for some reason, got south of the North Fork Falls. When we saw the sign, "1-1/2 miles to North Fork Cabin," we made a U-turn to get back to the falls. I guess I'd been talking to Doug and lollygagging, which got us onto the wrong trail. A few more miles in that direction and we'd have been completely out of the wilderness.

Because of the time wasted, we could only go by the falls. I was sorry I could not let the guys stop and explore this spectacular place, but we had to continue on, looking for a campsite.

We found a decent grazing area, but the spot next to it for camping was on a side hill, and there was a steep grade to the stream. We decided to stay, anyway, so the horses would have good grazing.

Our wrangler eased his way to the edge of our campfire circle tonight. He didn't say anything during devotions, but he was there listening.

Saturday, August 14, 1986

There was much bed roll slipping down the side hill during the night. At least those in the tent had the wall of the tent to stop their slide.

We got a decent start and reached Carmichel Cabin at lunch. There was a nice meadow surrounding the cabin.

On the way, our wrangler was leading most of the pack string. He went the wrong way but got back to us again. We then went up to the Tobacco Valley Trail, turned left to the Debrota Creek, crossed over the stream (where I had passed just a week and a half ago), and up a hunter's trail.

We went practically to the top of Scapegoat again, just below the huge 50-foot tilting rock.

We then went down Cave Creek Trail to the Dearborn River and camped at a site we had used a week and half ago.

Sunday, August 15, 1986

Layover day. I climbed to the mountain top before breakfast. From that vantage point, I watched the others finally getting up, getting their gear together, and preparing breakfast.

What a spectacular view. I took a picture of the camp from up there, but I suppose I was too far away for anything to really show up clearly. It was fun to sit there and watch the men (who look so small from that distance) get up one by one and get moving.

Ran across a male Fools Hen (Franklin grouse). I was faced with a dilemma. I had one picture left on this roll (since I had given my last roll to Franz, who had run out of film). Should I use my last shot for a photo of Scapegoat or of the grouse? I chose the grouse.

When I got back to camp, the men went fishing, and I took a nap. Martin got the biggest fish, and of course Doug (the competitor) couldn't stand it. He had tried and tried to catch one bigger but failed. He then kept ribbing Martin about how small his fish was. Franz was by far the best fisherman. One of his innovations was catching live grasshoppers on the bank and using them for bait. The fish surely go for them.

It was a good day for lengthy discussions. Doug had a long talk with our wrangler. He has a great influence on people; apparently our wrangler's heart is starting to open. Doug even invited him to be his guest at the next National Prayer Breakfast.

Today our dinner was steak, mashed potatoes, fish, and onions, carrots and tomato sauce mixed, with jello for dessert. Setting a kettle of jello in the stream (with a rock on the lid to hold it in place) firms up the jello in short order because the water is so cold coming out of the mountains.

The most spectacular thing happened just after dark as we were getting ready for bed. Somebody said, "Look at that!" and pointed to the sky, where a falling star or meteor burned so long we all could see it. Usually shooting stars are seen for only an instant. This one seemed to sweep across the heavens, and looked like it might even hit the mountain we saw in the distance.[14]

I'm beginning to see a change in our wrangler's demeanor, and it seems his relationship with himself as well as with God is changing. He seems more pensive, and is starting to ask me questions about God and the Bible. It's a thrill to see the hand of the Lord at work in this person.

Monday, August 16, 1986

Up at 5, worked 'til 6 and then got the others up.

Last night's camp had poor grazing, so this afternoon we took time to let the horses graze when we came upon a good spot.

Some of us wanted to look over some of the Scapegoat trails, so I told our wrangler to take the pack string and cut across to the campsite we had designated for tonight; we would meet him at camp in the evening. I was a little worried over whether we and our supplies would meet up tonight. I found out that our wrangler had gone to the wrong place, and after spending some time there, realized it, and then made his way to the right campsite.

~ ~ ~

When we collected the horses just before dark to tie them up, Dick's white Arab mare was gone. With hoof marks of 18 horses and mules on the trails, it was impossible to figure out where she had gone. Could she have known the direction to the trailer? Had she gone on the backtrail or climbed off on the mountain somewhere by herself? She had never before strayed from the camp while grazing. Dick went off to find her, and the rest of us looked for a while, too, but could not find her.

None of us knew which direction Dick had gone. We called for him but got no answer. I'd previously told Dick that when horses leave, they usually go on the backtrail, so maybe that was the direction he went.

Pretty soon it was plumb dark. I didn't think a horse would stray off by herself too far, but now we began to worry. We sat around the fire waiting and praying (including our wrangler), and after a while Dick came into camp with his horse in tow.

Dick had gone on the backtrail, and guess what–he found his horse way back where we'd stopped to graze this afternoon. She had remembered that succulent grass and had gone there to partake of it all by herself.

It will be on to the Benchmark Trailhead, and then we'll trailer to Augusta tomorrow.

Tuesday, August 17, 1986

When we got out of the wilderness and into Augusta, a number of our wrangler's friends were in town. He was to wrangle another trip (for another outfitter), but this would be a layover day for him. He immediately headed across the way to the bar to spend time with his buddies.

I was crestfallen. But what could I do about it? It is between him and the Lord.

To my surprise, it wasn't long before he came back out again, so I went over to say a formal good-bye. There was no smell of liquor on his breath. He looked up at me and said, "I only had a soft drink, Mr. Quie."

I also heard the voice of Jesus: "Oh ye of little faith."

I smiled back at him; we shook hands and said good-bye.

1987

Southern Wyoming
and
Northern Colorado

Atlantic City

Great Divide Basin (Red Desert)

Sweetwater

Oregon Trail

North Platte

Encampment

Buffalo Pass

Arapaho National Forest

Rocky Mountain National Park

CHAPTER EIGHTEEN

A promise to care for the 'inexperienced'

Thursday, July 9, 1987

Anticipation for this trip was great again this year. I began planning back in January!

We're now headed for the Divide area on the south end of the Wind River Range in Wyoming and the Red Desert of Wyoming.

I was 15 minutes late picking up Monroe Larson at the Amoco station in Burnsville, Minnesota, this morning–arriving at 5:45. His son told him he must have made a mistake "since Al Quie is never late." But this time I was.

One evening last winter, when Monroe (a good friend who serves with me on the board of the Search Institute) and his wife Esther were having dinner for Gretchen and me, I shared about my trips and showed some pictures. I suggested Monroe should consider coming along some time. He laughed and said, "I drive Buicks, and don't do very well driving horses!" We all laughed at that, and while Monroe did say it sounded like an exciting adventure, such a trip into the deep wilderness of the mountains was probably more than he could imagine because of his fear and inexperience with horses.

The extent of his experience with horses could be pinpointed to one time in his life–when he was five years old. He said he'd been cornered by some horses and was panicked by them.

About a month after dinner at our home, I called Monroe and encouraged him, once again, to go on the trip. He said he'd talk it over with his wife, who knew of his fear of horses. But she encouraged him to go, so when I called him a couple of weeks later, he said yes. "Esther encouraged me. She has great faith and confidence in you, and she really wants me to do this."

So here we are with Monroe quite anxious about what he might encounter. But I've assured him that I'll take care of him.

~ ~ ~

Monroe and I went on to Faribault to meet Al Severson, who is loaning me his mule, Gyp, for this trip. Bob Cashin and A.M. Lips (riding partners from years past) were also there to see us off. What a treat to see them.

Then Monroe and I went on to the Happy Chef at Owatonna where we met up with Hank Pederson.

I got to know Hank, chaplain at the federal prison in Rochester, Minnesota, through my work as Area Director of Prison Fellowship. He asked me one time to come and speak to prisoners. I thought it was challenging that he asked me to speak on "what Jesus has done in your life in the last week." He has some experience with horses, but nothing that would prepare him for this ride.

The three of us then drove on to Worthington where Lynn Street joined us to form a caravan heading for Gillette, Wyoming.

~ ~ ~

We're staying at the home of Bill and Sue Todd tonight. I got to know Sue through her Prison Fellowship volunteer work in Colorado and Wyoming. At a recent PF meeting in Reston, Virginia, she invited me to stop at her place in Gillette. She and her husband arranged for our horses to be stabled at R.C. Stables tonight at no charge.

After supper, Sue played the piano, we sang, and we talked. Sue is a unique musician. The Lord has gifted her to sit at the piano and compose songs–on the spot–using Bible verses as the lyrics. She said she feels God wants her not to be a performer, but to play, sing, and befriend the less fortunate.

Friday, July 10, 1987

After breakfast at the Todds' home, we drove on to Lander, Wyoming, Lynn doesn't like to drive as fast as I do. Luckily, we had agreed to meet at the McDonald's in Lander if we got separated (which we did).

While waiting for Lynn, I drove over to the Forest Service Station and got some good tips on our trip from a ranger there. It helps to talk to someone who knows the area.

Then we headed up to Northern Meadows on the east side of the Wind River Range–a very rough 24-mile trek, especially since it had started raining.

We set up the tent and tarp in the rain after we strung up a high-line rope between two trees and tied up our horses and mule. We ate stew late.

Lynn, Monroe, and Hank are sleeping in Lynn's new trailer–a four-horse gooseneck with living quarters. I'm outside in the tent.

Sometimes the sound of rain falling on a tent can be peaceful. Tonight–in concert with the wind–it was miserable.

Saturday, July 11, 1987

Thank goodness there was no rain this morning. Lynn and the others stayed in camp to organize things for our trip; I left about 9:30 for Pavillion, where I rented a couple pack horses from Lonnie Mantle of "Wyoming Horses" for this party. Lonnie has a business of renting horses to outfitters when they need extra ones for a trip.

Bill Bontrager is a judge who resigned his position after he'd stood up for a person who, he thought, should not have been punished the way he was. Chuck Colson wrote, in his book, *Loving God*, about Bill's experience. When Bill left his judgeship, he began working in Christian mediation and conciliation. Our paths crossed because of my PF involvement and his interest in prison ministry.

As we were having dinner one night late last winter, his wife, Ellen, said she'd always had the dream of one day going on a pack trip in the mountains. So here they are.

On the way back from Pavillion, I bought some perishables, rubber footwear for Hank, and a pair of boots and a shirt at a western store for me–$74 for the boots and $9.95 for the shirt, both good buys. (I had left my rubber-soled boots at home. It seems each year I forget something.)

The Bontragers, who drove their van from Minnesota, were waiting for me at the saddle shop in Lander, as I'd instructed. They followed me the 24 miles up to camp, arriving about 3 p.m.

Our original plans had been to sleep at the trailhead, but I wanted to get started since we had so much territory to cover.

So we packed up and took off from Northern Meadow Trail about 5 o'clock, heading to the Middle Fork of the Pogo Agie River where we're camping tonight.

Our trek this evening was not without incident, however.

Bill was on Coco (a dun mare I borrowed from Pastor Paul Nelson of Northfield), Ellen on Dusty, Hank on one of Lynn's horses (Maynard, a very stable, dependable and gentle Quarter Horse gelding), and Monroe on another of Lynn's horses (Chubb, a flighty mare less responsive to the rider and that Lynn's wife, Jean, usually rides). Lynn rode his big gelding.

We found a bridge that we used for crossing the Middle Fork of the Pogo Agie River. It was a good thing we came across it because the river was way too deep to ford. After we'd gone another couple miles, we came to a small bog. The bridge, constructed to enable people to cross the bog, was out, so Lynn, who was in the lead, went around the bridge and into the bog. Bill's horse Cocoa followed. She stepped in gingerly, then jumped forward and went down. She then lunged up, throwing Bill into the bog and kicking him in the knee with the next lurch.

We re-grouped, with Bill crawling out of the mud, dirty and in quite a bit of pain, and we continued on. It was then I noticed Monroe riding off center to the left. Before I could say anything to get him to "right" himself, his horse, Chubb, stumbled as she went over a log, corrected herself to the right, and threw Monroe off to the left. Monroe. The one whose great apprehensions did not prevent him from coming on this trip. Monroe. Whose fears were assuaged when I told him I'd take care of him. Monroe. Who was now on the ground.

Thankfully, he was not injured; we re-grouped again and made it into camp without further incident. (Monroe told me he thought he was going to die when he fell off his horse.)

Tonight's camp is just adequate for feed.

Sunday, July 12, 1987

Before taking off this morning, I led church services, using John 3:21, talking about how living by the truth brings us into the light, and how the story of the Samaritan women in John 4:23-24 ends the same way.

~ ~ ~

Monroe had the same problem today of riding off center. I asked the person riding behind him to help watch and remind him when he was leaning off to the side, but no matter how often he righted himself, he kept slipping right back to the side. Finally I called to him and said commandingly, "Monroe, you are going to get in trouble if you don't sit straight on your horse." I was worried.

Ellen, too, developed the same problem of riding off to the side. Riding behind, she called out to me, and when I turned to respond, there she was, tipped way over to the left. I quickly turned back to help her back on top of her horse, balanced.

I can't understand why people don't right their saddles so they won't slide to the side. I guess it is just something one learns with enough riding. Maybe it comes easy for me because we were too poor to have saddles in my youth, so I always rode bareback on the farm. I rarely rode in a saddle until I bought and trained horses after Gretchen and I were married.

I told Ellen and Monroe to think of having an eye screw in their heads, and pretend they are dangling from sky hooks–that's how centered they should sit. (I learned this by reading Sally Swift and Mary Twelveponies.) They seem to be learning, which makes me happy.

~ ~ ~

We headed up the trail today, going through the Lower Hudson Meadow, Upper Hudson Meadow, Shoshone Basin, and along the east side of Shoshone Lake. Apparently, the Forest Service allows four-wheelers in the Shoshone Lake area. We found tracks of motorized vehicles in the area, which totally changes the wilderness experience. With motorized vehicles around, there is no sense of being "away from it all."

There is something in the wilderness experience that tests one's mettle. I deal with God differently here than elsewhere. My dependence on other people ceases to exist out here; I'm more on my own mettle and, in a sense, in the hands of God.

Being in the wilderness also impacts my relationships with others. It's not a secret that I enjoy my alone-time. Some of my riding partners would say I'm ignoring them, but my relationships with people come into my meditation and thought. When I come out of the wilderness, I seem to relate to people better than before I went in.

I think this is Biblical. Jesus went up by himself to lonely places to be closer to God. I think it may be hard for some Christians to say He was better when He came out, but I think the wilderness experience changed Him. When you look at Him as true God and true man, the true man part of Him must have felt pulled away from God and drawn to the wilderness to get close again. Otherwise He would have just been moving along with God, "at one" with God, and never felt the need to talk special to God. I think it's important that we talk special to God, too.

~ ~ ~

After having lunch at the south end of the lake, we turned west and went up to the High Meadow Trail, crossing the North Pogo Agie River, and then on to Sanford Park where we had planned to camp. The park shown on my map, however, had overgrown with alders and had little space for camping. I spotted what looked like a great meadow for camping across the river, and I figured that must be the park since the name refers to a large native grassy area in the midst of trees. The river appeared to be quite deep so I decided to test it. I urged Spanish Bull to jump in, and I tried to hold my feet above the water.

It was deeper than I thought. My boots filled with water, as did most of the stuff hanging from my saddle.

Lynn found a place downstream to cross, which wasn't as deep, and the others followed. Once we were across, we walked down river another 1,000 feet to set up camp–a beautiful view. Monroe was ecstatic. I laid my stuff out to dry.

There is hardly any grass at this camp, but what there is, is nutritious, so the horses are doing well.

Using Psalm 139, Monroe led devotions tonight, telling us about an 83-year-old woman who said, if she could live her life over, she would take more chances and do more things. He said he feels like he is fulfilling this urge for himself right now.

Monday, July 13, 1987

We headed south this morning for Tayo Park. The trail was terrible–lots of rock, which is difficult for the horses to traverse. We stopped to change our pack horses to saddle horses; the packs seemed to be making the horses sore.

While having lunch at Deep Creek Lakes and adjusting our packs some more, two rangers approached us. First they asked for our horse permit. I had left it at the truck but had remembered the name of the ranger who sold it to me. I guess that made me seem believable to them.

They asked me my name, and when I told them who I was and added that I was the former governor of Minnesota, Bill jokingly said, "I hope you don't believe that." I was not happy with Bill. I don't like that kind of humor at such a time.

One ranger then wanted to know if we knew Garrison Keillor personally. Garrison had performed at my Inaugural Dinner, so I told them about him, our conversation, and his shyness.

Then their questions returned to the missing horse permit. "What is printed on the top of your permit?" one asked. I hadn't really read it all, but remembered that we were to keep our horses 200 feet away from the trails, lakes and streams when we camped. Evidently, that's what they were looking for, because they didn't say anything more. I guess the USDA is catering to hikers more than horse people. (But I have no problem with these rules.)

I guess not having my permit in hand made me a little nervous because, when we took off after lunch, I did not look at my compass. Consequently, we made a wrong turn, going east instead of south. When we got to Pinto Park Lake, we saw three hikers who told us where we were.

Instead of turning back, we went down Pinto Park Trail (rough, steep and rocky) and camped–at Three Forks Park–a long way from the trail and water. So I chose Dusty–the most reliable pack horse–and, riding Bull, headed to the Bosco Creek nearby to get water. I used two hard plastic panniers and found pieces of wood to lay on top of the water in the panniers to keep the water from oscillating too much. I had watched women in Africa do this when they carried pails of water on their heads. Dusty is a pretty stable horse, but I wanted to take these precautions anyway. It's a good thing I did because, with the water sloshing around on the way back, he wanted to buck and bolt. Nonetheless, Dusty, Bull, and I managed to bring about 25 gallons of water safely back to camp.

We are two miles from Sweet Water Pass, and we can see lots of snow on majestic mountains to our southwest, including Atlantic Peak at 12,700 feet, which is five to six miles away. The temperature during the days has been perfect–in the 60s–and the sun is shining.

Bill led devotions tonight using Luke 4 where Jesus announced His ministry. I like it best when the leader draws us out for discussion about how we can personally relate to the scriptures. It takes a while for this type of discussion to get going, though. Hank has been quiet, and Lynn is pretty quiet, too.

~ ~ ~

Breakfast food so far has been bacon, pancakes, and fried eggs, or Swiss cheese and onion omelets. We also drink lots of Tang. For lunches, we've been having sandwiches–cheese and sausage or peanut butter–with an apple and granola bars, raisins and trail mix. Our dinners have been chicken breasts, pork chops or steak, potatoes, and onions and carrots. I sometimes bake Bisquick bread in a jello mold so the heat comes through the middle as well around the out-side–it bakes faster this way.

And one night I made fruit soup, a Norwegian delicacy. I had planned for this, as I had brought various kinds of dried fruit along. No whipped cream, though, for topping. I also make jello–which, according to Garrison Keillor, is a Lutheran delicacy–but only when we have a layover day or when we arrive early in camp, when there is extra time for the jello to firm up in the cold water of the streams.

Tuesday, July 14, 1987

We set up camp this afternoon at a site that was more than 200 feet away from the trail we'd been on. But on closer look there seemed to be another trail nearby. At first, I didn't pay much attention because I thought that this other trail was one hunters used. But when Lynn and I took a ride up to Sweetwater Pass this evening, we noticed that it was the trail to Tayo Lake.

At Sweetwater Pass, Lynn and I tied our horses to trees and hiked as high as we could with the time we had. I told him that, other than Doug Coe, most people are not willing to climb with me.

Wednesday, July 15, 1987

At 6:30 a.m. this morning–before breakfast–Lynn, Hank, and Monroe saddled up and headed for Tayo Lake. They took a pack horse with them and some food, but said they would be back for lunch. I knew it was a 4-1/2 mile trail and told them it would be a two-hour ride up and a two-hour ride back. They still said they would be back by noon.

Bontragers slept until 9 o'clock. About 11:15, the three of us left to ride up and meet Lynn, Hank, and Monroe, who we thought would be on their way back from Tayo Lake.

Instead, we came across Lynn–on foot–about one quarter mile west of Poison Lake. By the long look on his face, I seriously thought that one of them had been killed by a Grizzly, the other maimed and he was the only one who got away. No one could look as desperate as he over lost horses. But it turns out that was the source of Lynn's despair.

He explained that they had hobbled Hank's and Monroe's horses and left his horse and the pack horse loose while they went fishing. When he had fished and caught five cutthroat, he glanced up and couldn't see his horse or the pack horse anymore. He left Hank and Monroe fishing while he went to find his horses, which, he figured, were on the backtrail. I knew, however, that if they had gone on the backtrail, we'd have come across them.

I believed the tracks Lynn was following were old, but he was convinced they were the tracks of his horses. So Bill gave his horse, Cocoa, to Lynn, who continued on his way, hunting for his horses, I got off Bull, and Bill and I walked as we searched among bushes and behind rocks for tracks. Nothing. Bill and I decided to climb a mountain and look down to Coon Lake (where the three had been fishing) to see what we could see. Still nothing.

So we went to look for Hank and Monroe at the lake and found them coming toward us–on their horses and leading Lynn's gelding and the pack horse. The two had simply been hiding behind rocks.

Hank and Monroe said they thought Lynn's departure had meant he was testing them. They were real proud that they had enough knowledge to saddle up correctly. They even packed the fishing poles on Chubb properly. I could feel their joy of accomplishment.

We all made it back to camp (except Lynn) in the early afternoon and spent the rest of the day hanging out, talking, and waiting. Lynn didn't make it back to camp until 9 p.m. We cheered for his safe arrival; he was relieved that his horses were safe, but that relief did not hide his chagrin. He'd ended up going all the way to Three Forks Park, where we had camped Monday night, looking for his horses.

Chapter Nineteen

A leather-y miner offers her help

Thursday, July 16, 1987

We decided to ride up to Sweetwater Pass again today. I wanted once more to climb to the top like I'd done a couple days ago. But sure enough, when we got there, none of the men wanted to climb with me. Ellen said she would, however, so the two of us started hiking. About half way up, she ran out of energy. I, on the other hand, was determined not to go back. There was more I wanted to explore than Lynn and I had time for last night. There was beauty to behold. And I felt it was too dangerous for Ellen to go back alone; I would not forgive myself if something happened to her.

Unless a person is fully aware of one's surroundings, which usually happens only if he or she is in charge and experienced in the mountains, it is easy to get lost. I've seen people get disoriented right in my sight, and as they are trying to find their way, they come upon me, not knowing I was so close.

Anyway there Ellen and I were, halfway up the mountain, with Ellen wanting to go back. But because I was determined to go on, I told her she had to stay put while I proceeded to the top, that I didn't want her to start thinking about going back alone, or waiting for me in a different place. "When I come back," I said. "I want to find you right here. I don't want you to move." I just looked her right in the eye and said, "You're gonna be here when I come back."

I was firm with her because Ellen is a person who expects to be in charge. It is interesting how I react when she tells *me* how to do things in the camp kitchen. And whenever she does, I'm always sure to do the exact opposite. After all, I'm the one with the experience here. Besides, the way to get a man to do something is to pose the request in such a way that, after he has time to think it through, it becomes his idea.

Men don't like jumping up to do something they've been told. It's true, men like to fix things, but women don't always want us to fix things for them they just want us to listen, and then at least to say, "Uh-huh," so they know we might have listened. We humans are surely different from each other.

So I went to the top alone, hoping Ellen would follow my instructions.

It was exhilarating to be all alone on the top of the mountain. The view was gorgeous. The sun made pools of water that were trapped in the hollows of rock look golden. Wind-swept trees were trying their best to keep footholds in rocky cracks. I could see 30 miles away at this altitude to the Pinedale Valley. Not many people make the effort to climb that high. I feel closer to God up there.

And when I came down, I was grateful to find Ellen right in the spot where we had parted.

~ ~ ~

We all rode to the west side of Sweetwater Pass and had lunch in a most beautifully flowered area. We spent extra time there because of the beauty and because we were finally having some good discussions. The troupe hadn't clicked too well the first few days, but now we are doing fine. It seems always to take a few days for bonding to happen.

Monroe is the least adept of the crew, but he has a great spirit, and he is a wonderful companion. He has seen the West in the past from motels and automobiles. Hank is resilient. He quickly adopts necessary skills but sometimes stands back rather than pitching in. I'll admit it is not always easy to see what needs to be done. Ellen is always eager and pitches in all the time. Bill is a better horseman than he lets on. He works hard and learns fast. And Lynn, of course, is a very necessary part of this trip with all his packing, mountain, and horse experience.

Friday, July 17, 1987

We packed up and got out at 8:30 this morning. It had already started to rain. We took the tough trail towards Northern Meadows where we'd left our rigs last week. It would have been a beautiful trek if it hadn't been so cloudy and rainy.

Today was the end of this leg of the ride. Bontragers took Hank and Monroe in their van (which had been parked at the trailhead) as far as Casper Wyoming. Hank and Monroe will fly back to Minnesota from there.

I brought the rented horses back to Pavillion and got my $500 refund from Lonnie Mantle. Also got my tire fixed at the Phillips 66, and got back to camp at Northern Meadows around 6 o'clock. Lynn and I loaded up, and we drove to the rodeo ground pens where we left our stock. Then we checked into the Holiday Lodge Motel in Landers. It's good to have a chance once a week or so to get cleaned up at a place like this.

Tomorrow morning, Lynn will begin his drive back to Minnesota.

Saturday, July 18, 1987

I called Gretchen before leaving the motel; then headed over to the Coast to Coast to buy a new axe and saw blade before taking off for Atlantic City, Wyoming, where I'm to meet Doug Coe and where we'll begin the next leg of our ride.

Atlantic City is practically a ghost mining town just east of South Pass where the Continental Divide becomes a big high-altitude desert basin. There is a north and south ridge defining it, and it is different from the rest of the Divide, as no water can go into either the Atlantic or Pacific from this Great Divide Basin. Doug and I will ride closer to the north ridge, hitting a little oil drilling village at Bairoil before heading south through Sinclair and on to Encampment.

The drive to Atlantic City from Landers was all up hill and steep; my hay net and buckets blew out of the back of my truck. It was dumb of me not to secure them better. I drove back to pick them up, but they were gone.

~ ~ ~

Atlantic City is a real old town with very few people and fewer working establishments. I looked around for Doug, not really knowing where I was going to meet him. When someone from Minnesota and another from Washington, D.C., make plans to meet on a certain day at a certain time on the Continental Divide at a town neither has been to, it makes one wonder how and whether the two will connect. But since Atlantic City was so small, it didn't take long for me to determine that Doug was nowhere to be found.

So I went into the TNT Cafe (which seemed to be the only establishment left in town), and I walked up to the bar looking for someone in charge. There didn't seem to be a proprietor, but there were eight people sitting at tables.

When I turned and found them all staring at me, I felt like I was in an Old West movie. I announced that I needed a place to store my trailer while I traveled across the desert. All but one looked at me suspiciously. One woman, old and lean, spoke up. I could tell by her leathery, weather-beaten skin that she spends a lot of time outdoors. This woman had the look of a strong-willed, independent person, and I found out soon enough that she was the type, if someone needed help, who would offer assistance, not caring what anyone else thinks or says. Barbara Cole had compassion for other people; she told me I could keep my rig at her place and to just follow her.

I did follow her out of the cafe, thinking I needed to find Doug before we could head out to her place, wherever that was. What a relief when Doug drove up with a friend who had given him a ride from some nearby airport. We threw his gear in my truck and took off after Barbara.

It didn't take long, once we'd arrived at her place, for us to find out she is, in fact, a prospector (jade was her mineral of choice), living alone in a long-used trailer. This character was one who wanted to share her life's stories with all those who crossed her path. Among the stories she told us was one about her daughter, who didn't want Barbara at her wedding. "I guess she thought I might scare her husband-to-be away!" she laughed, as she gestured toward clothing that her daughter would likely have viewed as unseemly garb.

I relished visiting with this old salt, so it took us until 5:30 to get out of her place. The weather was cold and threatening rain as we mounted up and headed out.

After a couple of hours on the trail, a pickup honked at us from the dirt road. A rancher by the name of Finlayson (with his wife and daughter) stopped to greet us. When we told him about our riding plans, he said we'd likely be riding on his land, which didn't seem to be a problem for him. They moved on, but it wasn't long before Finlayson came back, found us, and invited us to his home for dinner. He also encouraged us to camp that night on his property.

Over supper, we had a great visit. The Lord seems to put us in touch with people like this all the time. Doug told them about the National Prayer Breakfast and some of the work of the Fellowship.

Mrs. Finlayson boldly asked, "If you are such praying men, why don't you pray with us?" We proceeded to spend a wonderful time in prayer with them. (Two men in the prayer fellowship movement were not inspired to suggest prayer, but the Spirit touched Mrs. Finlayson.)

At the end of the evening, he directed us to an area on his property for camping. He had four camping trailers, a building, and a partially built cabin there. We slept in their uncovered cabin using my tarp; I put Bull in the grassy corral and let the other animals run.

Doug is riding Dusty on this leg of the trip, and we are packing the dun mare, Coco (whom I borrowed from our former pastor, Paul Nelson), and Gyp, the three-colored mare mule owned by Al Severson.

Sunday, July 19, 1987

We were up at 5:30, ate breakfast of scrambled eggs, bread, sausage and cheese, were out by 6:30, and arrived at Strawberry Creek by 10 a.m. We hung out there for a few hours and, after lunch, headed north from Strawberry Creek, looking for the Sweetwater River. We saw huge numbers of antelope and some cattle (the cows seemed overly fat), and came upon Lubestand Lakes.

The lakes indicated we were further south than my plan, so we headed back northeast. Finally, we came upon the Sweetwater River, and followed it for about a mile, looking for a place to cross. There were so many alders it was difficult to find a spot. Plus the river was deep. I didn't want to have Bull swim and get the packs wet, so we turned around. We moved back a half mile and then crossed, even though the alders were still thick.

When we got through, Doug noticed he had lost his camera. So we went back across the river, and followed our tracks, looking for the camera. He first looked on foot and then he rode Dusty back to where we tried the first crossing. I rode up on top of a 20-foot hill with a cutback on the river side giving me a good view. No camera in sight for either of us. We gave up and will depend on my camera.

We then climbed up trying to find Barros Springs. After much riding, we came upon a spring in a large muddy area. I've concluded that where we were was not the Barros Springs but instead just a muddy spring as identified on the topo map. The area smelled bad, so we moved on, approaching a bend in the Sweetwater River, where we are camping tonight.

There are some alders on the opposite side of a fence that I'd like to tie the horses to, but there is no gate to let us through to them, so we tied to sagebrush along a bank. Bull handled it well as did the other horses, but the mule got into trouble. She pulled up every sage bush I tied her to and walked off with it. So I tied her to some sagebrush right near our tent. The others I let roam.

We cooked spaghetti and meat sauce, green beans, chocolate pudding, and more sausage. Portions divided out great.

Had a long discussion with Doug about buildings for the work of the "fellowship." When I became involved there was one home where leaders met for prayer, Bible study and discussion–often with a meal. Now a couple more sites are coming into use. I'm not enthusiastic about owning buildings.

Al packed and ready to ride. Note the axe and saw secured on the outside of the packs. 1983.

Follow your senses. *"My senses told me the sign was pointing the wrong way....we contemplated turning it 90 degrees to point the right direction..."* Al (center) with Jeff Hoeffner and Doug Coe. July 11, 1983. (Chapter 3)

Daily weigh-in. *Al and Mert Schwarz conduct a daily weigh-in of the packs. It was important for the packs on each side of each pack horse to be of equal weight to prevent fatigue and saddle sores on the horses' backs.*

Some of the 'first year guys.' *Bill Starr, Doug Coe, Jonathan Coe, Jeff Hoeffner, Mike Dudley and Ben Quie.*

Some of the 1984 crew. *Outside of Monida, Montana, August 15, 1984: A.M. Lips, Bob Cashin, Al Quie, Mert Schwarz, Norm Madson and Al Severson. (Chapter 9)*

Morning routine. *Every day, all equipment from the smallest spoon to the most bulky tent had to be packed. Here, Al teaches A.M. Lips how to lash a mantie to a pack saddle.*

Above:
Packed and Ready to go. *Al, Bill Starr and wrangler Jeff Hoefner with some of the horses packed, ready, and waiting. 1983*

Cold but beautiful.
With coffee heating near the fire, Al writes in his journal and Bill Starr studies his Bible. July 4, 1983. (Chapter 2)

Finding the way through snow. *"It was a beautiful morning as we left camp on the Sun River and rode up Open Creek to Kevan Mountain, then near Table and Pentagon Mountains." July 5, 1983. (Chapter 2)*

Friends on the '84 ride. *Rob Linner, Fred Quivik, Darrell Cade. (Chapter 8)*

Rocky terrain. *Horses quickly wear down their shoes going over rocky trails. The Wind River Range was one such area. July 10, 1987. (Chapter 18)*

North Fork Falls. *"I listened to the roar of the water, which was almost over-powering. I looked down the gorge as the water splashed against rock precipices on its descent–it had to have been at least a 500-foot drop." July 12, 1983 (Chapter 3)*

At the top.
The minute figure at the top of the cliff is Ben Quie–at the top of North Fork Falls.

At the bottom.
Ben Quie at the
bottom of North
Fork Falls.

Looking down at Johnson Lake. *Riding in the Pintlers, Lynn Street takes a look to the right where Johnson Lake lies below. Note the fine trail behind Lynn's horse. July 24, 1984. (Chapter 7)*

Dark Horse Lake. On the Montana-Idaho border. Read about the lake in the August 2, 1984, journal entry. (Chapter 8)

Glacier Falls.
*Dean Cates
and A.M. Lips
before the falls.
August, 1986.*

Unexpected water fountain. *Water running down the side of the mountain and hitting a ledge created a fountain effect so Dean Cates and A.M. Lips could fill their canteens. Glacier National Park, 1986.*

An itchy back. *Escrow decides to roll–with his pack on. "When I tried to get him up, he couldn't make it...he was just like a gangly kid who could not get back up with his backpack on." Al and Mert Schwarz unpacked and repacked him. July 9, 1988. (Chapter 26)*

The Mountains of Glacier National Park. *1986.*

Sunset on the Idaho-Montana border. 1984.

Out where the fish are. *Al making a catch in Glacier. 1986.*

Who got the bigger one? *Al shares his catch with the ever-competitive Doug Coe. 1983.*

Riding in Glacier. _A.M. Lips on Goldie and leading Dusty. 1986._

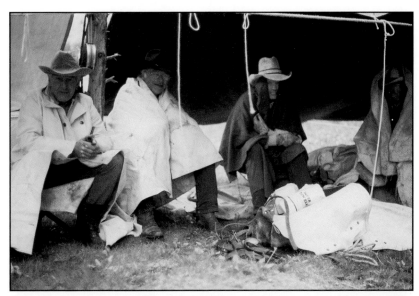

Wrapping in tarps to stay warm. *What a cold layover day! Mert Schwarz, Al, Al Severson, A.M. Lips. July 28, 1985. (Chapter 11)*

Coco gives in to being packed. *"I first tied up one of the mare's hind legs so she would be standing on three legs and couldn't buck or even shy away." July 27, 1985.(Chapter 11)*

Natural obelisk. *"Cigarette Rock – about 50 to 75 feet high and about 10 feet across – pushes majestically up and out of the mountain, demanding that we take note of it in its position of grandeur." Aug. 6, 1986. (Chapter 15)*

Eight horses in the pack string. *Bob Marshall Wilderness, 1986. (Chapter 16)*

Catch of the day. *Whenever the crew camped by a stream that had fish, they knew what they'd be having for supper.*

A first look at the Chinese Wall. *Ben Quie in the foreground; the 15-mile, 1,000-foot high Chinese Wall in the background. July 6, 1983. (Chapter 3)*

Goats on the Chinese Wall. *The second visit to the Wall: July 14, 1986. (Chapter 14) [Photo by Suzy Erickson Johnson]*

Typical camp. *Each night the crew unpacked the panniers and mantie packs, and then stretched canvas between trees creating a lean-to for their "kitchen." Ben Quie and Bill Starr are shown in this 1983 photo.*

High-wire act. *Mert Schwarz lashes a rope to a tree in preparation for setting up a lean-to for camp.*

Crossing the Red Desert. *Encompassing about 600,000 acres, this high-elevation desert in southwestern Wyoming supports wildlife, including wild horses, livestock and a large elk herd. 1987*

Getting to know flowers

"One thing (of many) that these rides are teaching me is to appreciate the flowers. For the first time in my life, I'm learning their names. I used to know only a geranium." July 21, 1986 (Chapter 12)

Asters

Lupine

Beargrass

Elephant Head. *"What a beauty you are; what a unique thing you are; you bear the symbol of the Republican Party!" July 21, 1986 (Chapter 12)*

Indian Paint Brush.

Crossing the North Pogo Agie River. *Al is leading the way; Bill Bontrager is following at the left. July 12, 1987. (Chapter 18)*

Springing from the ground. *Hank Pederson gets a drink. 1987.*

Typical New Mexico wooden windmill. Al Severson. 1991.

Like an obstacle course. *Sometimes the Aspen were so close together that the packs hit against the trees, making it frustrating to get through. July 25, 1985. (Chapter 11)*

Cooling off. A bull moose takes a swim in the Encampment River. August 1, 1987. (Chapter 22)

Antelope Wells Custom Station. *"When I asked if we could park our trucks and trailers at the customs station, he responded that he didn't run a parking lot." [Note the American flag in the foreground and the Mexican flag in the rear, just across the border.] March 25, 1990. (Chapter 32)*

Cumbres Depot. *"It took two steam engines to get the passenger cars up the steep grade from Chama." August 17, 1989. (Chapter 31)*

Watching branding. *March 26, 1990. (Chapter 32)*

The Colorado Rockies. Al on Bull outside of Buena Vista. July 16, 1988. (Chapter 27.)

The hand of God. *"It is amazing how God has developed (the mountains) over time: through eons, the earth's plates have moved together to push the mountains up and create the tilt of the rocks – in seemingly unexplainable formations. Some would say it's because of 'chance,' but I see the hand of God in it all." July 12, 1983. (Chapter 3)*

Gila River Crossing. July 13, 1991. *(Chapter 38)*

CHAPTER TWENTY

Wonderings about prayer

Monday, July 20, 1987

The horses acted up until about 12:30 last night. We had seen six wild horses in the distance yesterday, which probably agitated them. The mule had pulled loose from the sagebrush I'd tied her to last night, but thankfully was still in the vicinity when I got up a little before 5 this morning.

We were ready to ride and on the road in less than an hour (intending to stop for breakfast later). We rode east, hoping to arrive at Barros Springs where we could get water.

About 8:30 a.m., as I was riding along, lost in my thoughts, I stopped at a stream and looked back to find Doug re-setting his saddle. He confided that he was trying to get his saddle back in place and get on before I noticed (I understand the feeling). He'd stopped Dusty to look down at a dried up sole and heel from an old shoe. His grandmother had come west on the Oregon Trail and his thoughts were on her as he wondered, "Could this have been hers?"

His cinch evidently was loose after a 2-1/2-hour ride, and, as he leaned over to look, his saddle slipped and he'd toppled to the ground. He said he fell on the right side, while his left foot was still caught in the left stirrup. In order to free himself, he reached up to get his foot out. Holding the reins complicated his task, so he said he dropped the reins, which spooked Dusty. (The only fault Dusty has is, when something wiggly drops in front of him, he reacts quickly. He must have had a bad experience with a snake at some time.)

Well, apparently Dusty reared up and jerked backwards. Doug got his foot out, but since his left hand was clutching the stirrup, his shoulder was wrenched. He seems OK, but both his feelings and arm hurt.

We finally found Barros Springs and an abandoned cattle camp. The water was good, but we decided to go southeast to the Alkali River–a peaceful setting–where we stopped to have breakfast of pancakes, dried eggs, and bacon.

There are many antelope in this area. One came right up by us to drink in the river.

We started out again about 11 a.m., following a trail which the immigrants used. I have read that wagon marks still show in some places. Occasionally we saw four-sided markers stating "Oregon Trail" on two signs and "Pony Express" on the other two sides.

~ ~ ~

Doug had some more issues with Dusty. While riding, he dropped his left rein, and when he leaned forward to grab it, Dusty stepped on it. With Doug leaning over, Dusty threw his head back and hit Doug in the face, breaking one lens of Doug's dark glasses and cutting his cheek.

People might give me a hard time about putting Doug on a horse that isn't one of the more gentle ones. But Dusty is about as gentle and trustworthy as can be. People can make mistakes on a horse even when one is standing still!

~ ~ ~

We tried to locate trails that had been drawn on the topo maps, but we couldn't find them. In the desert they seem to get blotted out by people driving around in four-wheel vehicles. We ended up going too far south. I then decided to use the lay of the land to determine our route. We found Happy Spring and building remnants of an old sheep camp. A fence also enclosed about three acres of green grass, which was good for the horses. The grass was green due to its proximity to the spring. It was amazing how quickly our horses filled up. No wonder the cattle on the desert are fat where there is moisture.

~ ~ ~

Doug and I had a long talk on prayer tonight. For quite some time I've been wrestling with the question, "What happens when you pray?"

Doug and I have done a lot of praying together over the years. Once, when he and I were sitting in the hospital room of Senator

Harold Hughes, we prayed for Harold's healing, even though I was reluctant to join in. It wasn't that I didn't *want* to pray; it's just that I didn't believe that praying was going to heal Harold. And I felt that the prayers of an unbelieving person could prevent the prayer from having its effect. It troubled my mind.

I've also been wondering why we think God needs instructions from us. Isn't He capable of accomplishing what He wants without our asking?

And then there's the aspect of faith. When Jesus came down from the Mount of Transfiguration, and his disciples asked, when they couldn't cast the demon out of a young boy, "Why couldn't we drive it out?" Jesus said it is "because you have so little faith." (Matt. 17:19-20)

That means you can't just sit down and dash off a prayer and put your hand on a guy's head for healing. It takes a lot of prayer and a lot of faith. Does one have to check up on one's faith?

Doug and I didn't come to any grand resolutions to answer my wonderings. We just chewed on them.

Tuesday, July 21, 1987

The wind buffeted the tent much of last night; it was hard to sleep. Toward morning, one of the aluminum poles bent, and the back side of the tent came down. This would not have happened had I put up camp where I thought best. But every once in a while I'll say to one of the people traveling with me, "Where shall we put up camp tonight?" Yesterday was one of those days.

Doug had said, "Right out there." Well, I knew where the prevailing wind was and would have chosen a different spot for more protection. But since I'd already let Doug choose, I figured I'd better stick with his decision. That's the way people learn. I've made enough mistakes to learn a lot. Why not let others do the same.

~ ~ ~

We'd eaten breakfast and were packed up and ready to leave by about 7:30. With only two people it does not take long to make or break camp.

While it had been nice to have a fence around our camping area last night (the horses could stay in and all eat at the same time), the fences (which are always at the edge of the desert or at springs) sometimes make it difficult to continue in the direction I want. The area to the north of us is also fenced, so we tried to go east first, and then north between two sharp hills. Bull would not go when we got to some rocks. So I left him and went down to investigate on foot. I'm always amazed when Bull's instincts are better than my logic. Had he obeyed me, we'd have been in an area that would have been impossible for horses to progress, and even if we had progressed, it would have been difficult to turn around, maybe impossible.

We then proceeded back west and over the smaller hill, hopefully to avoid the fences, which we did. Then we could proceed east again.

After about a mile, I began to see where wild horses had marked their territory with manure. Some spots looked like they had occurred as recently as yesterday. We must be in wild horse country. Anticipation was building. I have read a lot about wild horses, but I have never been in their area before.

When we had gone about three miles, I spotted what looked like horses in the distance. I stopped, brought out my binoculars, and could see three dark brown or black adult animals, a yearling and a colt from this year. When we got within three-fourths mile of them, the stallion spotted us and came at us full tilt.

As quickly as I could, I grabbed for my saddle horn, taking off the lead rope, canteen, nose bag and finally the lariat that was on the bottom–all the while holding Bull's reins and my pack horse's lead rope. Clumsy, but I wanted to be ready if he charged us.

When that stallion came to within 50 yards, he stopped, looked us over for a few moments, charged to our left, saw what we were, wheeled around, and exploded back toward his band. It was not until then that I started getting my camera going.

This stallion was a beautiful black. As soon as he turned back to the herd, they seemed to know there was danger and bunched up (previously, they had stayed spread out, grazing). When the stallion reached the two mares and two colts, they all stayed bunched as they looked at us.

We rode toward them, and they held their gaze until we were within 100 yards. Then they charged off to the north and did not stop until they reached the horizon. There they halted momentarily and looked back at us; then disappeared.

What a thrill to see wild horses and to be approached by a stallion. Apparently he had no intention of attacking.

~ ~ ~

About noon, we came upon a sheepherder's wagon and a horse on a long picket line. The horse had a large white mark on his back and a rather large scar on his left hip. An old saddle with a high cantle and with a blanket flopped on top was leaning against the wheel of a trailer. I surmised someone was inside, so I called, "Hello."

A deeply tanned man came to the door. Besides the effects of the sun and weather, he had many missing teeth. He was either in his '70s, or he was a 50-year-old who'd lived a hard life. He spoke in broken English, and I could tell he was not too anxious to make conversation. He did answer when I asked what he was doing. "Sheep," he said.

I asked him the way to Arapaho Creek, and he pointed southeast, so I knew he could understand. We decided not to try anymore conversation with this man. We went up to a meadow just out of sight of his wagon and had lunch while the horses ate. We spent the afternoon watching antelope on our way to Arapaho Creek and decided to camp there even though it was early.

After an early supper, Doug and I talked in the tent (since it had started to rain lightly) while Coco, Dusty, and the mule grazed, and Bull was tied.

Soon I heard Coco squeal. I thought she was coming in heat. She quickly squealed again, and then I knew right away what it was—a wild stallion had come for her. I certainly wasn't expecting that. All the manure piles we'd seen this afternoon had seemed old, so I didn't think we were in the area of wild horses anymore. I unzipped the tent entrance, beat it out of the tent as fast as I could, and ran around the alders to where the noise had come from.

Sure enough, there was a Roman-nosed white stallion, and Dusty was fighting him off on one side of the creek while the mare Coco and the female mule were on the other side watching. I ran for Coco to catch her, but she ran away. They all did—the stallion with both mares and Dusty after him.

The thought of them all following that stallion and being corralled as wild horses crossed my mind. I ran for the nose bags (which thankfully I had recently filled with their feed ration), grabbed them and shook them. It's a sound horses like to hear. They made a swing around to return when they heard me shaking feed in the nose bags and as I called to them.

They came running. I put the nose bags on the horses and put the lead rope on Coco, calling for Doug to come out with his shoes on to help.

I gave Coco's rope to Doug and tied the others up. Then I started after the wild horse on foot to get him away from us. He kept a quarter to a half mile ahead of me. After I had gone a half mile, I stopped, and so did he. He soon began moving to my left. I made a couple steps to the left, and he turned to the right. I stepped to the right, and he moved left again. Soon I was driving him in the direction I wanted—and I was a third of a mile away from him all the time I was driving him. After moving him far enough, I turned and went back. Then he swung around and went way around us, and kept going north.

He must of have been a lone stallion out to pick up a companion. He had a scar on the back of his right hip as though he had been kicked. I'm glad Coco was not in heat.

CHAPTER TWENTY-ONE

Encounters with wild horses and rattlesnakes

Wednesday July 22, 1987

We broke camp early this morning because we knew we had a 25-mile ride ahead of us.

Little did I know that I would see an additional 50 or so wild horses today. Just before noon we spotted a small band of them close enough for us to approach–including a gray stallion and two dark mares and one foal. When one of the stallions moved toward us to check us over, his mare followed, keeping close behind. And as soon as he sensed our human presence, he whipped around and they all took off.

~ ~ ~

By following a couple of geological survey points, we found our way precisely to Harsell Spring, which turned out to be not much of a spring. We decided we ought to go on to Daumday Basin, about 4-1/2 miles northwest. On the way we spotted a grulla wild horse–all alone. It didn't take him long to get a glimpse of us, and when he did, he fairly flew off into the distance.

I am fascinated by the seldom-seen grulla. It has the color of a gray mouse on the coat, but has a black main and tail. When I was young, I read the book, *Smoky*, by Will James, a story of the training and life of a grulla horse that started out wild. I'll never forget today's sighting of a wild horse fleeing around a butte with mane and tail flying. Just like Smoky.

Daumday is a great campsite with trees and spectacular grass but no running water. From a high hill, we can see the communities of Bairoil and Lamant.

July 23, 1987

We skipped breakfast this morning and rode right into Bairoil where we met the postmaster, a friend of Sue Todd. Then we ate breakfast at the town's only (little) restaurant, which is located in a trailer. We also bought lip salve for Doug at the one-and-only store.

Doug surely is a city person, but he does handle the wilderness with humor and curiosity.

~ ~ ~

Instead of following the highway out of Bairoil to Lamont, we wound our way on side trails through sagebrush. We saw horse and antelope carcasses before running into a fence that bordered Highway 287. We followed the fence south, expecting to go only a couple miles out of our way before there would be a gate. We came, instead, to an overpass where we decided to stop and rest for lunch. There were trees for shade and grass for grazing. From there, we went under the overpass straight east to Big Sand Spring, but found it dried up.

Our final destination for the day was more than an hour further to Little Sand Spring. I wondered whether it, too, would be dried up. We found it and were able to water our horses in a muddy patch. We also found a broken down bed spring, broken down cabin (called the "Ohio Camp" on the topo map), and lots of abandoned oil well drilling equipment.

As we were deciding to camp by the spring, a pickup came by. The passenger appeared to be holding a pistol out the window and aiming into the distance. After they were out of sight, we heard two big rifle shots. I figured he poached an antelope.

Later, when we were nosing around the Ohio Camp, we found about 10 antelope hides hanging in the old cabin. Wonder if they have any connection to the guys we saw in the pickup.

~ ~ ~

It looks like we'll be riding across pretty dry desert tomorrow. It will be a challenge after watching and setting our sights on it for the past three days.

Doug and I are sleeping outside the tent tonight. The sky is full of diamond-like stars.

Friday, July 24, 1987

Sure enough-we rode with no sign of water today. We even crossed a sand dune that covered a very large area. Its terrain resembled a huge sand trap on a massive golf course (but no greens!). It felt strange to be going over a dry mountain after so many weeks of trekking, in past years, across the rugged and mostly lush terrain that one typically associates with the Rockies. The days are hot, hot and dry.

We headed for Ferris, which the map showed was five to six miles east of Little Sand Spring. When we got there, we found the place to be nearly a ghost town. There were oil wells pumping away, but other than that, only a few broken down buildings. Doug and I guessed there might be a total of 30 people living there.

We came upon three rattle snakes on the trail today. The first one curled up and began to rattle as soon as it saw Bull, so we backed off and so did he. I'm glad I noticed him; otherwise, he would probably have struck Bull. A little while later we came on another one, but this one did not even curl up. And then later, there was one that rattled by Bull's feet; but instead of striking, he went down a ground squirrel hole.

From Ferris we went on to Saltiel (which had some water), and on to Ranking Creek where we are staying tonight. The map said we would find some ruins here, but all we found were some pretty good-sized, run-down corrals.

It appeared that someone had tried to get a spring going, but about all that was recognizable was a dry spring bed. The horses aren't eating much. Either the grass is bad, or they are too tired. The water is bad, too.

We set up camp by the corrals to cut down on the wind, and shortly after, it began raining. We just took cover in the little tent and ate supper between showers.

Here's the way I developed for cooking a good supper: I first get the water to boiling. Then I cut open the dessert package, vegetable package, and main course package, and pour boiling water into each, stirring each with a fork. Then I fold the tops down and let them sit.

For potatoes, I put dried milk, a tablespoon or better of margarine, about a quarter teaspoon of salt–measured by guess–and about 1-1/3 cups of boiling water into a pan. Then I put that pan on the fire and bring it back to a boil and add about a cup of potato buds.

When I take it off the fire I pour in the contents of a dried vegetables package and stir. It sets up great.

This year, because the desert lacks firewood, I switched to a gas stove rather than a collapsible wood stove. Also, I decided to use packages of dried food since there were only two of us and we are in the heat of the desert.

~ ~ ~

We've decided that traveling in the heat of the day is too taxing. So we plan to head out right away tomorrow and travel first in the cool of the morning.

Saturday, July 25, 1987

When we got up, we immediately saddled, fed pellets to the horses, packed up, and got out of camp by 6 a.m. Coco didn't finish her feed pellets before we left and was acting sick, but we set out, anyway. I wondered if a rattler had bit her. She didn't eat all day and passed little manure.

By noon, we'd found and set up camp way up in Wild Horse Draw by a wonderful spring. I praise God for this spot. Wild Horse Draw is a deep canyon and very rocky at the lower end.

All the horses–except Coco–ate with relish. She lay down when unsaddled, which I thought might do her good. But she rolled in a way that told me she was in pain. I was afraid she was going to twist a gut, so I tied her to a sage bush so to prevent her from rolling. The sage bushes are tall here, near water.

It rained again today so it was difficult to do anything. But the rain is good; it was cooler because of it.

About 8 o'clock tonight I took Coco on a long walk. I prayed much on that walk (as Doug had done at mealtime). When I brought Coco back, she lay down again and tried to roll. In order to stop her, I lay beside her along her back, and she stretched out for about 15 minutes. Then she prepared to roll, so I spoke to her and poked her; she rolled back and lay on her side for 20 more minutes. I lay there and prayed. I took this position since I was too tired to stand by her, and I figured, even if I fell asleep, her rolling over on me would wake me up.

I became alarmed that she lay so long, and her breathing at times was shallow. I wondered how I was going to tell Rev. Paul Nelson that his horse had died. About 10 p.m., I nudged her, and to my joy, she got up, took a few mouthfuls of grass, and showed interest in all the other horses! The crisis was over and my prayers had been answered in the affirmative.

After that I washed in spring water (I was getting pretty filthy riding in the dust these days and then lying around with Coco), and now I'm off to bed.

Sunday, July 26, 1987

Today is a much-needed layover day, but I got up at 5 anyway so I wouldn't get out of the habit. I let the horses out to graze, hobbling Bull and Dusty. They moved up the draw under the instigation of the mule (that I now call Mildred), which I never tie. (The sage I must tie to is too weak, anyway).

I then meditated and began walking. I walked over many peaks in the next 2-1/2 hours while Doug slept. The early morning beauty in the desert mountainous area is better than the elaborate setting of an opera, and the sound is better than a Brahms symphony.

I got close to some antelope. No rattlers showed themselves even though they were probably there among the rocks. I decided that even if I saw one, I would not kill it. They should be able to live, too. Men are more killers than rattlers, any day. So preserve us both.

I found a 30.06 shell, and as I came over the mountain around 8 o'clock, I could see down below that Doug had just gotten out of the tent. I blew the shell like a whistle, just to fool with him. Big mistake. Instead of startling Doug, the horses got scared at the sound of my whistle. With Mildred leading, they jumped up a steep bank and went part of the way up the draw. Bull, however, who was still hobbled, could not make it up the bank, and he fell over backwards. What a shock to be watching this from afar! He managed to right himself, and I ran down to rescue him, all the way talking to him to sooth him down, to get him to stay put until I got there. And he did. Praise God he was OK. He could have broken his neck. Sometimes I wonder why others do dumb things around horses. Now I did. Live and learn.

After breakfast, we led the horses and went down the draw to some Juniper trees where there was shade. As we passed a huge rock, Doug wondered out loud whether Sampson could have turned it over–and if any man today could.

~ ~ ~

Doug read from St. Francis this afternoon as we lay under a tree. I let Bull and Mildred graze first, and an hour later tied up Bull and let the others (Coco and Dusty) graze. The horses really needed the rest; the feed was great. Doug and I stayed under the trees until 5 o'clock talking about the "fellowship," how to keep people accountable, and the importance of being honest and a good listener.

Monday, July 27, 1987

I woke up at 3 this morning, tied up Bull, and let the others out, then went back to bed until 5. We were out by 6, heading for Sinclair (about 18 miles away). We cut across country rather than follow the Seminoe Road. And when we came to the North Platte River, we were faced with a real precarious descent. Doug went first, leading Dusty, and did fine.

We then ran across a crew digging up a pipeline that needed replacement. I asked about Sinclair and was told it had no restaurants or stores–just two bars, one of which opens later in the evening.

When we got there, (shortly after noon when it was starting to get really hot), we found that the town was fenced and even had cattle guards at the entrances. It appeared we would not even be able to get in. We worked our way around to the west of town, though, tied our horses to a fence which had a gate, and walked to the K-C Bar about a block or so away. There we ate a double hamburger each and had some pop.

I called Gretchen. She told me about the 12-inch rain in Minneapolis. She was real smart in the way she handled getting home and taking care of water in the basement of our home. And, truth be told, I'm sure she'd rather weather a storm in Minnesota than be with me on one of these rides.

In fact, Gretchen has made it known that she very much does NOT want to go along on any of my trips to the Rockies. She's been in the mountains with me before, so she knows there is a lot of pain involved. And she also knows that she can say "no" to my invitation to come along and still be assured of my love.

On our 25th wedding anniversary, she "turned in" her sleeping bag because, she said, she didn't "want to be even tempted to go out there again."

She is a great sport, though, and has tried and done all kinds of things with me.

I also called Ted Schnell when I was at the bar. Ted writes for the Rawlins newspaper and had asked me to call when we were in the area. He had interviewed me by phone a while back when I was in the Prison Fellowship office in Reston. I had written letters to all the weekly newspapers in this area, telling them I was planning this trip across the Red Desert. I figured I'd probably have to go through quite a bit of private ranch land, and I believed any publicity we could get would help smooth the way with the local ranchers. Ted was one editor who followed up by writing and calling. When I reached him by phone today, he said to stay put; he was driving over to do another interview. So we waited.

In the interview, I found out a lot about Ted. He graduated from St. Mary's College in Winona, Minnesota; has been living in Rawlins for three years–and loves it; married a gal from Rawlins; has been tramping the hills for three years trying to photograph a rattler. (We saw two rattlers later today. Too bad Ted wasn't along.)

Doug invited Ted to the National Prayer Breakfast. Doug extends that invitation to many, many people.

After the interview, we mounted up, and Ted photographed us as we headed south of Sinclair.

Doug and I crossed some railroad tracks that we paralleled for about 1-1/2 miles. Then we went by a truck stop (bought two apple pies there!), and went over Interstate 80, traveling next to it another 1-1/4miles. We also went south past a petroleum pumping station. Way too much civilization for my tastes.

We had to go back east a little to get through a gate. Then we were able to go south again, over a rimrock and back into wilderness areas more to my liking. We saw that a storm was coming, and we wanted to get over the top and to the other side hoping we would not be hit by lightning. With the storm approaching, we decided to lead our horses down the slope. Then we mounted and trotted a mile, looking for a road that cut to the east.

We found one (a jeep trail), and followed it. We hunted all over for the springs that the maps indicated were in the area. It was after 6 p.m., the horses were exhausted and it was beastly hot, so we decided to make camp in the lee of a knoll next to some sage brush and other shrubs.

We unpacked the horses and let them eat sparse grass, and we drank from our canteens, ate granola bars and peanuts, and Doug had some sausage. With nothing to tie the horses to (except sage brush) and not knowing what was in store, I ate little and took a nap to conserve energy.

In about 45 minutes, all the horses had filled up, and Doug suggested that we lead our horses to Corral Spring, which we guessed was about three to four more miles southeast. The storm had passed, so I agreed. It was something I would do, but I had not suggested it because I was concerned about Doug's energy level. He has not, it seems, learned how to take cat naps, and he always pushes himself. His first full day, he had not protected himself from the sun, and his face–especially his lower lip–was swelling up.

We packed the horses back up and began walking to conserve the horses' energy just in case we might have to walk through the night. After a mile or so, we came upon a stream. What a joy for the horses to get a drink after such a hot day, having had no water since about 9:30 this morning.

It was getting dark, and I decided we should make camp in an alkali area that had ample grass. The horses seemed to like it. I asked Doug to take first watch, since I can sleep at will.

Tuesday, July 28, 1987

Doug stayed up for only about an hour during his first watch last night. Then I took a turn standing with the horses to make sure they would not run out. When it got cold, I wrapped in canvas. It's amazing how cold it gets at night in the desert, considering how hot it is during the day.

After a couple hours of cold, I decided to hobble Bull and Dusty and let the others all drag their lead ropes. Then I could go inside the tent to get warm. I figured the backtrail was through sage, and if the horses decided to take off, they would get slowed by the brush enough for me to catch them.

I was restless the rest of the night. Every time I woke, I peeked out the small tent window–the only opening other than the door–to see if the horses were still there. I felt like a Massai Warrior looking out at his cattle from a round hole (something I had witnessed in Kenya).

We got up about 6:45, rode the rest of the way to Corral Spring, and made breakfast there. For a change, we had beef stew as well as scrambled eggs (both from a package).

From Corral Spring, we headed over a couple of ridges, looking for Sage Creek, which, according to the topo map, was near the Bolten Ranch.

When we had gone a couple miles or better, I noticed two huge animal-like shapes in the distance. I had read once that there was such a thing as desert elk; could this be what I was seeing? I had seen the manure for a couple miles and thought no deer or antelope could make such big raisins. I grabbed my binoculars, and sure enough, there were two elk bulls–one seemed to be a six pointer and the other a three. What a treat!

Then I saw the Bolten Ranch. Where it was appropriate to set up camp would have been about a mile or so from the ranch home–too close for me. I'm desirous of doing as much of this trip as possible without people seeing me. Besides, we'd have had to tie to sage. So I decided we ought to go another two miles or so to Johnson Island, which is at the North Platte River.

We crossed the shallow backwater and are now surrounded by water. There is great grass here.

Doug didn't realize the back water around one side of the island wasn't the main channel of the river. As he headed to jump in the stagnant dirty back water, I told him to look at the other side of the island for the river. He was thankful for the suggestion.

I got a tarp up for shade and then walked over to watch Doug who was having a great time splashing around in the North Platte. He has been a good partner. By himself I wonder if he would stay alive, but he is great companionship. He said as we rode one day, he did not care what happened to him. He was only worried if something happened to him.

Later, we looked around the island and found hidden seven Hereford hides. Someone evidently had stolen and killed the young Hereford stock. Rustlers work more efficiently nowadays using trucks.

Then it started to rain. What a delightful thunderstorm! Not much rain came down, however. Two of the lightning strikes were so close there was hardly any time between them and their thunder. And it was so loud, I went over to quiet the horses.

After dinner, we had planned to go across the river and look at a graveyard where we think emigrants–perhaps caught in some disaster at the river crossing–are buried. But we could not cross because, what had been a light rain for us, apparently, was a much stronger storm upstream. Our previously calm, shallow river was now deep and rushing and even had entire trees floating in it. There was no way we could get across.

CHAPTER TWENTY-TWO

Altitude sickness brings an understanding of prayer

Wednesday, July 29, 1987

When we rode south from Johnson Island where the water had receded this morning, we came upon a vast, lush area that was being irrigated, making it impossible to get through. So we tried going around it but were soon confronted by a locked gate. Thankfully there was a part that was only wired, so we unwired it to get through. In the distance we noticed someone operating a self-propelled mower, so we headed that way to talk to the persons we thought to be the property owners. Two ranch hands, who came to meet us in a pickup, told us we were on the Emberg Ranch, and they gave us directions to get across. They seemed friendly enough, so I was somewhat emboldened to proceed across private ranch land.

Unfortunately, their directions brought us to another ranch with gates tightly wired shut. Again, someone in a pickup approached as we were trying to unwire the gates. I wondered whether we'd be accused of trespassing.

Instead, we were greeted by a woman who said, "You must be the famous Minnesota Governor we've been reading about." Apparently the Rawlins newspaper had arrived, and this woman (Marilyn Walch) told us we were front page news. She and her husband Gene chatted with us for quite some time. They run 250 cows on 1,200 acres with some irrigated land. They certainly are friendly people, which gave me cause to be even more bold about crossing private property. The two of them called Marilyn's brother, Dick Mawry, who ranches a little to the south of them, to let him know we'd be coming across his property–probably tomorrow.

Marilyn also imparted an interesting fact about rattlesnakes. She said we would not see anymore; that nobody has seen any south of Sage Creek, which we already crossed.

The next ranch we came to–another big one–we discovered belonged to the Bergers. A hired hand cutting hay spotted us. These ranchers and ranch hands are certainly observant, yet welcoming. He gave us directions to get out as easily as possible. We went only as far as the south end of their hay field, where we're camping tonight–Snow Creek. There is great grass where they haven't cut yet. I'm leaving all the horses untied again.

Thursday, July 30, 1987

We packed up early today and left without breakfast, wanting to get to the town of Encampment by 2 p.m. It's our last day coming out of the Red Desert. It has turned out that my anxiety about going through the desert was unnecessary. Because of the helpful ranchers (as a result of Ted Schnell's article in the Rawlins newspaper), we've been able to travel easily when we came out of the desert onto ranch land.

Coco bucked off Doug's duffle and bucked around the hay field right before we were ready to ride off–don't know what her problem was. Thankfully the panniers stayed on.

When we reached the Mawry place, we were invited in for tea and a good visit with Sue, Dick, and son, Shane. They then directed us to the Bath Ranch where we found the owner, who also gave us directions across his property.

On the way there, I saw tracks of a horse and colt–unshod–and another shod horse. I thought to myself, "A brood mare and foal came up this road day before yesterday, and someone rode up on a shod horse to fetch them." I was guessing, of course, but based my assessment on my what I have learned about tracks. I've always been intrigued by people who are able to track animals, so I've worked to develop my knowledge over the years.

In this instance, it appeared the tracks of the adult shod horse were coming purposefully and hard enough so there was likely a rider on the horse. And looking at the age of the tracks, I tried to estimate when all this happened.

Wanting to test my ability as a tracker, I asked the owner of the Bath Ranch–when we were getting directions from him–about the tracks I'd seen. The rancher confirmed my analysis: a mare and foal had gotten loose the day before yesterday, and his daughter saddled a horse to go after them.

When Doug heard this conversation, he figured I had used my binoculars to watch all this happen from the mountain. "No," I told him, "I read it in the tracks." He was amazed.

We then had Calf Creek, Otto Creek, Terry Creek, and Cow Creek to cross–and more fences to get through. When we thought we had it made, and Encampment was in sight, we went through one last gate which put us into a difficult wooded area with thick undergrowth that was hard to get through. We must have picked the worst place to get into town. We made it to the city limits at one minute after 2 p.m., though, and set up at the rodeo grounds. Then we went to find Doug Vogel (Gretchen's second cousin and school teacher in Encampment) and his wife, Joy, and kids, Matt and Alexandra.

Doug Vogel drove Doug Coe and me up to Atlantic Gulch by Atlantic City to get my truck and trailer from Barbara Cole's place. A friend of Doug Coe picked him up from Encampment and also took Dusty back to Montana.

Before heading back to Encampment, I visited with Barbara again and heard about her daughter's wedding to the lawyer in Washington, D.C. Barbara would honor her daughter's wishes and not attend the wedding.

I'm now back at the rodeo grounds in Encampment. Al Severson, Bob Cashin, A.M. Lips, Dan Stine and Mert Schwarz will arrive from Minnesota tomorrow morning to join me on the last leg of this year's trip. I met Dan about a year ago in Fargo, N.D. He is a friend of–and used to work with–A.M. He was on oxygen, then, due to his cancer treatments, and has been ever since–until about a month ago. He carried an oxygen bottle on the back of his saddle when he rode last year. I pray he stays healthy on this ride.

Saturday, August 1, 1987

Before heading out today, we spent some time teaching Dan's young horse, Chief, to be packed. We used the fenced corrals at the rodeo grounds so he would not get away if he got upset and bolted. He was pretty upset, but after a while calmed down enough for us to start.

We got out about 11:30. It was beastly hot–a thermometer I saw in town around 9 a.m. said it was 100 degrees F. We rode through town and via a road for a couple of miles, then a cattle guard blocked us off from the trailhead. You'd think the Forest Service could have put a gate next to the cattle guard, but they hadn't. We decided to just stop there and eat lunch, and while the others ate, I rode until I found a gate. I also found a place to ride and lead our pack horses and mules up a mountain, down again through a rough, wooded, steep area, and finally onto the trail, along the beautiful Encampment River.

After lunch, we rode 13 miles along this scenic trail; saw a cow elk and calf. At about 2 o'clock this afternoon, we came to a great meadow where it would have been nice to spend some time. But it had taken us so long to get to the trailhead outside of Encampment this morning that we needed to press on.

There is poor grass where we are camping tonight. It's difficult when grazing is poor. Not so bad for the new horses, but after three weeks, my horses need feed whenever they can get it, in order to keep going. Still, figuring the new horses might run back for better grass, I put ropes across the back trail (between two trees) to keep them in camp. There is a steep bank up on one side and a steep bank down on the other into the river. Mert's saddle horse, Gunther, is the most likely to attempt to return to the trailers.

Sunday, August 2, 1987

Our animals' antics made for a restless night for most all of us. I let both Coco and Bull loose on hobbles last night, and at 2 o'clock there was such a ruckus and squealing that I had to get up to check. Goldie was making love to Coco, who was in heat, and Bull was trying to run him off! I tied up Goldie and Coco away from each other, so it was quiet from that section the rest of the night.

Cashin and Schwarz, on the other hand, had tied their animals near each other and by the tents. There continued to be noise and kicking sounds from that area.

The problem was Cashin's mule, Maynard, who was beating up on his saddle horse, Prince. So Bob got up and let Prince loose with hobbles. "Now that I'm up, I've got to go to the bathroom," Cashin said. Evidently, he is a regular and his body thought he'd gotten up for breakfast!

Then Prince grazed right next to the tent that Al and Mert were in. Chewing that close to one's ear can be very loud.

And as I guessed, there were tracks this morning that showed Gunther had tried to get to the backtrail by going around my ropes and down one of the banks. Luckily, he came to his senses, realized the bank was too steep, and came back to camp.

~ ~ ~

It's hard to get out of camp before 9 a.m. with so many riders. We made it about 9:30 and followed the Encampment River again today. It is a stunningly beautiful river–so much to delight the eye and ear that it is hard to absorb it all. There is virtually no valley–just 800 feet of mountain continuously on both sides–until we came out of Wyoming into Colorado, where the river widened a bit at Commissary Park.

We made my planned camp on the West Fork of the Encampment River, near its source. There is a large meadow with fantastic grass here; the horses filled up easily.

~ ~ ~

I've been watching everyone's horses the last couple of days and find it interesting how they adapt (or don't). Bull, Coco, and Gyp (the mule I call Mildred) were hardened from the weeks of riding. Dan Stine has two quiet, soft Quarter Horses, Dusty, 13, and Chief, 4. The first night, after 13 miles, Chief was so exhausted he could hardly eat and just wanted to lie down. He also was so unsure of himself he would stick close to Dusty; and if Dusty was not tied where there was grass, Chief would still stay close, rather than move off a little and eat.

Also, when Chief gets into trouble, he bucks–which he did when I first put the panniers on in Encampment, and again along the trail when his pack lost an overshoe which had been tied on top.

Cashin's mule is small–under 14 hands–and I think more difficult to pack. Cashin always brings much personal gear with him, so the mule is packed high. Cashin's Prince is a good walker.

Severson is riding Misty, a sorrel mare. She sores easily behind the front legs, but Al uses a britching on his saddle to hold the girth back; it works well. The male mule, Jake, isn't shod on his back hooves. That may cause some trouble out here. Al's farrier said he doesn't like mules, and Jake probably could tell that. So when Al brought him to be shod, Jake fought too much. That's why he has only his front hooves shod.

A.M.'s Goldie is tough and dependable. So is Joe, the Appaloosa he packs. Mert has a beautiful pair of buckskins that are probably the best looking of the bunch. Gunther takes quick, short steps when walking and really moves out.

Everybody seems in good health except Dan. He has breathing problems when we get over 9,000 feet. Otherwise he's doing OK.

Monday, August 3, 1987

Had some trouble finding the right trail to go over the Continental Divide today. Once over the top, we went from 10,000 to 8,800 feet to the Elk River. Worked around the Sawtooth Mountain and then looked for the Mica Basin Trail.

We moved through a large flock of sheep (which had a Peruvian herder) to a camp where there were a few cabins. There we met Ray Corbett, owner of the land, and a friend of his. Both were very talkative, and they invited us in for a cold drink of water.

As we talked with Ray and his friend, they soon learned that all but one of us were from Minnesota. Ray's friend–a policeman from Denver who was there visiting–told us about his "Minnesota connection." His grandfather once had a ranch in this area, and one summer Butch Cassidy worked for him. At the end of the summer, when Butch was paid, he took off, but not before stealing 17 horses. Ray's friend said Butch probably stole the horses because his grandfather owed more money to Butch than the horses were worth. His grandfather, I guess, paid very little.

Anyway, his grandfather went after Butch, trailing him to Casper, Wyoming. Butch was not around, but the grandfather found that Butch had sold his horses, and they'd been shipped to Minnesota!

~ ~ ~

I asked Ray about directions to our next campsite. He said our map was right, pointing us to the east, but that would force us to cross a boggy area. I decided to tackle it alone on Bull, anyway, and was able to find my way across. But in coming back to get the other guys, I became over-confident and I went into a quicksand-type bog, going down deeper than Bull's belly. I threw my self off of Bull and rolled up to a tree. (I had read that it's best, in quick sand, to stay horizontal and roll to safety.)

As soon as I was safe, I turned and saw Bull, in one continuous motion, raise his front end out of the depths of the quicksand, turn his body to the left, hook his hoofs in the tree roots, and pull himself out! As he stood beside me, trembling from his exertion, I could see by the water and sand marks on him that he had sunk half way in from his belly to his back. And when he made his move to get out, his rear end sank so low that the cantle of the saddle had gone under. What a powerful horse! (I surely feel bad when I get my friend in such danger.)

When I got back to the group, Ray told us a better way to go, even though it took us out of our way to the south for miles. We found a great campsite at Lost Dog Creek, which is at an elevation of about 8,200 feet. It is about eight miles from where I wanted to be by this evening.

~ ~ ~

Cashin received a wood chopping lesson–sort of–from A.M. tonight. (Or maybe it was A.M. who got a lesson in humility). I and a few of the others watched Cashin as he swung his axe, over and over, striking the wood. Most of the time the axe just bounced off; some of the time it made a dent. A.M. told him he simply wasn't doing it right, and that he'd show him how. Then A.M. picked up the axe and demonstrated how to hold it and swing it. As A.M.'s axe landed on the wood, it bounced. He tried again, and again. Some wood is just too tough.

Tomorrow will be a layover day. We need it, as do the horses.

Tuesday, August 4, 1987

First thing I did today was to go for a walk and explore our trail since it "Y'ed" where we are camped. I passed the Feed House Campground as I walked to the Feed House Guard Station, a mile away going south. We are six miles from Slavania.

I got back at 7:30 after a three-mile hike, and we had breakfast.

I am concerned about Jake's unshod back hooves. We will have to travel more roads in the days ahead, and his hooves are already down to the sole. Al wanted to get out to a phone to call a farrier. I don't think a farrier would come to us anyway. My suggestion was to pack Jake light and not lead him, but let him find his own way. That way he can choose not to walk on roadway if he wants.

After a lunch of soup, sausage sandwich, and hot chocolate, I studied my maps, took a nap, and learned to play Whist. The Norwegians around my home on the farm always played this card game, but I never learned.

We all showered, and then I took time to write in my journal. Our shower is the kind where the sun warms the water in a plastic bag we hang in a tree.

This group is fun due to their compatibility and Cashin's and Severson's senses of humor. We don't spend time in organized discussion and spiritual fellowship, but on Sunday, I led them in a worship service, which they said they appreciated. We talk horse and mules a lot since we think of these animals first and foremost.

It is Gretchen's birthday today.

Wednesday, August 5, 1987

Dan Stine was up soon after me, got the fire started, opened the bacon, and got breakfast started–all before it was fully light. He was played out trying to breathe in the high altitude; he said he wanted to be able to do something worthwhile. He asked me how to mix pancake batter, and I knew after showing him that he would also be making our breakfast pancakes.

After we were on the trail for a while today, I was not exactly certain of where we were. So when a Forest Service pickup truck came by, I hailed it to ask the workers for directions. They didn't know where they were, either!

They did have a Forest Service map, however, which they gave me. With that and my topo map, we all figured out exactly where we were. I found a trail which wound to the right, and which appeared like it would save us two miles of road travel–very hard on horses' shoes. My speculation turned out to be right, and we climbed the Three Island Lake Trail up to 10,000 feet. Once again, spectacular beauty.

After this, we climbed on a very rough trail over Lost Ranger Peak at 11,932 feet. Instead of following the trail, I cut off a mile of our journey by cutting across and going down a very precarious-looking steep grade on rocks. If the men hadn't followed me before, they may never have trusted and followed me now. Interestingly, Dan followed first.

I wondered, when we were at Lost Ranger Peak, how Dan would do at that altitude. I didn't tell him how high up we were, but he did ask me tonight about the altitude of where we are camping–Lake Elbert at 10,200.

We have great grazing again. We're getting water from a small, nearby waterfall.

Thursday, August 6, 1987

I was awakened this morning–about 5 a.m.–by Dan who was rattling around, looking for things to make for breakfast again. Once again, he said he couldn't sleep well.

I got up to turn the horses out and discovered Chief, Coco and Bull, who were out all night, were nowhere in sight. So I saddled Dan's horse and went on the backtrail to find them. There they were—just over the hill grazing on better grass.

When I got back, Dan said he wasn't feeling well; he didn't eat anything but maybe one pancake.

We got out of camp on this high mountain trail heading for Buffalo Pass (about nine miles away). After a mile or so, Dan began vomiting. But not having eaten much for breakfast, he had little to throw up. I knew we needed to get him to a lower elevation, but there was no way to get him lower in this rugged mountain range. We had to stay on the trail and get to Buffalo Pass and down to Steamboat Springs 16 miles farther. The rest of the ride would continue in high elevation. Rather than tell Dan he needed to leave the ride, I asked him to make the choice. I knew how his heart was set to make this ride, but his life was at stake.

He said he would leave the ride—a tough thing for a man to say. He looked down when he said it.

We rode on to the trailhead, hoping to get help, but I know full well that we wouldn't arrive until noon at the earliest. At that time of day there wouldn't be anyone there. Even if there were cars there, the owners would be up in the mountains doing their hiking and exploring. No one comes into the trailhead at noon—it's always early in the morning or later in the afternoon.

But I didn't know what else to do. And Dan's altitude sickness was getting worse. He was having even more difficulty breathing, and the dry heaves continued. The thought crossed my mind, "What if he dies up here?" So we headed out for the trailhead, anyway. It seemed to be our only option.

I began to pray for Dan's life and wished that someone would be at the trail head. But as I did, my wonderings about prayer entered my mind again: How should I pray? And what happens when you pray? God is not our errand boy. He knows all. He is love. Is it right to pray for something specific? What happens when you do?

Certainly He's capable of accomplishing what He wants without my asking specifically. The prayer questions I discussed with Doug just two weeks ago flooded my mind again.

All this was so reminiscent of the feelings I had had when we were praying in the hospital for the healing of Senator Harold Hughes those many years ago in Washington. Back then, I was worrying that my lack of faith in prayer actually healing would stand in the way of helping Harold.

I was also reminded today of a fellow–an insurance agent in Washington, D.C.–who was brought to me by some friends. They wanted him to tell me about how he came to believe in Jesus Christ. He told this marvelous story about his daughter going to college in the Midwest, where she came to believe Jesus is the Messiah. He said he started studying the Bible so that when she came home on spring break, he'd have enough information to prove the error in her thinking. And as he read the New Testament, he began to feel guilty. So he called a rabbi friend in San Francisco to discuss his concern about reading the New Testament. The rabbi encouraged him to read it as well. He did, to prepare himself with persuasive arguments to convince his daughter she had come to the wrong conclusion.

In reading both the Old Testament and the New Testament, he came to believe in Jesus as his Savior. He then led his wife to Christ, and what a reunion they had when his daughter came home for spring break!

He also had led a young man in his 30s to Christ about a week before his visit to me. And he'd invited his young friend to my office, as well. But the new convert hadn't shown up on time. When he arrived about 10 minutes later, full of excitement, he bubbled, "I gotta tell you what happened! I know I was supposed to be here on time, but it was raining, and there were no taxis around. I thought, 'Well, I'm a Christian now. Maybe Jesus will help me'. So I closed my eyes and I prayed that a cab would come and take me to the Hill. While I was praying I heard the sound of tires. So I opened my eyes, and there was a cab pulling up along side of me! The taxi driver rolled down the window and said, 'Do you want a ride, buddy?'"

With stars in his eyes, the young man looked at each of us and exclaimed, "It works; it really works!"

My only response to this young fellow was, "I hope you still believe in God in the future when you pray for a taxi and it doesn't show up." I was basically telling him that God doesn't always answer our prayers the way we want. But my prayer question was evidently haunting me back then as well.

Then another thought came to me as I was riding along today, worrying about Dan. I was reminded of Eddie Rickenbacker's experience alone in a life raft in the Pacific with no food or water. He prayed specifically for both. As he was praying, a bird came and sat on his head. He reached up, took it by the legs, and with a little effort made it his meal and supply of liquid. It sustained him until he was rescued.

I thought, those two men prayed specifically, and it worked. People in the Bible prayed specifically, too. And I don't think God wants us to NOT pray specifically. So I prayed specifically that, when we got to the trail head, someone would be there to take Dan down to lower elevation.

Then I put it all in God's hands, determined not to worry any more.

At 12:30 p.m., as we came over the rise overlooking Buffalo Pass, I could see the trailhead. There was a gooseneck trailer. No vehicles. Nobody. We would have to continue riding down the road to Steamboat Springs–16 miles more (the number of miles we usually ride in a day).

But as we rode closer, we could see a winding, gravel road leading up to Buffalo Pass, and there was a vehicle coming up the road! Hope rose within me.

I instructed Mert to dash ahead, cut this guy off, and see if he would give Dan a ride into Steamboat Springs.

When we reached the car, we found out the driver was a young family man, but alone today–and willing to help us out. We chatted for a while, and then I waited with the horses as the others rode with Dan to town.

All alone and taking shelter under the gooseneck trailer from a light rain that had started, I began recounting in my mind our experience from the time Dan got up this morning. When my thoughts came to the part where I had prayed for someone to be at the trailhead, I realized that, with all the action, it totally slipped my mind that I had even prayed. I felt terrible that I had forgotten all about it; I wasn't praising God. I confessed this to God and shared with Him my sorrow that I had forgotten about the prayer.

Then I got to thinking about what I'd learned about this young fellow who was giving Dan a ride. He was born in Trinidad, Colorado; is a coach in San Diego; had come back to Colorado to vacation with his wife and two sons who were on a fishing outing today. He said the entire family had started out together on that outing early this morning. He'd given the fishing equipment to his sons who ran off to the stream, handed his wife's fishing rod to her, and turned back to pick up his own when it flashed through his mind that he hadn't been up in Buffalo Pass for a long time.

He'd said to his wife, "You know, I'd sure like to see what it looks like up there." And she had responded, "You go right ahead. The boys and I are going fishing!" So he put his gear down, got in his car, and headed out to Buffalo Pass.

When I sorted through all of this, I all of a sudden realized it was a *good* thing that I had forgotten about my prayer. Otherwise, I might have thought that I had *prayed* this guy into Buffalo Pass. In reality, God was answering my question, "What happens when you pray?"

When you pray with faith and humility, you can be a part of His plan. God revealed His truth to me and I was blessed by it. When you submit yourself as I did–in honesty and helplessness–our loving God reveals what we could only hope for. When I prayed, "Lord, the only way I can figure this out is for there to be a car there. I can't figure any other way to get Dan down where his life can be saved," even that was the Holy Spirit within me.

I had laid it out in honesty to Him and had no control over the events.

The point at which this young coach had decided to come up to Buffalo Pass was before I even prayed. God had His plan in place long before I prayed. Dan would have been taken care of, undoubtedly, whether I had prayed or not. And God combined all of this to bless me and help me see and understand that prayer is not only speaking, but listening to God.

An amazing experience. I have concluded from this experience that one of the reasons Jesus commanded us to pray and set an example of prayer is so we will pay attention to God. "Praying without ceasing" must mean we should pay attention to God at all times.

CHAPTER TWENTY-THREE

Spelunking becomes a spiritual experience

Al Severson went into Steamboat Springs with Dan. The plan is for Al to get Dan back to Encampment to retrieve his motor home and trailer, to come back to Buffalo Pass to get Dusty and Jake (I'm keeping Dan's pack horse, Chief, for the rest of the ride), and for Al to rejoin us tomorrow morning. A.M., Mert, Cashin, and I continued on.

I tried to lead Chief behind Coco. Since I had led a mule behind Coco in the first three weeks, I didn't think there would be any problem with this arrangement. But there was.

Maybe it was because Coco was just getting over her heat, but she was upset with this new arrangement. Over and over, she tried to kick Chief. So, after about a quarter mile, I decided to lead Chief and put Coco behind him. I originally was reluctant to do this because Chief had been hanging so close to Dan's Dusty the first five days that I thought, being in the lead, he might not follow well. But he did.

We traveled only four more miles to Grizzly Lake where we are camping tonight. There is good grazing here and, of course, plenty of water from the lake. Adequate wood, too, a flat place for shelter and trees to string the high line for our horses to be tied.

It looks like it's going to rain tonight. Mert said his pyramid tent sheds water and is the greatest thing to sleep in when it's raining. So A.M. moved his posturepedic sleeping pad into Mert's tent and is sleeping in there with him tonight.

Friday, August 7, 1987

Sure enough, it rained last night. A lot. A.M. got up this morning sputtering and mad as a hornet. It seems Mert's pyramid tent wasn't such a good tent in the rain after all. A.M. walked out of the tent, carrying his foam pad. And steaming.

He yelled at me (as if this was all my fault), "Al, look at this!"

I turned to see water–not dripping, but pouring-from the side of his pad. It had soaked up water all night–and he had been lying in it!

The rest of us got a great laugh out of it, which did not help A.M.'s mood. That pad is something I told him we couldn't pack, but he said he needed it for his back. So he's been rolling it up every morning, stuffing it in a duffle, and carrying it hung from his saddle horn.

A.M.'s sleeping bag was wet, too, as were most of his clothes. This can be worrisome in the mountains because of the risk of hypothermia. Thankfully, A.M. has other clothes in a waterproof bag.

I saddled up and rode out to meet Al Severson, who was on his way back from helping Dan. I guessed he would be about half way between Buffalo Pass and Grizzly Lake. When I met Al, he told me that when he and Dan called Doug Vogel for a ride from Steamboat Springs to Encampment yesterday afternoon, Doug was not available to help out. So Al and Dan rented a Ford Bronco and drove up to Encampment to get Dan's motor home and trailer. Al slept in Dan's motor home last night and then brought Dan's brother, who lives in the area, back to Steamboat Springs and Buffalo Pass this morning to get Dan's horse and the mule.

~ ~ ~

We left Grizzly Lake, traveling along Wyoming Trail and then Percy Lake Trail, where we hit an unmaintained trail. For a time, we followed a rancher and his two children as they moved cattle up a road. They stopped, gave us directions, and showed us White Slide and Harrison Hump.

We then moved south and east to get back to Colorado Creek. On the way, we went through an old logging and sawmill camp, and we saw an elk cow and two calves.

At about 5 p.m. we came to a corral and loading chute near Highway 14. This let me know, unfortunately, that we probably were on private land. When I'm riding in the mountains, I try, if at all possible, to avoid private land so as not to be unnecessarily around other people. My cohorts don't understand this. When they see an opportunity to turn into a town to buy some pop, I want to turn the other way and head back into the wilderness. I guess I just want to be alone in the mountain experience. To be at one with nature is such a rare and beautiful thing that I just want to stay away from civilization. On a ride like this, it takes about three days to begin getting civilization out of one's system. I don't want to ruin the experience by letting it creep back in.

Besides, since I am from a farm background, I'm especially conscientious about being on private property. I wondered whether we should try staying in the rancher's corral and explain who we were if he showed up or move to a stand of trees on the other side of two gates that would camouflage our presence. In either case, we'd be on private property. The guys and I talked it over, and we decided to stay in the corrals.

A.M. walked down by the bridge over the creek where there was a padlocked cable across and a sign that said, "No trespassing. Violators will be prosecuted." We had unpacked by then, so we nonetheless decided to stay. Anyway, I've learned that ranchers out here generally don't consider people who are traveling through on horseback as "trespassers." Horsemen, unlike some backpackers and hunters, are people who respect gates and don't break down fences. Something about our being on horseback brings out the hospitality of the ranchers.

Soon it began to rain and we knew no ranchers would come out in this weather.

Saturday, August 8, 1987

We ate bread with cheese and peanut butter for breakfast this morning so we would not have to wash dishes and could get out of camp quicker.

We went through the creek to get around the padlocked cable and rode five miles toward what looked like a jeep trail on my topo map. As we were getting close, a jeep pulled up alongside us on the wrong side of the road. He introduced himself as being from the Murphy Ranch, and then he told us we couldn't go across Murphy's private land.

I then introduced myself, explained what we were doing, and respectfully asked about the best, alternative way to get to our destination. After chatting with him a while, he said the Murphy Ranch owned all the land around, and he supposed we could go across, after all. Then he told us the best way to do it, and he even told us the padlock combination to get into the forest land at the boundary!

At about noon, we came to the edge of Murphy's property and tied up at an aspen grove for lunch. When we had finished, we saw a lone rider on the other side of the fence. When it didn't look like he would stop, I bridled Bull and rode over to him to talk. He seemed a little nervous as he saw me coming.

It didn't take long, however, for him to warm up. I found out this young man was a hand for the Myring Livestock Co., was originally from South Dakota, and was married with three little boys, the oldest being eight. He and his wife had taken this job just a few months ago, and though he loves the country, he was considering an offer from a 72-year-old man in Nebraska to take over his ranch of 2,300 cows. I bet he takes it. Nice guy.

He invited us to travel with him to talk to his boss. Though it was a mile out of the way, the trek was well worth it. They gave us great directions for the best way to get to Flat Lake and Bundy Park, and pointed out Spicer Peak, Hyannis Peak, and Arapahoe Ridge, plus they told us how to get to a good campsite on the Middle Fork of the Arapahoe Creek on Hyannis Peak Trail. We're at another great camp where we can layover tomorrow.

Sunday, August 9, 1987

We saddled our "misfits" (as Al Severson calls them)-the pack animals–and rode up to Hyannis Peak today. I rode Chief, whom I've been using as a pack horse since Dan left, and who has turned out to be a good pack horse. Mert rode Joe, and Al rode Gyp. Bob did not ride his pack animal.

We had a tough climb to the top of the peak where we had lunch. From that vantage point, we could see much countryside, and we could pick out landmarks and mountains we had traveled days ago.

We also had church services there. I read John 15, and then shared the story of my first spelunking experience.

It happened when I was still in Congress. Several people were having dinner at our home in Silver Spring, Maryland, when the conversation turned to spelunking. It sounded like a dangerous activity to me. And it certainly would not be a sport for a claustrophobic like myself. After some sharing, one of the guys, who was an experienced spelunker, said, "Hey! Why don't you come along?" Without adequate forethought, I–the claustrophobic one–had committed myself to a spelunking outing.

The next Saturday, I found myself on a narrow country road in West Virginia. We stopped and parked the car, got out, and crawled under a barbed wire fence. Now, being a farmer, I worry about being on someone else's property. But our leader said, "Come on! See that mound over there by the rocks? That's where the entrance is." We walked up, and to my surprise, there was a hole, and it was not much bigger than a large man could fit through.

Giving me no time to back out of this expedition, our leader immediately instructed us to don our helmets with carbide lamps. He proceeded down the hole via a fairly long ladder–already in place for spelunkers. I and two others were close behind.

We ended up in a domed, cave-like a room. I started to gaze around, using the light from the lamp on my helmet. To my distress, I saw that the domed room from about five feet up was totally and thickly covered with bats.

Two weeks prior to this, I had read in the *Washington Post* that people had contracted rabies simply by inhaling the fumes from bat manure. My anxiety shot way up. "Let's get out of here!"

Before I had a chance to retreat, our leader quickly pointed out the hole in the wall across the way; there was a short ladder leading up to it. He went first. Since being near the leader brought some security, I went second, with the two others in our party following. At the top of that ladder I climbed through the hole into a tunnel that, I soon found out, was about 150 feet long. This passageway was so small and so narrow that I could not crawl through it on all fours. I had to lie down on my stomach and wriggle like a snake. It did not help that the floor of the passageway was covered in greasy, slimy clay.

When I came to a curve in this tunnel, I began to panic and stopped. "Am I going to get stuck going around this curve? I'm thicker than these other guys. What am I going to do? Two people are behind me!"

Our leader sensed my hesitation. "Are you having trouble?"

I had to admit I was.

He said, "Come a little further and you'll be able to stand up." Taking his encouragement, I did wriggle a little further where I was able to stand–very near a 50-foot drop.

Our leader tied a 50-foot-long rope onto a stalagmite, and went down. Then it was my turn. I hung on and rappelled down. I came to the end of my rope and to my surprise I wasn't at the bottom! I realized that this 50-foot rope, tied to a stalagmite just a little back from the edge of a 50-foot cliff would not reach the bottom.

Then I heard a voice a little below me saying, "You're close to the bottom. Just let go." I trusted him and dropped. Into a creek.

We then followed the creek, which got narrower and narrower. To make matters worse, the creek walls were at an angle. I couldn't walk straight up and had to lean on the wall as we progressed.

Could anything get worse? Yes. The creek bed and ceiling began to drop, with the water of course staying the same level. And, looking ahead, I could see the tunnel we were following was completely filled with water.

Our guide explained that what I had to do to get through this section of the cavern was to put out my lamp and follow the tunnel while under water. "Just hold your breath," he said. "You will come out on the other side before you have to breathe."

Did I believe him? I had no choice. I was glad he had done this before and knew me.

So everyone turned off their lights; it was pitch-dark. The air was a deep, inky black. I discovered nothing is as dark as the black of a cave. You could have touched your finger to your eyeball and not seen it coming.

I took a deep breath and moved forward in the 4.5-foot high tunnel, (now completely filled with water), following our leader. The creek water surrounded me. In my childhood I dreaded having my head under water. My feelings haven't changed.

When I came out of the water, I saw the light of our guide's carbide lamp. Boy! Was that sight gorgeous. It was just a little light, but any light seemed miraculous after being in the depths like that. And our leader was right. I was able to hold my breath until the ceiling rose enough for my head to be exposed above water.

We later came to a chasm so deep that, as we looked over the brink, the light from our lamps did not reach the bottom. I found a pebble and threw it down. We couldn't hear it land. This chasm was awfully, awfully deep, and we had to get to the other side–about 15 feet away.

Our leader made a bowline in the end of his rope, formed a lasso, and lassoed a stalagmite on the other side. Then he instructed us: "Hang on tight. As you swing across, throw your feet up when you hit the other side so you can cushion yourself. Otherwise you might lose your grip and fall into the abyss." He added quietly, "And there wouldn't be any way for us to get you out of down there."

I was quite confident about performing this feat because of the rope and rock experiences I had had while in the Navy. But I feared for the safety of my companions, even if they had done this before.

With the chasm about 15 feet across, I guessed we would each land about that many feet below the ledge across the way. Then we would have to climb up, hand over hand.

My attention focused on what needed to be done.

We succeeded. But we still weren't out of the cavern.

We came to something similar to the inside of a chimney. It was very narrow, but once through, I knew I would be in the real world again.

I was instructed, "When you go through this, it is better for you to hold your hands down at your side." And I thought, "Naw, I can do better with my arms up so I can help pull myself up."

This time I went first. I reached my arms up, and I got only part way up before the passage got so narrow that I couldn't get a grip on anything. I could go no further. My arms were useless above my head.

As I edged my way back down, my belt got caught on a rock that was jutting out, and there I hung. I couldn't get a grip on anything to pull myself up with my hands; my feet were dangling, but too far up for anyone below to help me.

The only thing I could do was to slowly and methodically feel around with my feet, searching for any rough spot on the rock surface that I could hook a toe on and push myself up ever so little. I finally found one. I lifted myself up, wiggled myself over so that my belt would unhook, and then I managed to get down the rest of the way.

Trying once again–this time as originally instructed with my arms at my sides–I worked my way up the "chimney" using my shoulders, arms, and toes.

When I got out, there I was, standing in sunlight as glorious as the resurrection. Soon standing next to me was my high-school aged son, Dan, who had been my guide. At home I could tell him what to do. Here, I trusted and followed him.

I've thought a lot about this spelunking experience over the years, and I told the men this morning that it reminds me of one's relationship with God's son, Jesus Christ. As we go through life, we sometimes feel panicky and can't move on. In God's Son there is hope. When we come to the end of our rope, the only thing left is to let go and trust God's Son. In life, as in spelunking, follow the One who you trust, the One who has been there.

When I share about this spelunking experience, I hold back, until the end, that it was my son leading me because I want people to have respect for the person who guided me through the frightening unknown. Good advice for all of us: "listen to the voice of the One who has been there."

~ ~ ~

When I finished "preaching," we all prayed the Lord's Prayer. Later, Mert told me our church services out here are moving, spiritual experiences for him. He said he never feels this close to God when he goes to church back home.

I think there are two situations that contribute to our being close to God. The first comes when we are alone. Jesus went up into the mountain so He could be alone with God. But we can't stay on that mountain top forever, anymore than he did. In fact, most of the time, as we work our way through life, we are in relationship with others. And so God also makes it possible for us to get close to Him through others, including children, people who are different from ourselves, and those who are consecrated to Him. Someone who came to know Christ later in life told me that within five years, his closest circle of friends was composed entirely of other Christians. Previously, there were none. I think this is God's way of revealing Himself and helping us to feel close to Him through His people.

And when God's people come together there is a bonding that allows the Holy Spirit to work among us. Being "religious" sometimes hampers this.

~ ~ ~

On the way back to camp, I led with Chief so he would learn to walk fast (he did) and gain courage and confidence going over streams. It was a good training experience for him. Should I buy him and keep him for future rides? I think he's as close as I could find to what I am looking for in another horse.

When we got back, Mert checked all the horses' shoes and discovered Bull had lost both of his in the rear. Mert had some extra shoes along that fit Bull, so he put them on, and now Bull is back in shape again. Mert also is good at fixing things.

We all took showers this afternoon. Ahh, refreshing. The water in the black plastic jugs gets warm while hanging in the sun. Mert's jug–with a pull-out valve–works better than mine, which has a clamp like one finds on an enema tube.

We were out in the open when we took our showers, but there were no other people are around, so we didn't even need a screen.

CHAPTER TWENTY-FOUR

Another 'Lady Diana' experience

Monday, August 10, 1987

We left early and headed out on the Arapaho Creek Trail, known locally as the Hyannis Peak Trail. I asked Al Severson to lead us because he had hunted elk here, and I thought he'd be familiar with the territory. I think he got miffed at me when I said, "You lead. You know the country." He got us off in the wrong direction first and then took us down an almost impossible trail.

We missed the turn that would have taken us north to Arapaho Ridge, and we ended up instead at Poison Ridge–a short but sharp ridge. We worked our way around it on steep mountain sides to Troublesome Pass, which we expected to find in the first saddle; but it wasn't until the third saddle that we found it.

In Al's defense, I'll admit that it is difficult to know what an area looks like in the summer when you have only seen it in the autumn (as Al had done elk hunting). And when you ride with someone else who knows the territory–as he had–you don't pay as much attention to the area or directions.

I asked Al tonight if he was miffed at me for putting him in the lead today. He said he wasn't, but I sensed in his body language that he was. We Norwegians have trouble "fessing up" sometimes. I felt bad that I had offended him. He's such a wonderful, neat guy.

Tuesday, August 11, 1987

We got out at 7:30 this morning and rode until 11 o'clock, up and then down forest roads, past Parkview Mountain to Willow Creek Pass where we had lunch and grazed our horses for about an hour. My map showed that we could ride Highway 125 three miles north to a trail which would take us over a ridge that appeared to be about a mile away. Beyond the ridge would be Trout Creek.

We decided to cut across and go directly toward the ridge rather than following along Highway 125, but it required us to go over some pretty tough terrain. Going up a steep slope, I glanced back and saw Mert's pack horse Schatzi having difficulty breathing as she climbed the incline. She lost her breath (I think her chest strap was too tight), lost her nerve, fell, and started to roll down the hill.

I helplessly watched, praying she wouldn't break a leg. At this point the packs were not important. If they got smashed, so be it. I just was hoping nothing would happen to Schatzi. She rolled a couple times before becoming lodged next to a tree trunk. She couldn't move.

We all dismounted and scrambled down to help her. After we unpacked her, she calmly got up and trotted to the top of the ridge. We decided to carry her packs up ourselves and re-pack her on top. Thankfully she was not hurt and she did not panic.

Recovering from that incident took two hours, but if we had ridden along Highway 125 instead of cutting across, the time would have been the same. We eventually got to Trout Creek and then rode down to the Illinois River where we are camping tonight.

Wednesday, August 12, 1987

Woke at 5:10 this morning–later than I wanted, even though I didn't sleep well last night. The moon, which is more than half full right now, is giving off so much light that when I wake up at night, I think it may be morning. When I wake up, thinking it is time to get up, I check in the east to see if there is any light near the horizon.

And with the days getting shorter, it's staying dark longer in the mornings. I don't see rays of light on the horizon at 5 a.m. any more.

~ ~ ~

I couldn't find Bull this morning. Prince, who was hobbled, was nearby–probably because he is more interested in staying near Maynard, Bob Cashin's mule, than fraternizing with the other horses. Goldie, the third horse untied, also was missing. I thought of borrowing someone else's horse to go hunt for the missing animals, but it was too dark to do a search. I'd have to be too close to even see Bull's white hips, and I couldn't read tracks in the dark.

Then I hit upon a good idea. Coco, I reasoned, usually wants to be near Bull. So I turned her loose to see if she would try to find him, and I followed. She went to the next meadow and whinnied. No answer. Then she quickly ducked back into the trees between the two meadows, ran, and disappeared to the north.

I thought I'd lost another horse.

Not so. Coco apparently sensed or heard more than I could. Soon, Bull and Goldie came out to meet Coco from another line of trees. I walked over to Bull, took him by the halter, and led him back to camp. It is interesting how easy he is to catch first thing in the morning. Evidently he does not associate working with the early morning.

~ ~ ~

I knew we had a long ride ahead of us today, and I wanted Bull to get plenty of feed before we headed out. So when I got back to camp, I tried something new. I tied two lead ropes–one 10 feet and one 12 feet long–to Bull's rope. Then I tied a decker pack sling, about 55 feet long, to those ropes and anchored it on a log. It worked great for keeping him close by. It didn't take him long to fill up, and I had him right there when I was ready to saddle and ride out. I'll have to remember this trick for the future.

Thursday, August 13, 1987

For breakfast today, we tried to finish off some of our extra food. The ride will end a couple of days earlier than planned, and we have one less rider, thus the extra food. After breakfast we took utensils out of the kitchen and placed them in the cooler to equalize our loads. We shoved the heaviest stuff from duffels, which we pack on top, into the panniers in order to get the packs to have their weight low. This way they have a more stable ride.

We left camp following the Illinois River east by southeast. We came to a pack trail going off to the left and began a very steep climb. We soon had risen from 9,200 feet to 11,800 feet at Bowen Pass. Spectacular scenery: Ruby Mountain, Ruby Lake, Bowen Mountain, and Baker Mountain. Out of the mountains flow the Bowen and Baker Creeks, the first tributaries of the Colorado River, and a little east is the origin of the river itself.

From Bowen Pass we traveled down to Bowen Trail which was terribly rocky. We moved from the Arapaho National Forest into Rocky Mountain National Park, across Bowen Creek, then Baker Creek, past the ruins of the old town of Gaskill, and finally across the Colorado River.

On the other side of the river we came to a padlocked gate with a cable fence and plenty of signs warning us to "KEEP OUT." So we obeyed–sort of. We rode around and down a stream bank to get to where we wanted.

We saw what looked like a private home, so everyone waited while Al Severson and I rode up to the house. (Not knowing what kind of welcome we would find, we decided that only two of us would ride up.) When we got there, we decided Al would hold the horses while I talked to the owners.

Nice place–obviously a vacation ranch. I knocked, and an older man came to the door. It was about 4 p.m., and I could see I had awakened him from a nap. He went back for his shoes and then came out. He wasn't overly friendly and looked at me like I was some saddle bum. After being on the trail for five weeks, I guess I must have looked pretty bad.

He introduced himself as Fred Dick, and I explained a little about who we were and what we were doing, and I asked if I could use his phone. His reaction was reminiscent of the store owner in Montana, a few years back, who reluctantly let me use her phone. I'm beginning to think that having been the governor of a Midwestern state holds little sway with the locals.

Mr. Dick made it clear he wasn't about to let me into his house, but he had a phone jack outside–apparently for use when he was working outdoors. So he went into his home, got a phone, brought it outside, plugged it into the jack, and let me use it there.

I called Dick Reida (Area Director for Prison Fellowship in Colorado and Wyoming) to come and get us. (Reida had previously agreed to take us back to Encampment to get our rigs when we were ready.) He said he would leave right away from Colorado Springs. He reached us at the Dicks' Trail River Ranch about 8 p.m.

By then, Fred Dick had agreed to let us put all our animals (nine horses, plus mules) in his fenced-in grass enclosure, and he let us set up camp for the night.

His wife Betty had been in town when we arrived today, and when she came back, was she ever surprised to see all those animals in their pen. At first she said she thought her husband had gone out and bought a bunch of horses–but then she saw our motley crew.

This was the first time in 26 years, she said, that anyone had dropped in on them as we had. Unlike her husband's initial reaction, she was overjoyed with our visit, and rose to the occasion, which caused her husband to do likewise.

Friday, August 14, 1987

The Dicks were up to see us off today. After we fixed our breakfast, we gave Betty the rest of our eggs and our leftover bread for her birds. We chatted a while and learned that their 20-acre ranch had once been a 160-acre ranch, and that Fred was a retired banker from Illinois. They offered us the opportunity to stay at their ranch next year, leaving our rigs there as we would proceed south. This I will work on. We will start right after the Fourth of July next year, on the Green Mountain Trail, going through Grand Lake on the east side of Lake Granby and back into the Arapaho South.

After thanking the Dicks for their hospitality, we went south to Granby, visited the Forest Service Station to get some maps, and traced the route we traveled. We also stopped at an outfitters store and gabbed with the folks there. I bought some O rings. Who knows. I might need them for repairing or reconstructing packing and camping equipment.

On the way back up to Encampment, Al wanted to stop at the Homestead Ranch near Rand, Colorado., to see a friend who ended up showing us around an old-time barn. What a sense of history from old-time ranching. We also went to the camp where Al hunts elk so he could pick out his cabin for this fall's outing.

~ ~ ~

We got our rigs in Encampment, drove back down to the Dicks' place to get our horses, and headed for home. What I thought would be a direct drive through Wyoming was halted when I spotted Andy Hysong's saddle shop in Laramie. I just had to stop. Cashin kept going, but A.M. waited for Al and me at the gas station.

In the saddle shop, we looked at the owner's sizable bit-and-spur collection. Andy is a great craftsman, creating rawhide braided reins and crafting spurs and bits. He is a saddle maker, and he creates other leather and horsehair objects, as well. Al bought reins, and Andy measured me for some chaps. One might think my purchase to be a bit extravagant at $175. And I guess I have to admit I am indulging a fantasy I've had for a couple of years since I saw chaps just like these in Lander. I intended to order them in Lander this year, but the shop had gone out of business. Anyway, I need these chaps since my others are wearing out; these will probably be my last.

Well, we took 45 minutes in the shop, and A.M. seemed pretty frustrated by the time we arrived at the gas station. Al got in with him, and he seemed to settle down from his waiting peeve. I wonder what I would have done, if I'd been in his shoes. I probably would not have waited, and would have driven on, also a bit peeved.

We got to North Platte late, dropped our horses off in the rodeo corrals, and had quite a time finding a motel. All rooms were taken because President Reagan had been in town today to visit Buffalo Bill's Ranch. We found what we were told was the last bed in town; it was a double waterbed. They brought in a cot for Al. A.M. and I will sleep in the waterbed–each hugging the edge, I'm sure.

Saturday, August 15, 1987

After two nights of staying up 'til after 1 a.m. and getting up at five a.m., I was really groggy while driving today. It was agony to drive alone, fighting sleep. When Al rode with me, and when I gave a hitchhiker a ride outside Des Moines, it was easy to stay awake because I had someone to talk to. A no-doz pill helped, too, after it got into my system an hour north of Des Moines. It's dangerous to drive that way.

My hitchhiker was Erik Olson, 21, alienated from his divorced, adoptive parents for three years. An anarchist and poet, he seemed to have a hard time dealing with reality. I don't normally pick up hitchhikers, but he was scruffy and reminded me of one of my sons.

I talked about my sons and gave Erik advice on how to find his biological parents. Erik believed everything was hopeless. I told him I believed mankind could better the earth–as evidenced by the increased soil fertility on my farm and possibilities to produce food in Ethiopia. He said he believed that we're only mining the earth, and after a while we'll have mined it all out and people will starve. But I told him my farm is increasingly more productive. So is most of Europe.

He also wanted to talk about the "Harmonica Virgins." We got a laugh out of that one, because what he really had said was "Harmonious Conversion." The Aztecs had predicted this meteor shower, but nothing happened; I hope it wasn't too much of a disillusion to him that it didn't, and I hope he finds himself.

He obviously was moved by our conversation because he said he would take a different look at his paranoiac adoptive dad. I talked a little about God, but I didn't witness to him. I wonder if I should have. I don't like to buttonhole people; I'd rather listen to the Spirit and see how I am moved.

When I got to Northfield to let Coco off, I twice missed the farm (where she is kept) before I found it. The area was so brown, and the grass so dry and short when I left. Now it is green and lush, and the corn is tall. It is amazing how the countryside changed while I was gone.

At Messerli's in Minnetonka, where I kept my horses this past year, the road was out. Stakes were in the pasture so I knew he had sold the place and I'd be looking for somewhere else to keep my horses. I liked the convenience of keeping my horses so close now that Gretchen and I have moved from Rice County to Minnetonka. It's sad and a little disconcerting that I'll need a new place. A little like being homeless.

Sunday, August 16, 1987 (at home)

I called Dan Stine. He is OK. No after-effects of altitude sickness.

I also called Norman Inland, Chief's owner. He agreed to sell Chief to me. We did not settle on a price. Chief can be stubborn, but he has been good with children. Though he has a rough trot and canter, he has great potential for a soft jog trot and perhaps lope. He is smart and is responsive when he is relaxed.

~ ~ ~

Even though I was uneasy about riding the Red Desert in Wyoming this year, anxiety turned to confidence. I now have a great sense of accomplishment and fulfillment. I can read the desert now, which gives me great satisfaction. But I would caution people about going there unprepared or unable to protect themselves. The sun can burn you; the wind can dry you; the water is scarce; the rattlers are abundant. Yet the desert is beautiful and full of antelope and many wild horses. Nature that has been mostly undisturbed by humans makes me feel awe and danger; has majesty and beauty; presents a challenge; is unforgiving; and offers a sense of reward.

~ ~ ~

It is great to be home with Gretchen. She is warm and good-hearted, she cares about me and for me, and she is delighted about her pottery class at Minnetonka Art Center and her trip to Germany. She is brave and resolute to do her thing, and I love her for it and for herself. I'm a lucky man to have such a wonderful wife.

~ ~ ~

We had a picnic with our youngest son, Ben, his wife, Virginia, and their two sons, Samuel and Tanner today. The grandchildren enjoyed seeing my beard. I'm looking forward to seeing our son, Joel, his wife, Sarah, and their sons, Christian and Johan, too.

Each year I've done this, Gretchen has been unhappy before my departure–so much so that I often wonder whether I should sell my horses. I also continue to wonder if I am really committed to God if I keep my horses.

Frankly, struggles like this have been with me all my life. When I was a small child, I was worried that God would want me to go to the mission field in a foreign country (my sister went, however). Maybe it was my pietistic upbringing that brought these feelings on.

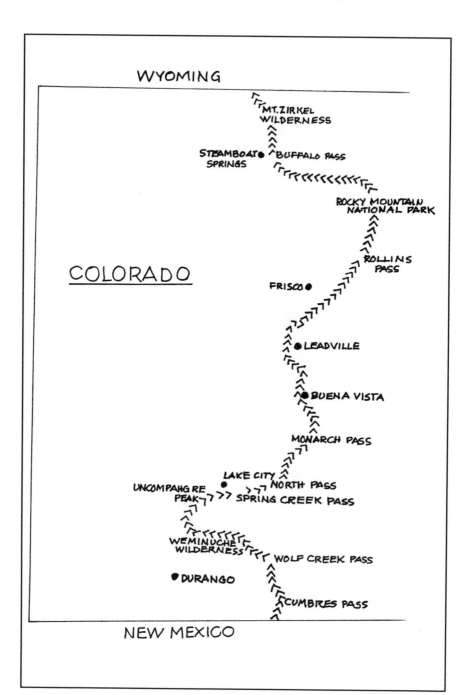

1988

Colorado

Rocky Mountain National Park
Copper Mountain Ski Resort
Mt. Elbert
Twin Lakes
Buena Vista
Monarch Pass
Cochetopa Pass
Spring Creek Pass

CHAPTER TWENTY-FIVE

Learning to share one's faith

Thursday, June 30, 1988

I got up at 3:30 a.m. to get ready for my drive out to Colorado and left about 4:30. Even though I was up so early, I felt more rested than usual. Maybe because the Lord re-energized me after I spoke last night at the Lutherans Evangelizing Together conference.

I shared with the group on the subject of Fear in Evangelism, which is something I personally experienced early in life as well as in my young adult years.

I grew up in the Lutheran church with its Scandinavian stoicism and reserved ways. So I was surprised when I first ran across people who were more open, not only in expressing their faith, but in living their faith and recognizing and articulating how God is moving in their lives.

Interestingly, this first exposure happened at a Lutheran Bible camp I attended with my family when I was about junior high age. It was there that I first watched as people prayed out loud, ad lib. I remember being impressed by it. And also scared to death that my parents might join in! That would embarrass me, I thought, plus, if they did it, I might have to do it, too.

The camp counselor in charge of games and activities for the youth also openly expressed his faith as he led singing and skits. By watching and listening, I came to realize that spiritual expression was not just a pietistic inner feeling or intellectual understanding. It was also physical, outward expressions. This was a real awakening for me. Never before had I realized I could act out my relationship with God, kind of like King David dancing when the Ark of the Covenant was brought back.

(People who don't know me well will find it interesting–maybe even surprising–that I found it to be pure joy, many years later in Israel when I got to dance the hora!)

When I went to Washington and became friends with Doug Coe, I was quickly exposed to the evangelical side where you are open to reaching out to people, sharing with them, and explaining what is happening in your relationship with God.

I worked with Doug in setting up various Bible study and prayer groups in Congress and various other places in Washington. But Doug was the type who could easily see my resistance to really opening up and sharing with the men in my groups. Doug encouraged me to go deeper.

The first time I tried it, I was a miserable failure. (Thankfully the Holy Spirit was not.) I had thought for some time that I'd like to draw closer to Congressman Mel Laird who, I thought, was the best politician in Congress. I wanted to ask him to get together with me for prayer sometime. But I just never got around to it. Until one day he sat next to me in the front seats of the House Chambers of Congress in the Capital.

I thought, "OK, God must want me to talk to him now." So I turned to him–and quickly lost my nerve. I turned away and silently composed, in my mind, what I would say: "Mel, we ought to get together to pray and invite some of our friends to pray with us."

But when I opened my mouth a second time, nothing came out. I lost my nerve. Turning back, I silently prayed, "God, I can't do this. You're going to have to get someone else to do it. I just can't do it."

At that moment Mel turned to me and said, "Al, I've been thinking we ought to get together some time for prayer and invite some friends to join us."

From that moment, I never again doubted the power of the Holy Spirit.

Mel and I immediately left the House of Representatives chamber and went to the speakers' lobby to talk some more. We agreed that we would each pick one person to invite to join us. He said he was going to invite Gerry Ford. My close friend on the Education and Labor Committee was Charlie Goodell, so I said I would invite Charlie. And Mel and I agreed we would pray for each other as we approached each of these men to invite them to be part of a small prayer group.

I then felt I had nerve enough to go and talk to Charlie. When I asked him, he immediately said, "Yes," which surprised me (though it shouldn't have).

Then I said, "Well, if we are going to pray together with Mel (who is inviting Gerry Ford), why don't you and I pray together right now?"

Charlie got up from his desk and walked over to close the reception room door and he locked it. I thought, well, he doesn't want to be interrupted, and that's OK.

Then he went and locked the door that led to the corridor. And I thought, well, I guess he doesn't want anyone coming in from that direction, either.

Then he went and locked the door to the bathroom! I smiled to myself. That is really rare. There is NO ONE coming in here from the bathroom! Yet, he wants to be totally sure there will be no interruptions.

And we prayed together. When we were finished, tears were coming down his cheeks.

The next night there was a big Chamber of Commerce gathering in town where we politicians go simply because people from our districts will be in attendance, and they are expecting us to be there.

Normally when you arrive at this huge affair, you immediately look to your right and left, scanning the crowd for faces of people from your district so you can be sure to shake hands with all of them; sometimes you even pretend to know people who think they know you.

But that night, as I entered that long, wide room, I instead began scanning the crowd for Mel. And I spotted him–coming in at the same time from the far end of the room. He must have been looking for me, too, because our eyes caught. We worked our way through that crowd not looking to the right or to the left (like normal) until we reached each other.

With excitement, he said, "Gerry said he would join us!"

"Charlie said yes, too!"

And Mel said, "This has to be of God."

That was the beginning of a small group that stayed together until Ford left the presidency. And after this group several other small prayer/accountability groups were formed in the Executive Branch.

There is fear in reaching out to people–especially those we know–mostly because we are afraid of rejection. It's tough to talk to your next door neighbor. And tougher yet to talk to a member of your family.

So I always tell people, "Just start with what is faith-sized enough for you. Develop a sensitivity so you can recognize how the Spirit is moving both you and the other person. Then, just take a chance on it. And what happens next is that you gain courage to take the next step because your faith becomes stronger and your faith-sized steps become larger."

~ ~ ~

My excitement for this year's trip began six months ago, growing in momentum each week until just a few days ago. That's when I really had to concentrate in order to prepare for the trip and get my life in order at home prior to departure.

It took a while to finalize who would be on the ride with me this year. I knew Al Severson, A.M. Lips, and Mert Schwarz would come, as would Bob Cashin. I expected Doug Coe for the second two weeks of this year's ride, but because of his arm injury last year, he decided against it. Later he had gall stones and his appendix out, so he wouldn't have been able to come anyway.

At the National Prayer Breakfast last spring, I saw Dick Whitmore and offered him another chance (he was with us for part of the 1986 ride). He plans to borrow another horse and drive out from Michigan next week.

I also invited Graham Purcell when I was at that Prayer Breakfast. He decided to come along, for which I'm thankful. He is such a good, long-time friend, and this will be an excellent chance to spend time with him. I truly love this man. He is a mirror of me in so many ways. Graham (a Democratic congressman from Texas) was in my small group Bible study, so he was among those of us who first met with Chuck Colson.

Graham came to Congress via a special election. His office was across the corridor from mine, and because my staff and I had been there for a while, we helped him get started.

Even though we were from different political parties, we became friends because of our mutual interest in horses. He had been a captain in the cavalry when WWII started and was also a polo player. One day, early in our friendship, he invited me to the polo grounds near his home at Mt. Vernon. Since I never would turn down a chance to ride horses, I went, but I made him promise not to take any pictures of me. I didn't think my constituents in the First District would think too kindly of me out playing polo!

I had to cut the afternoon short, however, because I had promised to share my faith story at a small prayer group. On the way back, Graham asked me why I had to get back early.

"Oh," I said, "I have a meeting I have to get back to."

"Why do you have to go to that meeting?"

"I have to give a talk," I said, trying to be intentionally vague.

"What are you going to talk about?"

"Oh, I'm just going to share some of my experiences with some people."

He knew I was attending the Thursday morning House prayer breakfast meetings, but I didn't really know where he stood spiritually, so I didn't want to tell him exactly what I was doing. I didn't want to take the chance of offending him and possibly losing this horse friend.

"Does it have anything to do with religion?" he pressed.

Now he had me cornered. I said, "Yes, there is a group of people with whom I'm going to share my relationship with Christ."

There was a long pause. Then these surprising words from Graham: "I don't want to push myself, but would it be OK if I came along?"

I thought, "What a reluctant person I am. Here I was trying to avoid telling Graham anything about where I was going, but even with my reluctance, the Holy Spirit moved Graham to invite himself to this meeting, independent of my resistance!"

I found out later that Graham was from a religious background, and that he wanted to associate with people who had a personal relationship with Jesus Christ. The Holy Spirit was working on him that day, in spite of my faltering.

~ ~ ~

I drove all the way to Fort Morgan today–75 miles from Denver. After calling Gretchen, I've settled in at the Hendricks Motel. My horses are resting in the trailer.

Friday, July 1, 1988

I had breakfast in Golden this morning, then drove on to Fred Dick's place just outside the Rocky Mountain National Park. He was at the gate waiting; Mert was there, too. We're taking Fred up on his offer last year to leave our rigs at his ranch while we ride this year.

Mert and I drove to where we planned to start the portion of our ride that will begin July 5 just to check it out. The first leg of the trip (from the Dicks' ranch) will last only three days–July 2, 3, and 4. We then drove to the Forest Service office in Granby. A guy there told us of a different place to start, where camping was permitted, and it was also a good place to come out from Devil's Thumb or Rollins Pass. We took his advice into consideration and went back again to the Dicks' place.

While we were gone, Al Severson, A.M. Lips, and Bob Cashin had arrived.

Barbara and Fred invited us to dinner, which turned out to be a party in our honor attended by four other couples who wanted to hear about our rides. We enjoyed regaling them with our stories

At the Dicks' we saw elk in the evening and early morning. What an experience.

Saturday, July 2, 1988

Before beginning our ride this morning, A.M. and I started out at 5:45 a.m. to drive his Suburban up into the mountains near Arapaho Pass so it will be there when we arrive on July 4. We parked it on a little-used road so it would be out of the way. I followed in my pick-up; the trip took us 2-1/2 hours, so we didn't get out of the Dicks' place on horseback until late morning.

We said our goodbyes and headed up the road shoulder about a mile and half to the trailhead of Green Mountain Trail where a ranger spotted us and stopped us. I told him the visitor center said we didn't need a permit. He said that was right for riding on the trail, but not for riding by the road as we were. He called his superior and got an OK, so we continued on to the Green Mountain Trail, turned right and traveled the Tonahuter Trail to Grand Lake.

We asked directions to get through town and over a bridge between Grand Lake and Shadow Mountain Lake. We went by Jack Fry's house who had been a guest the night before at the party at the Dicks' home. He climbed into his vehicle and led us to the trail. We followed Shadow Mountain Lake on a good trail, then on to Granby Lake by way of the Colorado River and Columbine Lake and camped high above the lake by a little swampy pond.

Somehow, Bull got sick today. I had wanted to get to bed early tonight, but I had to walk Bull, instead, to keep him from dying from colic. I heard a few rumbles in his stomach after much walking, so we left him for the night. Al Severson is a good-hearted person; he led Bull some of the time to give me a rest.

Sunday, July 3, 1988

As we ate breakfast, some of the horses meandered away, but we could see Bob's white horse J-J through the brush and figured the rest of the horses were there. After breakfast, Al Severson went down to take a look, and all the horses that had wandered that way were gone, except the white one. Al went off to look for them, and Cashin and I saddled up to help. Just then Cashin's mule, Maynard, came back, so I sent Cashin off with the mule following, thinking the mule would lead Cashin to the missing horses.

I rode down the backtrail to see if they'd gone around the pond. I heard Cashin yell, so knew he'd found the wayward horses. Nonetheless, I continued riding the Knights Ridge where they would likely have traveled because I wanted to practice my tracking. I did find their tracks where they had turned around. It seemed that going around to the backtrail was too much for them, as I could see in their tracks that they were trying to decide and then turned back.

I packed Bull light today so he could recover from his colic. We rode out of the Lake Granby area past Arapaho Bay and over to Monarch Lake where we got a pass to go into Indian Peak Campground. The ranger gave us the permit, directions, and some raunchy stories.

Monday, July 4, 1988

We got going at 8:30, heading for Arapaho Pass. When we got there, we discovered the trail went up a very steep mountain. I hung behind a little to take pictures. I hope they turn out well. The telephoto on my new Olympus camera really works well.

The trail up was easier than I thought it would be. Once at the top, we went over and by Diamond Lake. The rangers had said they wouldn't recommend this route to Devil's Thumb because it would be blocked by snow. I didn't believe them, so we tried it, anyway.

We got just about to the top on a very steep trail that had an equally precipitous drop off on the side and discovered the rangers had been right. A huge snowdrift prevented us from going farther.

I walked up the mountain around the snow but could not find a way to get the horses over. With boulders on both sides, there was no way we could work around the snow bank–and we were only about 50 yards from success.

We turned around and went down again, knowing we wouldn't be able to get over Rollins Pass and then back to the top of Devil's Thumb Pass and on to A.M.'s Suburban yet today. We'll have to do it tomorrow.

I am concerned that Gretchen would worry, since I told her I would call when we came out on the July 4. Now I'll be a day late.

We rode down the first trail that branched off to the right following Jasper Creek and then turned west onto King Lake Trail. The map didn't seem entirely right, but trails frequently do not show up in reality where they've been placed on a map.

We're camping tonight by a creek, and there is good grass. Bob Cashin revealed that he is losing the sight in one of his eyes, and he therefore is pulling out tomorrow. He had gotten bucked off his horse a week before coming on the ride, landed on his head, and experienced a stroke in his eye. I have two emotions: worry about his infirmity and disappointment in the loss of a rider.

Tuesday, July 5, 1988

We started out at 7:30 and headed further south to make our way around and back up to where we had parked Bob's Suburban. The trail we were on brought us out of the wilderness which didn't seem right. I finally realized we had made a wrong turn yesterday, which now put us just 1-1/2 miles from Eldora, Colorado. So we turned around and headed back up the trail to reach where we had turned west yesterday onto what we thought was King Lake Trail. When we got to the spot, we saw the sign pointing east to King Lake Trail. All five of us had missed it when we came down yesterday.

When we reached the outlet of King Lake, Bull leaned down to get a drink from the creek. Then he stumbled onto a boulder under the deep rushing stream, and his front feet dropped into a hole. His whole front end disappeared. When he reared to come out of it, he lost his balance and threw me out of the saddle. I didn't want him to come down on me in the water because, if he did, I might get caught under him and not be able to breathe under water.

So I threw my legs up against him and pushed back into the upstream, practically submerged in ice cold water.

My new expensive camera, strapped to my belt, went under, filled with water and was ruined. I'm sick about that.

Up there in the cold wind (it was about 40 degrees and windy) I stripped and got my long underwear out of my pack. This is the first time I didn't have a change of jeans or shirt readily available, so I put my chaps over my long-johns and I wore a sweater. I threw my jeans and shirt over the pack under the diamond hitch to dry as we rode on.

~ ~ ~

Turning right after reaching the top at Rollins Pass we followed the Corona Trail north to Devils Thumb Pass–here, 24 hours later, at exactly the same hour, we were only 50 yards further from where we were yesterday when we couldn't get through because of the snow drifts! Corona Trail followed the Continental Divide on the west side a few yards. Then we traveled down to Cabin Creek, wondering if we would be able to find the deserted road where we left the Suburban. We did!

We tied the horses in the woods so no one would see them, taking the packs off but leaving the others saddled. In the Suburban we set out for Fred Dick's place about 46 miles away where we'd put our rigs. Betty Dick said she was worried when we did not arrive on the Fourth as planned, and she said that if we had not arrived today, she would have notified the Park Service to come looking for us. They would have had a hard time finding us.

After driving back up into the woods to get our horses, we went to Fraser and ate at a bar and restaurant. Mostly bar. Three of us had creamed chicken, and Al and Bob had huge hamburgers.

After saying good-bye to Bob, we climbed into our rigs and set off for the trailhead–in the dark–and we couldn't even find where the road left town. We had to ask. We stopped a young boy who came by, and he said his parents, who had lived in the area all of their lives, would know.

We found out that the road had been moved, and that we had to go north of Fraser to get to the trail. No wonder we couldn't find it earlier. We traveled a ways per directions we'd been given, and still did not find the trailhead, so we found a turn-off where we could park, and we all are sleeping in our rigs tonight. Mine will be a difficult night since I have no bed inside my rig.

Wednesday, July 6, 1988

I slept on hay in the front of the horse trailer last night. Chewing horses and occasional stomping made it difficult to sleep. Toward morning Escrow, my new pack horse for this year, began to stamp and paw so I got up at 4:50 to give him some hay and to begin getting ready for the day.

I unhooked my trailer and jumped into my pickup to go find the real trailhead. It was not marked, so we unknowingly went on by last night in the dark.

~ ~ ~

We left our rigs parked and rode up the trail, but at noon we lost it again because of logging roads. We finally turned back and are camping at a lower altitude.

Thursday, July 7, 1988

Bull tried to leave last night. I knew because I had put a bell on him. For some reason, the gentle, constant jangle of the bell kept me asleep, and as soon as the sound moved off into the distance, I would wake up. I am as attuned to that as a mother who sleeps while her child gently breathes, but who is startled awake as soon as the breathing stops.

I jumped out of bed and got Bull twice; the second time I tied him up.

We rode back to the trucks today and then drove to Silverthorne where we showered and bought maps. Two of the Forest Service guys, Greg and Paul, told me a better way out of Frisco.

We went up Miners Creek Trail, and tonight we are camping at the most fantastic site. There is a stream nearby that is just the right width and depth so that we can stand at the edge and dip a full pail of water without getting our feet wet. And there is lots of grass for the horses.

We put up our camp among the trees. A.M. and Mert decided to sleep under the tarp, so Al and I moved out under the stars. Mert and A.M. offered to put up their tent if they were pushing us out, but I declined. I want to sleep under the stars tonight, anyway.

CHAPTER TWENTY-SIX

A call to a barred owl reaps a bobcat

Friday, July 8, 1988

Today we rode a rugged trail rising to a 10-mile ridge that was at an elevation of over 12,000 feet with numerous peaks. The climb getting to the trail was terribly steep, but even worse was that it was so rocky. Escrow really got pooped on the climb up. From the top we looked down 2,000 feet to Colorado's Copper Mountain Ski Resort right below us. I realized by the layout that the resort was just like it appeared on the map I was given by the Forest Service in Silverthorne. The map showed the route we ought to take through the resort–about a quarter mile long. We went from Miners Creek Trail to Wheeler Trail and made a rapid descent.

Going through the resort was an odd experience. People were crossing the streets as we rode through with our pack horses. Some of the tourists took pictures of us. Others stood gawking like they'd never seen horses before. Then out of one of the buildings came a guy dressed in a dark suit. He looked like a salesman engrossed in his next sale and paid absolutely no attention to us and our string of pack horses going through town–as if we were the most common, everyday occurrence. How different people can be!

We stopped long enough for Al to have his picture taken by the awning in front of the main three-story building. Then we boldly traveled on a well-marked service road that said, "Don't enter–wrong way." We even went onto a brick side walk and finally onto a bike path before we got to a stable on the other end of the ski resort.

A stable manager named Maggie gave us directions to get to the Colorado Trail going up Guller Creek. This is where I finally called Glen Roberts and made a decision on where we would meet.

Glen is an outfitter in Buena Vista, Colorado., who previously worked in the mines. He'd heard about my Continental Divide rides, and he wrote me, asking that I contact him when in his area so he could come and ride with us. He had said he would guide us along the Colorado Trail and onto Mt. Massive without charging us an "arm and a leg" like other outfitters might.

I had written back, told him when I was coming, and we worked it out that I would call him when we were at Copper Mountain Ski Resort.

In my call to him today, he said he will trailer to the west end of Turquoise Lake on Sunday morning, and then travel up the trail until he finds us.

~ ~ ~

We left the stable after making the employees there jealous of our trip.

While having lunch at the beginning of the Colorado Trail, Gunther, Schatzi, and Misty–carrying their saddles–tried to roll. We figured the mules carrying the packs might follow suit, so the only horses that we should leave to graze during lunch were my two, Escrow and Bull.

We went up Guller Creek, over Jacques Ridge, over to Kokomo Pass, and down to the timber again on Cataract Creek where we are making camp.

A hiker and his wife came by our camp tonight. He is a Spanish professor from the University of Hawaii who loves to hike. He has hiked in New England, the Appalachian Trail, and part of the Pacific Crest. He said he doesn't like Hawaii because the islands do not have enough places for hiking. His wife tags along. They have been married 15 years, and when I told her about Gretchen "turning in" her sleeping bag after 25 years, her eyes really lit up. I may have given her an idea.

Saturday, July 9, 1988

Instead of bringing the collapsible wood stove that I've used in years past, I again decided a gas stove would be better this year because we'll be going through areas in Colorado where there isn't much wood. Mert Schwarz brought a griddle and his two-burner gas stove, and I've got my small single-burner. Without a wood stove, we surely can get out of camp easier.

In the past, with our collapsible wood stove, we would have to wait until the firewood burned out and the stove cooled off before we could dump the ashes. Only then were we able to collapse the stove and put it into a canvas carrying case for packing on a horse.

We got going about 8 this morning and had a long ride, until just about 6 p.m.

We rode the rest of the way down Cataract Creek. To my delight, the new Colorado Trail took us other than by road to get over Tennessee Pass. Part of the way up yesterday, we were on the east side of Highway 24.

During lunch today, both of Mert's horses tried to roll, but after he intervened they didn't try again. When we were just about done with lunch, Escrow, with his packs on, looked like he was going to roll. I yelled and ran to him to try to stop him, but he went down anyway. When I tried to get him up, he couldn't make it. He appeared to be stuck. He was just like a gangly kid who could not get back up with his backpack on.

I asked Mert to hold his head so he wouldn't try getting up until I got his packs off. After he was up, we repacked him. For some reason, the pack horses' backs must be itching them a lot to make them want to roll like this.

We followed the Continental Divide, not far from Lily Lake, along Long's Gulch. It was a tough climb, but a fairly good trail into high country, sometimes over 12,000 feet. We then came down and stopped just short of Bear Lake.

A nice young couple who had been fishing came by us earlier today. The young man said the girl really loved horses so Al invited her to climb onto Misty to have her picture taken. As we rode the rest of the way into camp, Al said he could still smell the perfume...and said he wanted to sleep on his saddle tonight so he could keep smelling it! He has a good sense of humor.

Sunday, July 10, 1988

I didn't sleep well last night because I didn't level my cot well enough. All night I kept feeling like the cot would tip over. This left me sleeping tensely and therefore colder. Never again, if I can help it, will I not take time to dig in one side of the cot to level it when I have to sleep on a side hill.

We had a church service before leaving at 9 this morning.

I said a prayer and asked if anyone else wanted to pray, but they declined, saying they never learned how to pray in public. I read the 139th Psalm and a portion of James on the two kinds of wisdom.

I prayed another prayer, and then Mert asked if we could all pray the Lord's Prayer together. Afterward, they all said how much this meant to them. Mert had tears in his eyes and had to blow his nose.

Al said he got more out of our Sunday services than he did going to church back home. I told him the reason probably was because we were bonded as friends. The body of Christ is people bonded together in the name of Christ, and so, as we are bonded and turn to Christ, the feeling is stronger. We also talked about such things as anger and not holding it, as well as about enjoying each others' company

Later today, Mert told me how he has shown slides of our previous trips eight times. With each showing, he mentions we always have Sunday services and we don't have any alcohol along. Preachers who see his slide show tell him they are not surprised, since these rides are "Quie rides." But others, he said, are surprised.

~ ~ ~

Got up to Bear Lake about a half mile away, and then A.M. and Mert went ahead to search for a trail. They found none. I then left my pack horse with Al and went looking.

I knew the trail went between the two small Galena Lakes. The one we were beside, I believed, was the southern of the two lakes. I went to the south of it, found the outlet and checked through thick timber and rocks. When the stream plummeted down the mountain, I turned north around the west side of the lake and checked on that side. There I found the trail and North Galena Lake, and then I found a way to get the others over to me. Not easy because of downed timber and marshy ground, but we managed.

Together again, we traveled a ways and saw a pair of hikers in their camp; we asked if we were on the trail to the huge Turquoise Lake, where we are to meet Glen Roberts. They affirmed that we were, so we made a rapid descent. It was so steep, we decided to get off and walk down. We walked down 1,400 feet. When we neared the bottom, I saw two strangers coming up the trail. I didn't think either of them was Glen Roberts because neither looked the way I expected to Glen to look.

Then one of them spoke up, "Dr. Livingston, I presume?"

I smiled and responded, "You must be Glen Roberts!"

A friend had come with him to take his truck back.

Glen led us along the trail leading to the top of Mt. Massive where we are making camp. This time I dug down on the uphill side to make my cot level.

Glen has a shell that he slides his sleeping bag into that makes it waterproof on the bottom and repellent on the top. I think I'll have to get one. He also has an interesting lean-to type tent that looks like an Adirondack hut.

I found out tonight that Glen has volunteered in prisons and has a friend who is conducting prison seminars (Dick and Carol Gott). We shared a lot about our prison experiences; he has a deep faith and is quiet.

I learned from him about the area. He is a wonderful mountain man. He was kind of struck by the fact that I'd been riding the same horse all the way from the Canadian border.

Monday, July 11, 1988

We had ice on the tents this morning.

This morning, we went down off Mount Massive and to the base of Mt. Elbert–I think the tallest mountain in Colorado at 14,433 feet. We also crossed a bridge that apparently wasn't stout enough as A.M.'s horse Goldie went partially through. Goldie lurched to prevent going all the way through, nearly throwing A.M. He was hurt only a little when he was thrown up against the saddle horn.

Glen's horse shied away from the bridge. He said that she had had a similar wreck before and apparently saw the bridge as a danger. We are always concerned about bridges, because we don't know their stability until we go across.

We rode into the town of Twin Lakes about noon and found a park where we tied our horses to a baseball backstop while we had lunch under a tree. We bought pop and an ice cream bar at a little store and then we rode over to the home of Glen's friends, the Gotts.

Dick used to be a supervisor for the Climax Mine by Leadville and had to take early retirement when it closed. They now lead a Bible study and Sunday services in a number of prisons, in addition to instructing in-prison seminars. They have an old fashioned cabin furnished as if it were turn-of-the-century. What a charming couple who love the Lord.

After this, we rode to an old pre-1900 resort called Interlachen, where we're spending the night. It has beautiful New England-type architecture and is located right on the south side of Twin Lakes. We were told the Forest Service owns it, it was built in the 1800's and has not been used since 1910, and that the CCC's rebuilt it in the 1930's. There is no road in, so it is unlikely anyone will come while we are here.

The resort has a main lodge with a two-story out-house, an annex with eight bedrooms and a detached six-sided out-house, a big barn with grooms' quarters, a cow and chicken barn, the owner's cabin with a veranda all the way around it, two granaries, and a blacksmith shop. The dance pavilion was in a shambles, but I could tell it had been shaped like the prow of a boat.

I was intrigued by the two-story out-house, attached to the end of the building. It was built, I suppose, so that guests staying on the second level would not have to navigate the stairs in order to go to the "bathroom." One two-holer had been built on top of the other. No doubt the "business part" of the upstairs was offset from the one below. Usually these are just a joke, but this one was functional.

And in the six-sided outhouse six people could sit with the door open and enjoy the scenery with "privacy!"

We had a great supper tonight. Fried onion and raw carrots for the beginning, then steak, mashed potatoes, green beans, and peas. Pudding made our dessert. Fantastic.

At dusk, I decided I was going to sleep on the veranda of the owner's cabin. It was quite a ways from where the other guys were. I laid my sleeping bag out, and then took time to just admire the huge trees and kind of a silvery look that appeared through the trees–probably from the sun reflecting on some nearby sage brush. I heard an owl. I've learned how to mimic the 10-point hoots of the Barred owl while I was governor (what else do governor's learn at their country home on weekends?). So I called back to him to see if he'd call to me. I started to work my way into the woods toward the sage brush on its far edge.

There was no sound, then a hoot back to me. I waited on the owl's lead and then called to him again as I moved a little closer, trying to spot it. (Wild birds many times seem to have long pauses in their calls to each other.) I moved a little closer, trying to spot it.

As I progressed into the woods, I approached a large, downed tree, and around the roots of that uprooted tree came a bobcat stalking me! (From the sounds he'd heard, he must have been stalking the one of the two owls that sounded kind of sick!) We stared at each other momentarily. At first, he must have thought, that is the biggest owl I've ever seen!

Then he slipped around behind the roots of the tree. All I could see then, under the trunk of the tree, were his four feet. I stood very still–I was about 10 yards away–and he undoubtedly was looking at my big feet. I remained still for what seemed a very long time–probably a couple minutes–just staring at his feet.

I wasn't scared. Bobcats, no doubt, are more afraid of people than vice versa. After those minutes, I decided he apparently was waiting for me to make a move, so I decided to gently shift around to get a better look at him. When I got to what I thought would be a good vantage point, he was nowhere to be seen. He'd vanished without a sound a leaving no trace.

Tuesday, July 12, 1988

We rode with good trails today, but half of the day we were on a steady incline as we rode to Glen's cabin located in the last trees before the timberline. It is old and rustic with a dirt floor–built before 1900. It has four bunk beds, a pile of sacked alfalfa cubes, an old door for a table–one end attached to the wall, the other supported with a leg–a couple of benches, two carved wooden stools, an old rusty stove, old newspapers for chink, three windows, and a weathered, wooden door. Water is 200 yards away.

After supper, as we were making plans to trek up to the tundra before dinner to look at the elk, the horses we had turned loose to graze had disappeared.

I threw a saddle on Misty, whom we had kept tied up, to go look for them. I spotted them 1-1/2 miles away on the backtrail, drinking water in a mountain-side creek. When I reached them, the last horse was taking a drink and the others already had moved on. I kept trying to catch them, but as soon as I'd get close, they would run away. I was going as fast as I could on Misty and could not pass them.

The trail we were on had a big U-shaped curve with a deep gully to my right. The only way I could figure to catch the horses was to head down that gulch and head them off. So, I barreled down, with Misty jumping over logs and cutting across the ravine just like in the "Man from Snowy River." I made it to the bottom and up to the trail again, just barely ahead of all the other horses–except Gunther. So I whipped right up on the trail and stopped Schatzi who had been right behind him and who I knew was Gunther's buddy. I thought if I grabbed and stopped her, maybe Gunther would come back. All the other horses stopped, and Gunther apparently decided he didn't want to go off by himself, because he came back. What a wild ride. We all got back 1-1/2 hours later.

I'm going to have to pay more attention to the horses' need for water. If they hadn't been thirsty, they probably wouldn't have run away.

Even though it had gotten late, we all saddled up and went up to the tundra to watch elk. Glen showed us the way. When we got close, we went behind rocks so the elk would not be spooked. There were dozens of large elk on the mountain side. I could see one big bull through my field glasses and one bull lying down a long distance away. I wouldn't have been able to see him without the field glasses. But he apparently saw us. He got up. I sensed he was worried about us. He walked into the middle of a herd of cows for protection. The other bulls and the lead cow were keeping an eye on us, too. They seemed nervous trying to figure out what we were, and they didn't give up looking at us, even though only our heads were showing, for a full 20 minutes.

Wednesday, July 13, 1988

When I got up at 5 o'clock today, the horses I'd left out for the night were gone. So I saddled Goldie to go look for them. I figured they hadn't run out, but stayed in the high meadow, which is where I found them. As I rode toward them, I thought I saw the spotted white "blanket" on Bull's rump, but I soon realized I was looking at an elk. And as I got closer, I saw it was a bull elk. There were two bull elk grazing with our horses. I remembered from "Never Cry Wolf" that one should not stop, but keep moving in order not to alarm the wolves. It works the same way with elk. I saw two prongs at the end of the antlers on one bull, and then a bigger elk came into view. I counted four prongs on one side and three on the other of his antlers; because of the small prongs close to his skull, he would be classified as a 5 by 4. Glen had told me you can't herd elk, but I tried anyway. I rode around them to move them to camp to surprise my comrades, but they weren't about to let that happen. They headed slowly for the upper woods, so I rode parallel to them–15 to 20 feet away–for about 200 yards until I reached the timberline. What a thrill and how different from the elk who expressed anxiety last night.

~ ~ ~

We rode down out of the mountains today, and put our horses and mules in Glen's pasture. He then took us to Frisco to get our rigs. When we got back, we parked our trailers at his pasture and put all our gear inside. We had dinner tonight with Glen and his wife Connie at Casa Del Sol. She is very nice. A secretary for the parole board at the prison. I called Gretchen to let her know all was well and to see how she was.

Thursday, July 14, 1988

Dick Whitmore came in last night from Michigan. I got up at 5, fed our horses and came back for breakfast in town. I then took my truck to Salida to get the engine checked. A.M. picked me up, and we went to Leadville to see the old mining town.

Al, A.M., and Mert left for home in the early afternoon, but not before I gained another fascination for animals' behavior. When we loaded their animals for the trip home, I tied Bull to the side of the trailer by his bridle reins to hold him while I helped. Al's mule, immediately upon being loaded, started messing with Bull's reins, beginning at the end of one rein and snarfed it up right to the knot. No matter how long a person is out in the mountains, there is always another lesson to be learned.

Friday, July 15, 1988

We shod horses today. We knew Misty needed them, Dick had a horse barefoot in back, and low and behold, Bull needed his shoes replaced, too. This took until one in the afternoon. Glen then showed us where to start our trip tomorrow morning, and we went back into Buena Vista to meet former Texas Congressman Graham Purcell and buy some groceries. Then we packed the groceries when we got back to camp and got things ready for leaving on the next leg of our trip tomorrow. Didn't eat supper until 9 p.m. I also called Gretchen one more time when I was in town.

CHAPTER TWENTY-SEVEN

Head-over-heels down the mountain

Saturday, July 16, 1988

Got up at 5 this morning, fed the horses, saddled them, and got ready to go. Then we went back into Buena Vista for breakfast. I called Glen to find out if he'd had any luck finding someone to pick us up at Molas Pass at the end of our ride in 10 days. He hadn't, so I asked him to contact Shad, a former staff person of Graham, now a banker living here in Colorado. Shad had told Graham he'd help us out if needed.

After picture taking, we headed out at 10:20 and rode over to a gravel pit about 20 miles south of Buena Vista by the Deer Valley Ranch near Mt. Antero Hot Springs. There was a very steep climb right at the beginning, and Dick's pack horse Suzie, a pure-bred Arabian mare borrowed from the University of Michigan, became alarmed. The trail had a sharp drop on one side and a high incline on the other. That Arabian appeared to be scared to death.

She tried (I think for safety) to walk alongside Dick's saddle horse, so we stopped, and I tied her behind Gyp, the mule, instead. But she tried to walk beside her, too. In fact, she tried to climb all over her. I also tried leading her from Bull, and that didn't work, either.

I then asked Dick to stay on the trail and hold her still while Graham and I rode up to the top of the mountain–it wasn't too far away. I figured I'd leave Graham's and my saddle horses and mules with Graham, and I'd walk back down to lead Suzie up. When Graham and I were tying our horses at the top, we heard a noise like several thunder claps one right after the other.

Graham jerked around, "What is that noise?!"

I knew right away what it was—the rumble, rumble, rumble of a horse—fully packed—rolling down the mountainside.

I jogged back down as quickly as possible, and as we looked over the ledge, there we saw Dick's mare, lying up against a tree at the bottom. She'd rolled 100 yards.

I found out that Dick hadn't stayed put like I'd instructed. Thinking he'd help out a little, he had moved up the trail a little ways—where it was even steeper. That's when his mare slipped slightly over the edge, and when she raised her front feet up to get back on the trail, she went over backwards.

Miraculously, Suzie was not injured. When we got down to her, I could tell she didn't have her senses about her, so we turned her loose. I figured she'd find her way back to the trailer. I told Dick to follow, keeping an eye on her. "When she gets to the trailer, she'll get her bearings. Then lead her back here. Without anything on her, she'll be more relaxed."

I went back to the top, and Graham and I then unpacked my mule. We brought her down, and picked up everything that had been strewn all over and re-packed it onto the mule. But I could find only three of my cot legs. Without the fourth, the cot was useless. I looked all over. Then I thought, "What if, when this wreck happened, one of those legs came out and ran like a ski down the mountain." I calculated what its trajectory would have been, and, from that, figured out where it might have gone. Then I walked and walked and walked down that mountain along the sight line I'd predicted. At times I was ready to give up, but I kept walking. I finally came to some thick bushes, at least 100 yards further than where Suzie's fall stopped, and there, by a tree, was my cot leg—like an arrow stuck in the bushes.

Graham and I took my freshly-packed mule back up to the top of the mountain and I explained to him why Dick was following his pack horse back to the trailer. Graham was impressed. "You know, I was in the cavalry for a long time, and I never learned all this stuff about horses."

I teased him, "That's because you were a captain and had an orderly who saddled your horse for you, made your bed for you, and put up your tent for you! It is no wonder this is a new experience for you!"

When Dick reached us (he had followed the pack horse down the trail and back up the mountain using her tail as a tow line), Graham rode the wayward pack mare, Suzie, and we packed Misty, the horse he had been riding. We made the rest of the trip, about 3-1/2 miles short of our intended site at Squaw Creek. But where we are is a nice camp.

Ate beef chunks, mashed potatoes, green beans, and lemon pudding for supper. Started reading the Epistle of James at campfire tonight.

Sunday, July 17, 1988

Got up at 5 and did the usual chores. We left at 9:50 heading toward Squaw Creek and came down into the North Fork Valley. Dick thought the river we were by was the South Arkansas. At first I thought so, too, but when we started up the trail, I couldn't find Fooses Creek as shown on the map. Besides, the direction didn't seem right. I wasted two hours checking and going back, and I finally decided we were right where we wanted to be–on the Colorado Trail.

We climbed and then went down again and crossed Highway 50 further west than I expected. We found the Fooses and rode to the South Fooses. I didn't want to climb on top of Mt. Peck, which we would have had to do if we had ridden the North Fooses. To my surprise, the Colorado Trail went along the South Fooses also. We are camping toward the head of it tonight.

A very difficult day. Everyone is pretty tired. I told Graham to sleep as late as he wanted tomorrow morning. Dick has a hard time breathing, especially when he is lying down. Suzie seems to be doing fine. She is a little slow, but otherwise seems OK.

The stove stand isn't working very well. It would be a good idea if the stove bottom had a slot that the stand could stick into. I'll have to remember this for next year.

Monday, July 18, 1988

Graham has a great sense of humor. He has a mummy bag that he thinks is too confining, and woke up this morning feeling so crippled he said he thought he had polio.

He can be so funny. I remember the time early on when we were meeting with Colson. He said, "I sure am a lousy Christian. I never chase women; I've never been an alcoholic and never been in prison. I don't have anything to talk about!"

The two of us are pretty much together in that way. We both are straight arrows.

~ ~ ~

Got out by 9:30. No mishaps today, even though it was a steep climb up to the pass just east of Monarch Pass. What a splendid scene as we looked back all the way to Mt. Shavano. Graham was ecstatic.

We rode to the head of Green Creek Trail going north where an Adirondack cabin was located. We then traveled to Marshall Pass where we talked to a lady who was walking a little way off the trail. She was very interested in our ride. Her husband was staying back at the trailhead by the car watching their two young children. The family is from Florida.

We found our way around Windy Peak, and just as I came to a sign that said, "no motorized vehicles," a motor bike came buzzing toward us with a Forest Service employee aboard, evidenced by his uniform. I kidded him about being on a trail that didn't allow motorized vehicles, and he quickly said he had permission. He was supplying food and material for a group of teenagers who were a part of the Student Conservation Corps.

He gave us good information about the trail and said it was OK to camp near the students' camp. So that is what we are doing. Or at least what I thought we were doing. One of their supervisors came down and complained that we were in their camp area, the only level piece of ground, and that we drank out of their water can. (Horses like to do that.)

Once we got settled, a man by the name of Robert Frost and his wife came by us. They each were riding an Anglo-Arab and had a Quarter Horse pack horse with two beautiful German Shorthair dogs tagging along. The pack horse was not led, and he had a nose screen or basket to keep him from eating. The Frosts are from Longmount, Colorado, where they make saddles as a side business. He is a researcher for the Department of Commerce in Boulder. We had a good visit about saddles. Theirs are nicely made endurance saddles built on the principle of a dressage saddle. They are lighter weight and built with rider balance in mind, as opposed to jumping saddles that have a forward seat, or roping saddles built with special ruggedness.

When the Frosts left, our mules took after their dogs (as mules are prone to do) and one dog ran away–on their backtrail. He never came back, so they finally went back to look for him. Later Robert came up and said they found him. Nice of him to keep us informed.

In my dream of dreams, Gretchen and I would be doing this together like the Frosts–riding our horses, leading a pack horse, traveling through the mountains, having a trailer to camp in, and simply doing all of our vacations this way.

On the other hand, Gretchen is probably also dreaming, "Wouldn't it be nice if Albert would be an artist and would go to Italy with me to take in operas simply because he loved them so...."

We have very different interests, but the Lord put us together, anyway, because the Lord knew how incomplete my life would be if I'd been married to a woman who was a horse woman. What Gretchen has done for me–as an artist and as one who loves classical music and opera–is enrich my life in ways that never would have otherwise occurred. The Lord knows what is best for me. I suspect this is true for Gretchen, too.

~ ~ ~

After supper, Graham and I took the horses out north of camp and let them graze. A couple of the young men from the Student Conservation Corps came by–one from Nebraska and the other from Colorado–and we visited. They told about seeing elk on the slope in the mornings. They have been here a week, have four more to go, are working on the Continental Divide Trail and doing some backpack-

'The ridge on the Razor Back Trail dropped off 1,500 feet on one side and 2,000 feet on the other.' July 30, 1983 (Chapter 5)

ing. Finally I asked them who they thought would win the presidency in this fall's election. Both agreed it would be Dukakis.

As Graham and I brought the horses in, full and in good spirits, the young people's voices and campfire and party nearby excited them. Even Jake, the stoic male mule, tried to look like an Arab with his head held high, arched neck and tail up and flying. The other horses did too, except Bull, who I was riding.

Tuesday, July 19, 1988

I was up at 5, and didn't see Bull around. I didn't tie him up last night, thinking he'd stick by camp. Wrong. So I saddled Misty to go find him. Estereka and Suzie, Dick's two Arabians, followed. As we rode by the student camp, there Bull was, lying in the middle of the courtyard. The supply tent was on one side, the dining fly on another, and sleeping tents rounded out the other two sides of the courtyard. I first just rode by, and he simply stared at me. What a character. He must enjoy having more people around. Or maybe he likes the enclosed, "more civilized" arrangement of this camp as opposed to ours which are always "in the wild." After a while, he ambled out, and I changed the saddle from Misty to him.

I moved all the stock a ways up the mountain to give them some good grass for grazing and to look for the elk. I sat on Bull as he ate and just watched the others graze. Soon the mules acted as though they spotted something in the trees; 10 minutes later the Arabs did, too, and 15 minutes later, the others seemed to, as well. I never saw anything. The elk didn't come.

Then I saw a mule deer doe looking at us, then a yearling. Soon Misty walked over to a bed of two fawns. They were soon surrounded by horses and were startled by our presence. They didn't panic, though, and waited a little while before vanishing.

After the horses got their fill, they started moving up the mountain backtrail, so Bull and I caught up to them and put a lead on Estereka to keep them from going further.

Soon I saw a layer of white rolling clouds below me to the northeast. Every once in a while, cloud vapor will burst into rain. It didn't take long before the clouds were sliding toward me, so I hurried back to camp. We saddled all the horses, packed, and were out by 9:30.

While on the trail this afternoon, we were met with hail and thunder. At the first flash of lightning, I counted the seconds to determine how many miles away it was. There were fewer than five seconds, so

I knew it was close. Dick was riding way ahead and Graham way behind, so I waved Dick into the trees and called Graham in as he came by. Dick then started out again. I yelled at him, but with the rain and hail I guess he could not hear.

I was exasperated with him, but I couldn't go after him. So I said, "Lord, take care of him, or if you're gonna allow him to be zapped, zap him with as little pain as possible."

After the storm was over, I went up and explained lightning in the mountains to Dick and Graham. Neither knew when you're in a lightning storm in the mountains that you get under trees (not the tallest one); Dick thought you should stay out from trees like you do on a golf course in Michigan.

~ ~ ~

Supper was canned steak, mashed potatoes, peas, and pudding.

We had a great fire after supper to take the chill off. We read the second chapter of James and talked about "not doing" and what we "should be doing" and the difference between doing and being.

Wednesday, July 20, 1988

Around camp I need to tell Graham and Dick more than is usually is the case with riders who have been with me before; but they are quite observant and are picking up the know-how. They have been trying to help me with what I'm doing, and I am gradually getting them to do things by themselves, like repacking, weighing packs, bringing up pack animals, and loading them.

We got out at 8:30 this morning; good timing. Little did we know what a great day it would be. We rode up to Sargenti Mesa where we could see a great distance. Many beef cows with the VJ brand were grazing in this vast, lush area. I checked the way the rancher had set up their water system. There was a fenced-in catch pond, with a plastic pipe running from it to a big cow tank a ways away (and at a slightly lower level).

We rode on, taking much longer than we expected because of a terribly rocky trail–less than two miles per hour. (Bull's hooves hurt on rocks.) We just about went the wrong way on Houghland Trail, but a quick check of my wrist compass kept us going in the right direction. We found our way back on the Colorado Trail quickly and went over Mt. Baldy. Again, a gorgeous view and more pictures taken.

As we moved west we passed Middle Baldy, and in a park before Mt. Baldy we spotted three big bull elk with huge antlers flashing in the sun. There were at least 80 cows in the herd, as well. The elk weren't particularly afraid of us even though we came within 150 yards of them. What a thrill. I can't wait to tell Severson.

We then passed through Middle Baldy Park with its almost non-existent trail, and then came upon a luxuriant grazing area along Razor Creek, an intermittent stream. We went further than we expected, but I saw on the map a treeless area that I thought must be grassy and would be good for the horses. It was identified as "Shorty's Cabin."

When we came to a small clearing, I asked Dick and Graham to hold the pack animals while I explored. As I did, I found the "Shorty's Cabin" area and I saw an elk ahead.

With my binoculars I could see it was a cow, and that she was soon followed by a spike bull. I thought they were the only two, so I rode up an embankment to get to a higher meadow for a better look. There were 15 elk, with the closest one only 150 feet away, grazing and not seeing me. I gently turned Bull and eased back down to get Dick and Graham. When I brought them up, 25 more elk crossed the trail and went up into the trees by the meadow. We watched for a while, and then all of a sudden, all 40 took off with the crunching of timber. A little calf went off in the opposite direction. I hope she eventually finds her mother.

After supper, I went for a walk to see if I could find the trail we want to be on tomorrow. Dick's Colorado Trail map shows that it goes up to North Pass. I couldn't find it, but I did find where two trees were cut down. My topo map shows the trail going right on top of where the trees are down.

I walked back to camp–about half to three-quarters of a mile away–in the dark. I heard coyotes up the canyon where I had been, but I knew Dick and Graham couldn't hear them. There is a ridge blocking the sound from where they are.

It is interesting how your imagination plays with you when you are alone and in the dark. I thought about what I would do if I spotted a lone man coming toward me. It couldn't be, since I had seen no tracks or other signs, but just the same, the thought gave me goose bumps. I mimicked an owl a few times and then quit for fear I might call in a mountain lion, instead, or a bobcat as I did before.

These thoughts could be a bit unnerving, walking alone in the dark, dependent on one's own resources. I'd be pretty nervous, but with trust in God who has cared for me without fail, I talked with Him as I would another person and was able to accept "come what may." Then I remembered Saint Paul's words, "Whether I live or die, I am with Christ." What more could a person ask?

I went back to camp and told Dick about not finding the trail. He pulled out his map and poured over it with his flash light trying to find where we should go. I think we are better off with my topo maps, though. In fact, I think Dick would be lost if he depended solely on his Colorado Trails map.

When I told him I'd maybe bushwhack up to the top of the mountain, he said, "No, no, oh, no" over and over again. It seemed the thought of bushwhacking was foreboding to him. I hope it doesn't keep him sleepless tonight thinking about it. Well, I don't want to use up my flash light batteries.

Thursday, July 21, 1988

This morning I told Dick to ride ahead, since he was so sure his Colorado Trails map was accurate and that he could find the trail. It's better to let a person find out himself whether right or wrong. When Graham and I came to the place where I thought we should begin bushwhacking, Dick came back and admitted he couldn't find a trail.

I went into the woods and could not go very far before we were blocked. I asked Graham and Dick to wait while I explored. I went on the south side of Bear Gulch as I saw how impossible it was to get through in the north side (the terrain went practically straight up).

It was very difficult going, and I finally had to tie up Bull and climb. As I moved up Bear Gulch, I made my way around fallen timber until I reached the top. I found the trail and walked it north to see if there was any trail going down, but found none. So I went back and started down the way I'd come up. When I got back to Bull, I rode back on the north side–very steep–to get back to Dick and Graham. I was gone more than an hour. I gave them an option to ride the miles back up Razor Creek, and then hope there was a trail on top to bring them back. They chose instead to bushwhack with me; we worked our way up without having to cut many trees.

From then on we made good time. We came out on a trail west of the North Pass, followed the Lujan Creek and then up to the Los, and we're camping between the sources of the two tributaries. We turned the horses loose, and they all came back for feed at my call. They have finally learned the drill. Camp is now home for the horses.

Friday, July 22, 1988

We got out just a little after 8 this morning and covered a vast grassy area and then up the Cacetopa Creek, traveling about 20 miles. It was another hot, hot afternoon–92 degrees by our thermometer. Just road traveling is terribly boring. I got off and walked a great deal. If my feet didn't hurt, I'd do it even more. We finally came past a trailhead, saw a Colorado Game Warden and two helpers coming out on horseback, and we're making camp nearby. We went through a gate about 1/3 mile before setting up camp, so that fence will hold the horses and prevent them from heading down the backtrail tonight.

Saturday, July 23, 1988

Layover day today. I got up at 5:30 to go climb the mountain. Didn't get back for breakfast until 9:30. The route was more dangerous than I should have taken alone. Great sights, though, and a sense of accomplishment. At 11, we all saddled the pack stock and went for a ride. Then we took turns taking a bath by the creek and generally lolled around. It is clouding up and cooling off.

CHAPTER TWENTY-EIGHT

The legendary story of Deadman's Gulch

Sunday, July 24, 1988

We got out of camp at 8:30 after eating only eggs and bacon for breakfast. No pancakes today. The trail along Cacetopa Creek was long and between 10,300 and 12,600 feet in elevation. Then we traveled along the top and down over one mountain and then another to San Luis Pass.

There was a glorious view, so we took time for pictures. It was only about noon, and no storms seemed to be on their way. Usually they will wait until about 2:30 in the afternoon. Before we could get to trees for protection, we had to go through a long swale with no trees and then over another pass without trees. There seemed to be plenty of time.

But as I stepped into the saddle, I looked up into the sky and saw a dark spot to my right. The next thing I knew, not a hundred yards away, a bolt of lighting hit. Then another was right in front of me.

We were in a dangerous spot. I knew lighting could sometimes zip down rocks and then strike you as though you were its original, one and only, target. So I scrapped the plan to go through the swale and pass to the trees and just went down in the low gully with our animals. I told the guys to move fast. Thank God the storm went by quickly, because Graham was not making his horse move fast enough for me. He had his spurs on his saddle horn. I told him I did not mind his getting knocked off by lightning, but I did not want to be the one who had to call his wife, Nancy, with the news.

We then traveled over the next draw and to some trees where we ate lunch. When the weather cleared some, we headed out, going west of San Luis Pass, but could not find the trail. By then it was 2:30 and storms were railing north of us. We decided to just find a campsite and weather the storm under our tarps rather than endure them on the trail.

We found some trees in a flat area where we set up our tarp. It was cold, the wind was blowing, and then it rained and hailed. It even snowed a little.

~ ~ ~

Interesting. I found a big and bulky tree whose trunk is close to the ground. When I sit on the leeward side, it's warm. I'm sitting here now looking at the maps and writing. The coyotes are calling, and I just fed the horses. Dick and Graham have gone to bed to keep warm.

Monday, July 25, 1988

Got up at 5 and turned both of Dick's horses loose so they could graze a little. He had tied both up to keep them quiet. As they left in the beginning light of the morning, I could dimly see the form of Bull, Misty and the two mules, Jake and Gyp. I walked over, caught Bull and saddled him. I told Dick, who was now awake, that I would follow his horses and let Bull graze at the same time. Those Arabian horses can cruise all over the mountain. They are hardy, quick and brilliant. Following them gave me an opportunity to look over the countryside, searching for the trail we left yesterday–the one we intended to follow before the storms came up.

After two hours I caught Estereka and led all the horses back to camp. Dick and Graham had not eaten; I had expected them to have eaten and be partly packed by the time I got back. I thought I had them on their way to taking the initiative to get things done. Graham said they were unorganized while I was gone. We packed up after breakfast. I was disappointed.

~ ~ ~

We had some uncertain times today finding our way as we tried to stick close to the Colorado Trail. We first rode up on the south side of the gulch and then through some bent twig willows to get to the top of the mountain. I figured our camp last night had been along the Colorado Trail, but as we rode along the north side of the mountain, the trail branched, taking us down toward East Mineral Creek; we instead needed to stay on the part of the trail that would take us further up and farther west. It was rough going with rocks, downed timber, short steep downs and ups. I wish the Colorado Trail were better marked at some opportune times.

I thought we should be going over Snow Mesa, but we found that our trail went over the mountain instead. There was a sign indicating we were on the Colorado Trail, so we followed it even though the trail went down, which was against my instincts. But I was not too alarmed since we seemed to be going in the right direction.

We had come over an exceedingly rocky trail with huge boulders as well as smaller rocks that seemed strategically placed in our path—as though it had been a calculated thing on someone's part. The boulders hadn't been moved when the trail was made, and our pack horses could barely get through. After a while, I realized we were going down Timber Creek Trail.

Later, we came upon a tent where there were seven horses outside. I rode up to see if anyone was inside and found two men. The one who came out could not understand English—he spoke, and apparently understood, only Spanish. The second would not come out. I thought at first they were outfitters, but when I smelled sheep and discovered they did not speak English, I decided they must be sheepherders.

I asked if they had seen elk, and he motioned over the mountains and to the west. I then expected I might see some when we got over there. When we went, however, we saw only sheep. That's when I realized that the sheepherder didn't understand my question and depended on guesses. He must have thought I was inquiring about sheep. It was a nice big band, but there was no one caring for them. I was surprised at the number of Suffolk and Shropshire sheep. I expected Merino or Lincoln.

Toward evening we got down Tremble Creek and then to Cabella Creek. I saw some cabins, so I turned back into the trees to stay away from civilization.

I'm beginning to feel sick so I'm turning in. It is only 8 p.m.

Tuesday, July 26, 1988

I felt better this morning.

There is no way, in a day and half, that we can get to Molas Pass (where we are supposed to meet Shad tomorrow). I thought about going to Howardsville, instead, but it is up high in the tundra. The third alternative is to go to Spring Creek Pass just a few miles away, which I chose.

I went to the cabins that are near the Pass to see if anyone there had detailed maps of the area. I met a Zelda Blackburn and her three sons. The cabins belong to the Blackburns who have a ranch nearby. They call it Oleo Ranch—a poor man's spread. The Blackburns run a fishing camp in summer and an elk camp in fall, and they do bighorn sheep hunting. They also have a quail camp in New Mexico and a mule deer camp in Texas. They did have some maps which will show us the way past Dead Man's Gulch.

Legend has it that this gulch is so named because, back in the 1800's, there were six guys who went elk hunting in the area in the late Fall and got stranded. The next spring only one emerged from the mountains, and he was in remarkably good condition.

It came to light, as he was bragging in the bars to his friends, that he had killed and eaten his buddies to stay alive. He had said the freezing temperatures "kept" his friends' dead bodies, so he was able to eat them all winter while up in the mountains.

Needless to say, he was taken to trial. According to legend, the judge noted that all the men killed were Democrats and their county had had only seven Democrats to begin with! The surviving elk hunter, a Republican, was hanged.

(I don't know about the truth of all this, but I did read that students and teachers from the University of Washington got a permit recently to dig in the area. They found bones which had knife marks on them.)

~ ~ ~

We rode up to Skyline and looped south around some willows, about two sections of them. We also encountered storms today and had to take cover in the woods. While waiting out one of the storms, I saw a herd of elk nearby. When the rains let up, I rode to watch them, and Dick followed on Estereka. The elk did not spook for quite some time; they headed down a draw only to return again. I could hear by the barking that they had run into coyotes. I swung Bull around to see where they were going, but they turned again and went down the wooded gulch. What a thrill to see more than 40 elk close up; wish I'd had my Olympic camera.

While eating lunch today we listened to some coyote pups from a nearby den. Then we headed out. We are making camp tonight not far from where we were last night.

Wednesday, July 27, 1988

When we rode out of camp this morning, we saw gorgeous mountains toward Silverton and especially Uncompahge Mountain, which is shaped like a head in a bishop's hood. I tried to check where the trail would go, since I want to start in this area next year. We couldn't find the trail as it was shown on the map so we just cut across the willows on our way back to the Oleo Ranch.

When we arrived, we asked Zelda if she could take us to Buena Vista to get our rigs, but she was able to take us only to Lake City. We got a grocer there to take us to Buena Vista, and we called Shad to let him know he didn't need to help us out; we made arrangements to meet him in Denver tomorrow.

From Buena Vista, we decided to take a different way back to Oleo Ranch (where our horses were) since Slumgullian Pass was so steep. We came back south and east of Creede.

The Blackburns are putting us up for the night in one of their big cabins that sleeps 12. It also has a huge fireplace.

Thursday, July 28, 1988

Zelda fixed breakfast for us this morning. Her son Matt wants to fly helicopters, so Graham talked to him about the Naval Academy before we took off.

We drove through Creede Del Norte, Monte Vista, Pueblo, Colorado Springs, and on to Denver where we met Shad about 9 p.m. at the intersection of Highway 34 and Interstate 76. Graham and Shad are spending some time together before Graham heads back to Texas.

Friday, July 29, 1988

Dick was going to follow me to Lincoln, Nebraska, but he couldn't keep up. I went back for him once, but the second time he trailed behind, I just kept going.

I got to Severson's about 7 p.m. tonight; they were having corn on the cob, so I joined in. On the way home from Seversons I had a flat tire. I changed it and called Gretchen from a nearby gas station. When I got home, she was as glad to see me as I was to see her.

I lost about 15 pounds on the ride this year. I think I have giardiasis.

Saturday, July 30, 1988 (at home)

I called Dick tonight to make sure he made it home safely. His wife Ruth met him in Lincoln, and they did arrive home OK. He told me he got behind on the trip home yesterday because he had to stop and sleep t a rest stop.

Another year gone by. I got within a day of where I originally planned, but that's OK. Where I ended up will be a better take-off point for next year. It's nice to know people where you start.

1989

Southern Colorado

Spring Creek Pass
Uncompahgre
Wolf Creek Pass
Cumbres Pass
Chama

CHAPTER TWENTY-NINE

Altitude sickness strikes again

Thursday, August 3, 1989

I've been planning this trip since last year. I was going to leave Minnesota early on August 5 so I could celebrate Gretchen's August 4 birthday with her tomorrow. However, if I had waited until Saturday to leave I knew I wouldn't make Cumbres Pass by the planned end of the ride on the August 18.

Gretchen, the great sport she is, said it didn't matter when we celebrated her birthday. So we did it on July 30 with a wonderful picnic with Dan and his family, and Sarah and the boys who had arrived to be with us the day before. Joel is in South Bend where Gretchen and I had helped him and Sarah move so he could begin his study in New Testament Theology at Notre Dame.

I bought groceries for the trip yesterday, except food for the noon meals, which I left to A.M. Lips. As I was driving today, I realized I'd forgotten the fresh meat at home, plus my jacket. And tonight I realized I'd forgotten the coffee. I thought I'd learned my lesson about making lists, but I guess it didn't stick. No problem, I can get it along the way.

~ ~ ~

Mert Schwarz, A.M. Lips, and Dave Singer are on the ride with me this year. Al Severson was planning to come, but he had a heart attack this year, so he couldn't. Dave Singer does PR work for Prison Fellowship at the national office in Reston, Va.

He took my picture once and I commented that it would be great to have a photographer like him along on one of my rides. Later he asked if he could come, so I invited him. This is his first experience with horses. I told him what to bring and warned him that all he carries should fit into one duffle and weigh no more than 30 pounds, but that he didn't need to count his camera.

He flew to Minneapolis from Washington, D.C., so he could help me drive to the mountains. When I picked him up at the airport yesterday he was so proud because he had all his gear in one duffle weighing 29.5 pounds! He had another duffle along, however, and when I asked, "What's that?" He replied, "My cameras."

I asked how much the bag weighed and, with a slight smile, he said, "Forty-five pounds. You told me I didn't need to count my photo gear."

He had cameras and lenses filling that large duffle, and besides that, a back pack full of film. All the way to Colorado today I talked to him about what could possibly be left behind, but he felt he could not leave anything back.

Wanting good pictures, I finally caved in. I decided I'd give him my saddle bag to fill with some of his photo gear, and I'd carry it behind my saddle. We'd also fill a nose bag with his gear and hang it on the saddle horn, plus we'd have to fill a photographer's vest with the extra film. What we couldn't fit in that way, we would pack by leaving some horse feed behind.

Dave also proudly showed me his cowboy hat at the airport. It was a soft one with no leather sweat band inside. I would have offered him one of mine, but since his head was smaller, none of mine would fit. He looks like Napoleon when the part of the brim that turns up straight on the side turns to the front. Dudes are such a riot.

~ ~ ~

Gretchen fixed a great dinner last night for Dave and me. Earlier in the day I had loaded my trailer and took Bull to A.M.'s farm two miles east of Nerstrand, Minnesota, and 1-1/2 miles south. He had already brought his horses home from where he pastures them. Mert Schwarz also had brought his horse, Farah, over there. It's good to have the horses spend a little time with each other and get acquainted before the ride. It helps them develop a pecking order.

When we got there at 1:30 this morning to pick up horses, I saw that Farah had paced a circle in the barn yard. What a nervous (or maybe homesick) horse.

Dave and I are hauling Bull, Gyp the mule, and Farah, and A.M. is hauling Goldie, Tico (an Appaloosa) and Misty. I had the use of Severson's C-B, so we could talk between vehicles today.

We're staying overnight tonight in the fairgrounds in Goodland, Kansas. They are charging us $5 per horse to stay here. It's a good place to leave horses overnight.

Friday, August 4, 1989

Before leaving Goodland this morning, I bought a double hunting jacket to keep me warm in the mountains and enough canned meat to take care of us through the next couple of weeks.

We drove the rest of the way to Spring Creek Pass, altitude 10,800 feet, and met Mert and the two dun horses he had hauled at the corrals. I went down to see Dick and Zelda Blackburn at their Oleo Ranch, but they weren't around.

We fixed supper and made some preparations for tomorrow's departure. Though inexperienced, Dave is trying to his best to help out, which I appreciate. His efforts tonight, however, resulted in the skin on his hands being torn apart. When he was helping unload the horses, A.M. handed him Goldie's nylon lead rope and asked him to keep Goldie from backing out of the trailer when the back gate was opened. Dave's grip wasn't strong enough, and, when the gate opened, Goldie gave a mighty pull. The rope slipped through Dave's hands, burning the skin off the palms of both. He spent most of the evening with his hands in an ice chest, trying to sooth the burning and oozing.

~ ~ ~

I didn't feel like eating much or drinking water today. I wonder if driving so quickly into this altitude is affecting me.

Saturday, August 5, 1989

I awoke with the beginnings of an upset stomach this morning. I continue to wonder if the altitude is bothering me.

It took quite a while to get packed up the first time and Dave, of course, was totally green.

In order to make room for all of Dave's camera gear, we packed only 25 pounds of horse feed, and Dave put 20 pounds of his gear on the saddle horse. Since Dave was smaller, the total was no more than my total weight.

Before setting out, I showed Dave how to saddle and put the bridle on. When I told him how to put his finger in the horse's mouth to get him to open his mouth he said, "You've got to be kidding!" He could not believe such a thing, and he did not know that a horse has no teeth where the bit is held in its mouth.

I watched as he tried for the first time to bridle his horse. He had forgotten to hold the bridle by the crown with the right hand and the bit with the left hand. He held the bit with both hands and tried to shove it into Misty's mouth. Now, Misty is a rooter. She pushes her nose forward hard when she is exasperated. She did this then and knocked Dave over on his back. As he went down, his feet slid out from under him and down under her. There he lay, one leg on the side of her front legs, and one between them, still holding the bridle with both hands and looking up at her. I don't know if he was chagrined or not. I tried not to make anything of it.

~ ~ ~

We finally were on the trail at 11:30, and rode until 6 p.m., making camp at 11,000 feet after having traveled to 12,400 feet.

It was farther to Jarosa Meadows than I had remembered from last year. Dick Whitmore, Graham Purcell, and I had ridden up there and realized we would need to go back to Spring Creek Pass since there would not be enough time at the end of our ride to reach Molas Pass.

Coming up to Jarosa Meadows, I was remembering the great sight of the large elk herd we saw last year. Stalking them to get closer, we used the screen of pine trees. That is one of those memories that will last. This time, we saw some more elk, but they were further away and there weren't as many. But it is always exciting to spot elk, no matter how many are in the herd. They are such majestic animals. Freedom and beauty are exciting. Eagles, elk and the Statue of Liberty make the heart quicken. Freedom. That is probably the best word to explain why I find such pleasure in seeing a herd of elk. They once were plains animals, but because they were hunted, they became elusive mountain animals. Some species are obviously successful in their struggle to survive.

We cut across the south of the mountain, spotting a radio tower, but at the pass we tied the pack animals and rode up to the tower. That way we could see Uncompahge Mountain. Later we saw so many sights that we would not have needed that exertion. We then traveled past Big Bush Creek and on to Ruby Creek where we are camping tonight.

I didn't eat anything at noon today. Water tastes terrible.

Sunday, August 6, 1989

We left about 9:30 this morning, traveling at high altitudes again, and reaching 13,362 feet. (Are these high altitudes causing me to not feel well?)

We followed the Continental Divide on the Colorado Trail past the head of Lost Trail Creek. We saw the trail branch off to Heart Lake, which we did not take, but kept on going to the head of Pole Creek and followed it down.

We're camping on a high hill overlooking Pole Creek and Middle Fork. It was difficult to find a level spot, and there is no water nearby. We had to haul water up on horses. Mert and I carried a bucket each, and A.M. handed them to us after we climbed into our saddles. Tough going up a long hill carrying water on horseback, but it was a necessity in order to get water up to camp.

My stomach problems are getting worse. I feel especially terrible in the afternoons. Riding jiggles my stomach too much. I forced myself to eat a little bit at noon today, and my stomach kicked back like a bad ulcer and heart burn.

Water tastes so bad that it's hard to drink anything. If I sip even a little water, my stomach hurts even more.

By late afternoon today, I was very sick, but I didn't want to show it to the others. I wanted to do my part to set up camp. What made matters even worse is that Bull got colic.

When I first started these rides in 1983, I brought a syringe and medicine for colic, but I quit bringing that stuff when it didn't get used. Now I need it.

Sick as I was, I led Bull. The area was so steep I tried to walk on the contour. Oh, how I needed to go to bed.

Dave came over and offered to walk Bull for me, and I quickly accepted. I'm climbing into my sleeping bag.

Monday, August 7, 1989

It was next to impossible to sleep last night with my aching gut. I felt like I had the same problem Al Severson had just before his heart attack. I also worried that I might possibly have cancer.

Then, at 2 a.m., when I heard Bull thrashing on the ground, I got up and tied him high so he could not roll while I got dressed. I was too sick and weak to walk in the dark with him, so I saddled Goldie and led Bull from horseback. I got bored riding back and forth in our camp area, so I began to ride along the mountain, as much on the contour as I could, using my flashlight to see where we were going. After a couple miles, I decided to turn back. So as not to burn down the flashlight batteries, I turned it off. Goldie, I expected, could pick his way back to camp without the use of light. He did it well. Whenever I would turn on the flashlight to check on him, I saw the tracks, which we had recently made, right under him. Though I figured he'd be able to do this, it still seems uncanny. How does a horse retrace his steps exactly? Has he such a memory that he knows every bush and rock? If he were following a trail, I could understand it better. I know horses have a sense of direction, but to stay exactly in the tracks they made coming is awesome. It's just like a hound dog being able to stay on the trail.

When we got back to camp, I got off to see if Bull's stomach started to rumble yet. To my joy, it was now making noise and I knew he would be all right. I was also glad because I did not have to ride for several more hours. Then, the question I had was, will Bull be strong enough to keep up on the trip?

I went back to bed and slept in. Mert teased me when he brought me breakfast in bed.

~ ~ ~

Instead of following the Colorado Trail up West Fork, we took Pole Creek down to Bear Creek and took that up to Beartown Site and then found the La Ganita Drive–a pathway for stock going over the top. We were at 13,000 feet.

We're camping tonight a little before Black Lake.

Tuesday, August 8, 1989

I had the choice this morning to stop the ride and head home or go to Lake City where I can see a doctor. Even though I was not eating and water tasted terrible, I did not want to stop the ride. I'm also realizing I can't lick this–even though I think of myself as being rather tough. We decided to go back to Spring Creek Pass. We got part of the way back today; we'll make it the rest of the way tomorrow, and then we'll drive to Lake City.

CHAPTER THIRTY

'Phonetically, that would be spelled K-W-E-E. Kwee.'

Wednesday, August 9, 1989

We traveled Ute Creek today, went around the northwest end of Rio Grande Reservoir (which was dry), and found the trail as it left from Lost Trail Creek Ranch.

After following a park trail below Heart Lake, we went past Pearl Lakes and the lower end of Ruby Creek, up to Jarosa Meadows and then in to Spring Creek Pass where our rigs are. A most spectacular rainbow greeted us as we left the Jarosa area and rode down toward Spring Creek Pass. The sun broke out in the west during the middle of a rain shower, and to the east–the direction we were headed-a brilliant triple rainbow appeared.

We put our horses in the corral and drove in A.M.'s Suburban to Lake City.

We're staying at the Lake City Motel, and the others ate dinner in the restaurant. I tagged along, but didn't feel like eating. While in the restaurant, we found out Lake City has no doctor, but they do have a practical nurse in the auxiliary medical center. The other choice was to go on to Gunnison where there was a doctor.

I think my problem has been a combination of things: (1) Altitude sickness, which can be brought on by inadequate sleep before going into the mountains, and by lack of water. Before driving up into the mountains, one should drink water like one does with a cold. Using fruit juices to induce more liquids and drinking Gatorade, which adds electrolytes, really helps. (2) Activity upon reaching high altitudes that is too strenuous. (3) The excitement of the trip and having too much on my mind, which brings on stress (making lists would help in this area). I may have the beginnings of another ulcer.

The first time I had ulcer problems was back in 1956 right before I began working on the Eisenhower campaign in Wisconsin, and I have had ulcer problems ever since.

In the summer of '56 I was asked if I would come to Wisconsin and work on the agricultural issues related to the Eisenhower campaign. It was probably August–after we'd gotten the grain in. I wanted to do this, and the excitement of it all, the preparations, the conflict I experienced knowing I'd have to leave Gretchen for an extended period, all contributed to stomach problems for me.

I knew I would meet new people while putting an organization together and working with the congressional candidate in that area. And the experience would add to my political knowledge. (I was in the State Senate at the time.)

Stomach problems plagued me a couple years later when Gretchen and I were discussing whether to go into full-time politics or full-time farming. Farming as we had known it was changing and changing fast. And I knew if I stayed in farming, I was going to have to be a big farmer, which meant leaving politics. I couldn't do both.

Gretchen and I were sitting in the living room after lunch talking about this and decided to pray about it. Thankfully we had learned to pray together. (In our early years, being Lutherans, we hadn't learned to do it well.) Prayer, I think, includes listening to God. Therefore, the two of us were trying to figure out how to listen for direction from God.

That's when we heard a news flash on the radio in the kitchen. Congressman August Andreson had died of a heart attack.

I walked over to the phone and called Lionel Anderson, an economics professor at St. Olaf and asked if I could come in and see him for advice.

Taking challenges and stepping out in faith is not something I thought I necessarily was doing. But as I look back, for a little old country boy, I sure did it enough times. After mulling it over, and consulting with others, I decided: I'm going to go fly in the Navy; I'm going to run for the State Senate; I'm going to run for Congress; I'm going to run for Governor. When I look back on it, I wonder how I ever had the courage to do all these things. And the anticipation, preparation, and stress each time gave me stomach problems.

Thursday, August 10, 1989

We went to the motel restaurant for breakfast. We met the owner, Nancy Zeller, who also turned out to be the nurse! She seemed quite competent, so I went to her office when it opened at 9:30.

Nancy checked me over and drew blood for testing. She decided I did have altitude sickness; she prescribed Gatorade and Tums and said she would send the results of the blood tests to my home doctor. She said she thought I would have no problem going back into the high mountains. I said I would, nonetheless, call her back when I got to Chama, New Mexico, a to find out the test results.

When I wrote out a check to pay for her services, Nancy looked at the check and asked how to pronounce my last name. I told her, and she said, "Phonetically, that would be spelled K-W-E-E. Kwee."

Then she looked at me, and then back at the check. I was wondering if she thought my check was no good.

To my surprise, her next question was, "Do you know Chuck Colson?"

I was dumfounded. "Why do you ask that?"

She hesitated, and then said, "I just finished reading *Born Again*, and there was a Quie mentioned in the book who offered to serve the rest of Colson's sentence. Is that you?"

"Yes."

"Well, I think this is why you got sick. So you could come in here and meet me," she said.

As the story unfolded, I became even more surprised and saw the Lord's hand in this. Nancy has a son (from an earlier marriage) who is in prison at Pendleton, Oregon. She wondered if I could visit him.

As the Lord would have it, I had already been planning an October trip to Oregon to spend some time with the PF Area Director there, Mark Hubbell. I promised to visit her son at that time.[15]

To me this is a proof of the presence of the Holy Spirit in all we do, and how God constantly uses circumstance for His purposes. Most of the time, however, we are unaware of it. Occasionally, as in this case, He clues us in and makes us aware. That is exciting. Thanks be to God!

~ ~ ~

After stocking up on Gatorade and Tums, we drove back to Spring Creek Pass.

Friday, August 11, 1989
　　We drove down to Wolf Creek Pass today where we are sleeping in our rigs during rain. We will take off on the trail from here tomorrow.

Saturday, August 12, 1989
　　I feel quite well today. How blessed health is. I thank God for it. I know the point I started to get better. It was right after I decided I can't make this by myself no matter how tough I am. That's when I turned to God in a different spirit than I had in my earlier prayers.

~ ~ ~

　　As we left Wolf Creek Pass, we found our way around to the top of the ski resort where the tows drop off skiers. We passed a little "mound" [just my little humor] called Alberta Peak whose altitude is 11,870 feet. We kept seeing Alberta Reservoir as we followed the Divide, all the time at about 11,600.
　　We went by Silver Pass and Bonita Pass, and then dropped down to 11,000 feet for camp.

Sunday, August 13, 1989
　　We traveled past Summit Pass and Elwood Pass and then lost our way again looking for the Continental Divide Trail. We just plain ran out of trail. So we decided to stop and eat lunch overlooking Iron Creek.
　　Some places a trail is evident because there are slashes on trees. Other places, when no one has used the trail for long periods of time, we have to figure it out on our own. And most times the actual location of the Continental Divide is not obvious. If you don't have a topo map but are using only Forest Service maps, you just have to time yourself to determine when and where the Divide takes a turn.
　　Sometimes, on multiple maps–Forest Service, topo, and others–trails will show up going one way on one map and another way on another, or they may not even show up on another.
　　Some of my topo maps are 60 years old, but I still trust them the most. I got them from the National Geological Survey Office.

Forest Service maps are difficult to read because the scale is so small, and they do not show elevation. This is especially so when there are switchbacks that drop elevation fast.

We took off again after lunch and found a jeep trail, but didn't stay on it long. Figuring the Continental Divide Trail had to be up near the top, we rode up into the mountains a ways,, probably above the timberline. We kept riding until we just about ran out of trees; we were up into the Limber Pines, right before the tundra. We were tired and still hadn't found our trail. Traveling above 13,000 feet on a consistent basis takes a lot out of us, so we decided to make camp.

It looked like inclement weather was on the way. We put up the fly; A.M., Mert, and Dave were unpacking, and I told Dave to go ahead and rest. I saddled Bull again and went exploring up in the tundra to see if I could find the trail.

I did. Followed it a ways until it forked off. I saw some more elk, and then I came upon a fellow walking alone. To my surprise, he did not have a backpack. He was wearing jean shorts. He said he was from Pagos Springs and was just up for a hike.

"I notice you don't have a back pack," I commented. "How long have you been out?"

"Oh, my car is down by the jeep trail."

"Have you got the day off?"

"Oh, I just figured I'd take the day to hike around."

This guy didn't seem too swift. I went on my way and kept watching the clouds that were moving and roiling; I knew I was working against time. I wanted to get back into camp before the storm hit. So I was stepping off pretty good with Bull. I wondered how that single hiker was going to survive the storm.

As I reached camp, what did I see coming toward me but Dave Singer–buck naked!

"What are you doing without your clothes on!?"

Then Mert stepped out in similar fashion. They had decided to take a bath while I was gone. They'd gotten water from a pond, heated it up, and they were now proud of the fact that they were squeaky clean.

I told them to get dressed as fast as they could. "A storm is coming!"

I went over and pulled my saddle off. And just as I was putting it under the nylon cover, the rain started.

"We've got to get everything battened down," I pleaded.

Then it started hailing marble- to golf-ball-sized hail. All the horses that were loose tried to get under trees for protection. But Misty, still tied up, was getting hit hard by the hail. She couldn't go anywhere; she went right down on the ground.

Bull started running, and when he saw us under the tarp, he "bulled" his way in, hitting one rope the tarp was tied to and ripping out the end. The whole thing started to come down on us.

I kicked Bull out and ran and grabbed the rope to pull it tight. About then the hail turned to smaller hail, so the horses weren't suffering so bad. Mert drove a stake into the ground; I tied off on the tarp fabric and fastened the rope to the stake. We managed to save the cover so we could stay dry. Our long yellow slickers were life savers, as we worked through the storm to do the repair.

It hailed so much, though, that we had a 1.5 foot bank of hail as it slid off the tarp.

Just then, something moving in the bushes caught my eye, and when I looked over, there was the hiker, squatted, trying to protect himself from the storm. I yelled at him and waved him over.

He didn't wait two seconds before he came running in. After securing the tarp once again, we got the stove going and cooked up some hot soup for him.

I asked, "What's your plan? We don't have extra sleeping bags." He said he'd go back to his car, but we told him he had to wait until the rain let up.

We didn't have any extra clean clothes. Dirty, yes. Which was better than nothing, I guess. So we decked him out with dry clothes and, when the rain stopped, we sent him on his way. He said he'd meet us someplace by Pagosa Springs to return our clothes, but we said, "No, just keep them."

~ ~ ~

I love storms. Being up here close to the clouds, watching them, timing when they will hit, figuring out where they will strike, being ready.

Being responsible for others can be a bit heavy, though. For a few moments it was not very easy going. And normally Mert and A.M. would be looking at the skies, watching for storms. I guess they figured, since I was up there with the clouds, I'd recognize if there was an impending storm and would be back sooner than I was. They told me, however, that they had seen the storm coming and were a little surprised I was "out there" under such threatening conditions.

I'm happy I found the trail we can take tomorrow.

Monday, August 14, 1989

The pond that was about a quarter mile below us froze overnight. I have had water buckets freeze over while on rides up here, but never have I seen a whole pond freeze over.

We worked our way up into the Continental Divide trail, following the trail I found last night. We traveled past Montezuma Peak and Summit Peak, traveling at 12,000 feet, and made camp at Adams Fork.

Tuesday, August 15, 1989

We traveled much over 12,600 feet today, staying away from trails that would take us down. We ended up at Blue Lake, where we are camping tonight.

Wednesday, August 16, 1989

Again, we followed the Divide at about 11,800 feet today, going past Green Lake and Trail Lake. We dropped down by switch backs to Dipping Lake–11,200 feet–where we are camping tonight.

The ponds near our campsite are dried up, but I rode around until I found water. There are lots of streams because of water seeping out of the mountains, but the water doesn't stay in the ponds if there isn't muck there to hold it. Most of these so-called ponds look more like rock piles because they are either dry or the water has receded, exposing rocks and making it impossible to get to the water. And the rocks in the ponds have a blackish color compared to the more gray looking ones outside the ponds. This all gave me a feeling like being on the moon or in Iceland. I haven't been to the moon, but I have been to Iceland! It also makes me wonder what else is in store for us on this trip.

We saw more storms coming in as we were setting up camp. We got the kitchen fly up and our gear covered right before they hit. There was lightning and a little hail, but nothing like that which we experienced a few days ago. It passed over quickly, but the sky stayed cloudy for a couple of hours. This gave everything a gray and dismal look and feeling.

The men are really tired and so am I. Thankfully, I'm not sick anymore. First Mert and then the other two went to bed at 8 o'clock. We all felt great and relaxed in the sunshine as we ate our noon lunch today behind a rock protecting us from the cold wind. The events after lunch–taking so much time to find our way and the bleak camp–sure change my mood.

There is supposed to be an eclipse of the moon tonight. I don't think I'll stay awake for it.

CHAPTER THIRTY-ONE

Am I ready to go through the process of dying?

Thursday, August 17, 1989

We pretty much followed the Continental Divide today, saw coyotes and two bands of sheep. We talked to one friendly herder and his stepson, who, after some confusion on my part, pointed the way to Cumbres Pass.

When I asked, "Where's Cumbres?" he said, "Right here."

"No, no." And then I repeated my question, but more slowly, "Where's Cumbres?" Just as slowly, he responded, "Right here."

I paused in frustration but didn't repeat my question.

I think he realized, then, what I was asking and said, "Oh, you mean Cumbres Pass."

What I didn't know was that, in Spanish (these herders' native language), cumbres means peak. We *were* at the peak. We *were* at Cumbres. What I needed to be asking was, "Where's Cumbres Pass?"

I thought this young man didn't understand, but my question was perfectly clear to him. It was I who lacked understanding.

~ ~ ~

On our way to Cumbres Pass, we decided to take a more interesting route than the jeep trail–an abandoned pack trail. We also followed a logging road on which each log deposit site was numbered. We thought, since the first number we encountered was "55," and subsequent numbers were going down, that the road would lead us to the beginning of the trail. When some miles later we got to "1," we found we were not out, but way in at the top.

To get the rest of the way to Cumbres Pass we were going to have to go cross country through some rugged country. We soon found out that "rugged" was putting it mildly.

A.M. didn't want to cut across such craggy, rough terrain; Mert was doubtful as well. (They had done this with me before and knew the trouble they could get into!) But if we didn't cut across, we would have had to go back, and I didn't want to do that. We had gone all that way, winding around on the logging road. And even if we went back, there was no guarantee the other trail would get us any closer to the pass. From where I stood, I knew where I was going, and I wanted them to come to that realization, as well.

I asked them to wait as I explored a little. I went down through the trees and came out, but still high up on a grassy knoll from where I could see a highway. I established that it was Highway 17, and by the bends, hair pin turns, and location of the railroad, I determined exactly where I was on the topo map. I then went back up and showed the map to A.M. and Mert, which would hopefully give them more confidence in going cross country. Dave was going to cut across with no questions asked. He doesn't worry about danger. I discounted that because of his lack of knowledge of mountains and his inexperience.

A.M. and Mert agreed to do it my way. We started down by going to the right of where I had just explored. I figured there would be more open area at that point, and the men's spirits would perhaps be up if they were out of the trees and able to see their destination. Earlier, as the logging road was taking us farther south than I wanted to go, I was worried we might miss Cumbres Pass and go an extra 10 miles into Chama, New Mexico. If we had done that, I figured Mert could ride in and phone John, his son, asking him to meet us in Chama instead of Cumbres Pass. But after looking at the treacherous land we needed to cross, there was no way we could have done that.

What was especially tricky was not necessarily the steep mountainside–we could do switchbacks down it. Rather, getting across deep gorges or arroyos caused the most problems. There were drop-offs-sometimes 50 to 100 feet deep–making it almost impossible to get across. But we worked our way around each time until we found places where cattle had gotten across.

Our last hurdle was finding a gate to get into the large fenced area–at least a quarter section–around Cumbres Pass.

We found one–but it was wired up tight. My farm experience helped as well as my Leatherman pliers which enabled me to pull out a staple and unwind wire.

We had seen the steam train going up the grade, so we figured there might be an old railroad station nearby. We rode into the pass, took pictures of the station, and waited around hoping another train would come by.

It was great fun watching the next train pull into the station. It took two steam engines to get the passenger cars up the steep grade from Chama. The engine going on up the mountain was refilled with water for its boilers, and the auxiliary engine turned around on the round table to go back to Chama. I was reminded of the steam engines pulling freight cars on the long grade near our farm home when I was a boy. The sound, then, as now, conjured up visions of faraway places.

I let Bull loose to graze while we were looking around the area, but I kept my eye on him. He ambled to the station where there were some tourists, so I called, "Bull!" He stopped. "Bull!" He just looked at me. "Come back. You're not supposed to be there." He stared at me.

More emphatic this time: "Come on back here!" He did.

One of the tourists said, "You've got that horse trained like a dog!"

~ ~ ~

Back in camp, when we were putting up our tarp, John, Mert's son, showed up. We were so surprised. Mert had just given John's phone number to a lady tourist who was waiting for the train, asking her to call John for us. We wondered how he could have arrived so quickly!

Well, John had decided to come a day early to wait for us. He had with him wife, Debbie, his 14-year-old son, Ben, and 8-1/2 month-old son, Matt. After we got everything settled, John took us to Wolf Creek Pass to get our rigs.

John drove, Mert and Dave rode up front, and A.M. and I rode in back of the pickup on a cushion. In Chama, which is at a lower elevation than we'd been traveling, people were dressed in shorts and T-shirts. We felt out of place. West of Chama it started to rain, and the speed of the truck made the water fly over us and hit the back of the pickup bed just past our feet. We managed to stay dry, however.

We drove out of Wolf Creek Pass immediately, with me following John, Mert next, and A.M. bringing up the rear. We went down to Pagosa Springs and ate dinner there. It was after 9 p.m. (too late for me). I called Gretchen as soon as I ordered my meal. I was thankful to hear everything was OK with her (I hadn't talked to her for two weeks), but it was hard for me to talk and find out more since I was so hungry.

We got back to Cumbres Pass quite late–about 11 p.m. (Quite different from our 8 p.m. bed times in the mountains.) Dave and Mert are sleeping in his truck, A.M. is in his suburban, and I'll be under the tarp at the campsite.

Friday, August 18, 1989

I awoke in great consternation at 4 a.m. this morning. I was anxious and remorseful that I hadn't told Gretchen in my phone call last night that I would hurry home immediately. If I got home quickly, Joel might still be there and I could see him Sunday. Family responsibility and love flooded in on me.

When I was able to get back to sleep I had a dream (more like a nightmare) in which there was a lanky, Gary Cooper-type cowboy and his wife (who was blind). In my dream, this wife had a dream that she had gone crazy because of her handicap. I could relate to that–some handicaps would just about do that to me. Then a man came into their house intending to do harm to the wife. She remembered her dream and pretended to be crazy, just as David (in the Bible) had done, and the man left. I awoke in a sweat. I have no idea what this dream means, or why it would bother me so. Maybe my mummy bag is just too tight.

I got up, walked and prayed, and walked and prayed until my anxiety started to subside. Then I couldn't go back to sleep, so I walked over to the train station and read its history by flashlight. The plaque said the route had been scouted in 1776 by a Lt. Anderson who recommended the route be a toll road. The area was so rough that in some areas they had to let wagons down by ropes, and the slopes were so steep they would tie a tree behind the wagon for brakes. Initially, the toll was $1.25 for a team of up to 12 horses. Apparently the route was so steep they needed 12 horses on a wagon to pull it. Just as now the train takes two engines to pull up the rail grade from Chama to the pass (13 miles), and then one engine from the pass to Antonito (41 miles). The toll for a horse and rider was 12 cents.

~ ~ ~

We all got together–eight of us–for breakfast of fried eggs, bacon and pancakes. It rained all through breakfast.

I had told the guys earlier that I was going to hang around camp for an extended period before heading back to Minnesota, but I was changing my mind. I offered to travel back following A.M.; he said he could get along OK, so I let it be. I didn't assert myself and say, "I'm going with you." Was it pride? Was I too proud to let someone know I had changed my mind?

I am peculiar in that way. If A.M. had said it would be helpful for me to be with him, or, "I'd enjoy having you with me even though in another vehicle," I would have packed up quickly and would have been traveling with him.

Instead I'm traveling home alone.

~ ~ ~

Before leaving, I drove to Chama and called Nancy Zeller, the nurse in Lake City. She said my blood tests showed I had hepatitis. I had had it back in 1956. It always shows up in blood tests.

When I was done with the call, I walked across the street to have a look around the railroad yard. The auxiliary engine I saw yesterday was there, but not the tourist passenger train. Striking up a conversation with a couple of men in overalls, I found out that they and other railroad buffs and former employees volunteer to work on and run the trains in the summer. This was their vacation–working around steam trains. They loved it as much as I love horses and mountains. It is important to do what you love.

Saturday, August 19, 1989 (at home)

I was reminded today of how disturbed I was when I woke a couple nights ago with that nightmare. Was it altitude and lack of oxygen, a tight sleeping bag, worry and anxiety, illness? I didn't like it and it scared me.

Death came to my mind so much in the nightmare. Am I ready to meet Jesus Christ? I think so. But am I ready to go through the process of dying? It seems like an enormous struggle. I remember Dad.

He died two days after I was elected governor. About two weeks before the election, his word to his offspring, which he wrote in a note from his room in a retirement home in Northfield, was that he was going to die. He specifically told Paul (my brother who is a doctor) not to worry. "Jesus has redeemed me and I'm going to Him," Dad wrote.

We knew he wanted to go; he was ready, and we never wanted him to die like our mother had. She died in extreme pain with cancer of the liver.

I never talked to her about death. I was in Congress at the time and didn't see her a lot. I always regret not talking to her about it. So I decided I was going to talk to Dad about it. We had a marvelous time together that day. I remember his saying, "Albert, I'm so glad you're not afraid of death." (I used to have a terrible fear of death.) Some years ago I wrote to Dad that with my walk with Jesus, death was not something to fear. I'd come to that place with maturity and trust in Christ.

On the day Dad died, my oldest sister, Alice, and my brother, Paul, and I were with him. We knew by his breathing it wouldn't be long. I remember standing by his bed listening to his labored breathing. The three of us walked outside. I prayed, "Lord, take him; don't let him suffer."

We went back into the room to talk to him, and we watched him take his last breath. It had been excruciatingly painful for me. I loved this man. He was the first person I have watched die, and never before had I prayed that God would take someone.

~ ~ ~

I think often of Christ and his death. Christ took all the wrong of all mankind, all the sin. I've got all I can do to handle my own life. My own sins. Then I wonder if I am accepting grace. The forgiveness of my sins.

Christ's Apostle Peter amazed me. I can understand his weakness (when he denied Christ), but the legend of his wanting to be crucified upside down? That is bravery beyond what I'd be capable.

I didn't like the nightmare experience. It will fade in the comfort of my home, the lower altitude, and the companionship of sleeping with Gretchen.

~ ~ ~

I am bothered that the mountains don't have the same impact on me as they did when I first encountered them. I remember standing in awe of their majesty. Now I've seen so much majesty that I don't get the same sensation.

The mountains are still magnificent, especially when one is on top. It's true, if one gets a clear view of a spectacular mountain from enough distance, the view is awesome. But it's a view one can get from a car.

To get close enough to the mountain top to feel it and see it from that perspective, you have to be on a horse or on foot. Besides, on horseback, you don't have the noise and fumes and presence of vehicles and people (other than those with whom you have experienced the trek up).

The beauty of God's creation is in the mountains. It is my inability to still feel the awe of newness that concerns me.

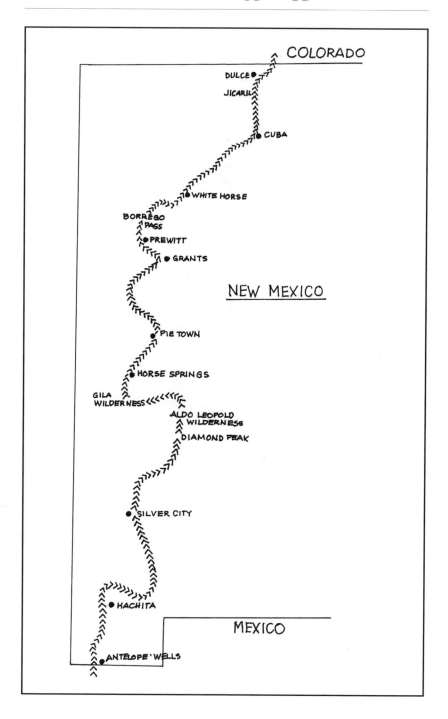

1990

Southern New Mexico

Antelope Wells
Hachita
Gila National Forest
Pinos Altos
Aldo Leopold Wilderness
Mimbres River
Diamond Peak

CHAPTER THIRTY-TWO

Riding the *roads* of New Mexico

Sunday, March 25, 1990

I arrived in New Mexico a week ago so I could spend some time working with Prison Fellowship's Area Director here. Plus, I participated in an in-prison seminar in Grants last night. Jeff Martin, Prison Fellowship Council Chairman and host while I did PF work in New Mexico, had arranged for my horses to stay at Alex Hudson's pasture this past week.

In addition to Goldie and Bull, I brought Hiker and Tico along this year to use as pack horses. Hiker is the son of Lace, who was my pack horse on the early rides. That would make him the "nephew" of Bull. Tico is a horse that belongs to Al Severson.

Glen Roberts, who was with me for a few days in 1988, is joining me again this year. He arrived in Albuquerque last night. I met him at his friends' house and showed him the way to Alex Hudson's before going to the seminar. On the way to Alex's, Glen made a notable comment. He said he got to thinking, coming from his home in Buena Vista, Colorado, that he shouldn't stay away from his wife (who has Multiple Sclerosis) for two full weeks.

I replied that the same emotions came over me as I left Minnesota each year. Though Gretchen doesn't have an illness, I still feel uneasy leaving her for such lengths of time. I touched Glen's shoulder, hoping my comment and touch would allay his concern, though I'm afraid they will not, and he will leave early.

Ray Seaver will also be on the ride this year. Ray is the Executive Director of the Minneapolis Heart Institute. Ray was asking me about my trips once, and so I said why don't you come along. While he does have experience with horses, it will be like having a dude along because he has neither experienced day-long horseback riding, nor used a pack horse to transport gear, food, feed, and camp necessities; cooked and slept outdoors for long periods of time; gained a destination in a linear fashion on horseback; found his way in strange surroundings without signs left by others.

Ray's flight was to arrive at 3:50 this morning; he said I could pick him up at 5:30, which would give me some extra sleep after leaving last night's seminar, but I felt guilty about leaving him alone in the airport for an hour and a half. I decided that if I woke up without the alarm clock an hour before plane time, I'd get up and go get him when he arrived.

This happened. And when I went to the gate to meet him, the passengers were deplaning, but I couldn't see him. When all had disembarked, I went to the baggage claim area to see if he was there, and he was not. I wondered if he had missed his plane, and I was contemplating how I would find out whether that was the case.

Then I saw a guy with a western hat. I had no clue who he was, but approached anyway and asked him if there was anyone else on the plane wearing a big hat. He said, "Yes. There was one other who wore a brown hat."

Then I knew Ray was around somewhere. Standing at the baggage claim perplexed, I was relieved to hear Ray hail me from behind. He had gone to the men's room, and that's why I'd missed him.

Our reunion complete, we went back to Jeff Martin's house for a short sleep, a bite to eat, and then on to the pasture not a mile away to meet Glen by 7 a.m. Glen was waiting at the gate when we arrived at the pasture about 6:40 a.m. First I fed my four horses as did Glen his two mules and pinto horse. His had been in the corral overnight so they would not be forced to get acquainted with Alex's buckskin horses, mules, and donkey jack, as well as my horses, which were running with Alex's. Glen tied his up and I brought mine into the corral for feeding to keep them away from the seven buckskins of Alex.

When it came time to load the two trailers, I started with Hiker. As I walked out the gate, Ray and Glen were standing next to it, so I expected one of them would close it behind me. They didn't. And Goldie, who had taken up with Alex Hudson's buckskins, sneaked out behind me and ran off to the east where they had disappeared over a hill. I certainly didn't expect this of Goldie; with grass so sparse in this desert country, I expected the horses would stick around. But I guess, for Goldie, being with his new pals at this point was more important than food.

Since Ray was not involved in the loading of horses, and strangers seem to be able to catch Goldie better than a person who had worked with him before, I sent Ray off to catch him.

When we got the rest of the horses loaded, there was no Ray in sight with Goldie, so I grabbed a feed bucket and headed off in the direction I last saw them. As I topped a rise, I saw Ray walking back toward the corrals and trailers, and about 100 yards behind followed the donkey jack. I wondered if Ray was chasing the horses ahead of him but there was no dust. From where I now was walking, I could see most of the area the horses could be in, yet I saw no horses. I decided they might be hiding behind some low trees and high bushes over in a draw. After another quarter mile of hiking, that proved to be the case. Goldie came up to my feed bucket with no hesitation. Food is still a strong motivator in horses.

To my surprise there was quite a bit of blood on Goldie, but I could see no cuts or broken skin. When I got back to the trailer, Ray told me that when Goldie had run up to Alex's horses, the donkey met him and they had a fight. Even dragging a lead rope, Goldie was the victor. He had kicked the jack in the face, giving him a nose bleed or a mouth bleed or something of that nature. It was good we got out of there before some equine mayhem occurred. What a beginning experience for Ray.

~ ~ ~

I've ridden with a single dude alone before when Doug Coe and I rode across the "Great Basin Divide" or "Red Desert" in Wyoming. But I feel more at ease if there is another experienced horseman around, so I'm hoping Glen will stay the full two weeks. Ray has owned two horses which he rode occasionally in the LeSueur, Minnesota, area, but he has not had the experience of extended trips.

I like to take dudes with me to give them a chance to have this marvelous experience. They will talk about it the rest of their lives. Many times, when I invite people and they say they are too busy, I say, "Whatever you're gonna do, make sure it is something you'll remember for the rest of your life."

~ ~ ~

I decided not to ride through the Jicarilla Apache Indian Reservation in northern New Mexico this year because of the necessity to ride on roads rather than in the wilderness. The Indians would not give us permission to be on the reservation other than on their roads. I think roads will be too narrow for all of us plus our pack horses, and besides, riding among civilization does not appeal to me.

So we're going south to the border to ride in that part of New Mexico first. Before heading out, we stopped at Smith's Grocery and bought some perishable food: two dozen eggs, sausage, American sliced cheese, onions, carrots, margarine in a squeeze bottle, and two loaves of bread. Also bought some Gatorade for me (paid separately), syrup, and another box of pancake flour (store had no whole wheat Krusteeze). Most of the canned and dried food I brought from home was left over from previous years' trips. Ray and Glen had the coffee responsibility.

We stopped for gas, and I called Gretchen and Ben one last time since we may not hit a phone again.

Then, finally, we were able to get started for Antelope Wells on the New Mexico/Mexico border. When we got to Deming we stopped for gas. I figured it might be our last chance to top off. On the way, Ray proudly announced that his duffle weighed only 29 pounds, which pleased me.

Even though I'm strict about limiting weight, I do bring along "just in case I need it" things. Glen, on the other hand, brings just the essentials. Of course, I have to bring all the camp necessities for cooking.

We got to Antelope Wells at 3:40. Good thing because the customs station closes at 4 p.m. and doesn't open again until 8 a.m. There is only one customs officer–Roger Morrison, an Hispanic who is bilingual. We found out he lives at the customs station with his wife and 13-year-old daughter. When I asked him about riding the Divide, he asked me if I had permission from the ranchers. Upon my negative response, he said I'd have to get it; gates are locked everywhere and ranchers don't want strangers on their property. He then told me about some hikers who recently tried to walk the Divide, and one of the ranchers had them arrested. It seems they had parked on some rancher's property, and even though they'd left a note telling what they were about, the rancher turned them in.

When I asked if we could park our trucks and trailers at the customs station, he responded that he didn't run a parking lot.

As I visited with him for a while, he relented and gave us permission to park there, plus he offered the names of two ranchers I could call on the phone. A broken down phone booth was just outside the building. I first tried William Hurt and got an answering machine; I left a message. I called later, but the person who answered did not speak English. We never got hold of Mr. Hurt, and I gathered by comments of the Morrison's daughter that Hurt wasn't the easiest person to get along with.

I next called Lonnie Moore, foreman of the Gray Ranch operation, and was able to reach him. The Gray Ranch, we found out, is mostly on the west side of the road we want to travel, Hurt's spread is on the east. But Gray does have one tract of land on the east with a 20-foot diameter windmill fan. I asked if we could water our horses there. Lonnie said OK, and complimented us on asking permission. I asked other questions of him, and could tell the Gray ranch would not be any use to us beyond watering there, but said we would ride over and say hello. It helps when I tell people who I am; a Governor and Congressman from a northern state may not impress them much, but coupling that with being a horseman who is capable of riding the Continental Divide seems to do the trick. I also figured out it was Lonnie who had had the hikers arrested.

The phone then went out at the customs station, so it's a good thing I had called Gretchen earlier.

~ ~ ~

Roger Morrison and family loaded up in an old '56 Chevy, which looked great and sounded terrible, and, taking along a Mexican cowboy friend from across the border, headed for church in Hachita. Roger, his daughter told us, was the discussion leader for the Sunday evening service at the Catholic Church. Roger half invited me to go with him, but I had to get ready for tomorrow's ride and care for the horses. Also, the services and discussions would probably be in Spanish.

~ ~ ~

For supper, I took soup starter and added some potato buds. It wasn't too bad. Ray and Glen said it was good. Evidently they weren't eager to be the cooks. We finished with canned fruit cocktail.

I notice that Ray was quite talkative when I picked him up early this morning, and now he is quieter. Either he is talked out or it was easier earlier to talk than to wait for me to talk. Glen also is a quiet person, but he did talk today about his Navy experiences and outfitting, and he shared a fascinating tale about how bull elk get into loco weed, develop an addiction, go blind, and die. Maybe that is why there are so few young bulls compared to young cows. Maybe it's only the teetotalers who grow to be old bulls.

Because we can't get through ranch land, it looks like we'll need to ride roads anyway from Antelope Wells to Hachita (47 miles) and then on to Separ (25 miles) where we will cross Interstate 10. I wonder how it will be to ride the roads. Can we make 20 miles a day with soft horses?

We all are sleeping in the gooseneck of our trailers tonight. I've never done this before, but the ground next to the customs station seems quite hard for driving in tent stakes. And I know, or at least I've heard, that poisonous things crawl around at night down here. Otherwise I would have chosen to sleep on the ground.

Monday, March 26, 1990

We got up at 5; it stays dark until 5:45. A truck came last evening to go south of the border and had to wait until the customs station opened this morning to be able to cross. Roger was a half hour late opening.

We worked hard to get everything ready for a 9 a.m. departure.

I thought I was now friendly with Roger since he was agreeable to our leaving our rigs at the customs station for a week. But when I asked him to come and have his picture taken with us, he refused. In the past, when someone has said no to such a request, I figured they were in trouble with the law, but I didn't think that could be the case with a U.S. Customs officer. Maybe Roger didn't want to be implicated if *we* got into trouble with the law.

The Mexican cowboy (who went to church with the Morrisons last night) took our picture. Last night he was all dressed up, and this morning he was in his working clothes. He must have brought them along, since he had yet to cross the border.

The last thing Roger told us before we took off was that he didn't think we could get to Silver City in a week.

The horses were full of energy. Glen's mule, Strawberry, which he rode, wanted to run. He held on for dear life and used a long-shanked bit to keep her in a walk. Bull was full of energy, too, and kept a fast pace for a half day with Hiker doing a lot of trotting to keep up, which also caused Tico to run.

Later I led Tico, who has a long stride, and tied Hiker behind; then Hiker trotted less and Tico seldom had to trot. Goldie, who Ray rode, did pretty well at keeping up, but it's hard on a rider when his mount has to trot to keep up.

When we got to the ranch with the big windmill, we rode in and watched some branding, dehorning, and the giving of shots by three cowboys, after first meeting Lonnie Moore.

I was really impressed by the coordination of the little cowboy who handled the chute gate or stanchion. He was one of the real keys to a smooth operation. As the calf bolts through, he slams the stanchion tight on its neck.

The calves looked pretty good for such dry country. Evidently that dry grass has good food value. They brand 700 to 800 head per day and did that herd in three days.

Ray took a lot of pictures, which I look forward to seeing. As we rode out, I looked back and saw a picture opportunity I'm sorry I missed–three roping horses were standing quietly in a large corral, hobbled and waiting. It would have been a masterpiece, but we had already said goodbye.

When we got back to the pack horses, I found Tico had pawed into a barbed wire and had it wedged between his hoof and shoe. Any violent pull and he would have ripped off his shoe. I got a wire cutter from a ranch hand who was fixing a trailer nearby and cut the wire loose. From now on I'm going to have my wire cutter handy and not packed away.

I'm glad I bought the small used horseshoe hammer from a farrier in Albuquerque last week. Even though he didn't need it, he charged me $5 for it, which was $2 too much. Oh well. I'm glad I have it. It fits perfectly in my saddle bag. With the hammer and nail cutter, which was on the other side from the hammer, I was able to tighten up Tico's shoe again.

~ ~ ~

We rode 24-3/4 miles today. Tough on Ray. Only the day before yesterday he was in Minnesota, and now he has ridden a good eight hours. He is pretty sore. He'll get over it, but I bet he's wondering why he came. I hope he'll get used to it. Others have, but we won't have much rest until we get to Silver City. We can't take layover days by the side of the road like we could up in the mountains.

We're camping just past an old abandoned ranch place with a cable across the driveway. This was the site we had hoped to reach but didn't realize it was quite this far. It is half way to Hachita, so we should make that tomorrow.

As we tied up, Glen jumped over the cable and went to look for a water tank. If he could find one, we figured we would take down the cable to get the horses in to it.

Just then a pickup truck came up. I was down the road looking at another gate on the east side and Ray was watching the horses tied to a wire fence. When the driver of the pickup got out, Ray quickly saw he had a big revolver strapped to his side; he had a friend with him and his little boy was in the back of the truck. He said he was the caretaker of the property and made a point of the fact that he hadn't invited us to camp at this site.

As soon as I got back to Ray and this fellow, I was informed that the ranch on the east side of the road belonged to William Hurt. I had seen the broken windmill, the downed electric wires, and a water tank, but I hoped there was water there, anyway, since I also saw cattle around. Needless to say, the gate I'd found was locked.

He said Hurt was a problem and we'd better not go onto his place or we would have trouble. We decided to go down there and get water, anyway.

Well, the fence was tight and there was no hill to take it down. (If I take the staples out of fence posts on a hill, the wires will lay flat on the ground on the top of the hill, making it possible to go across). We tied up my four horses on the locked gate so they would not put a foot over the wire fence. The gate had a metal frame and woven wire. Glen put his three animals out on long tether lines. It is great that roads have such a wide right-of-way on which to ride and graze.

We then took a pannier and a bucket with us to the windmill to get water. Glen figured out that the wires for running the pump motor were underground, and he guessed the pump was on a timer. With a ball-point pen, he made contact with electricity, and the pump ran. We made three trips using plastic panniers to bring enough water for thirsty horses, for our supper and dish washing, and for filling our canteens. Ray and I have five canteens and Glen has a plastic carrier. The tank was about 1/8 of a mile away; our fingers and knuckles hurt after that.

During one trip back to the horses, I saw Hiker chewing on his lead rope, so when I got there, I slapped his nose. I know better than to do that. He jerked back, pulled the gate off the hinges, and bent it. If it hadn't been for the chain which locked the gate, the whole thing would have come down, and the horses—all tied to it—would have run off and gotten hurt.

I know that it never works to slap a horse in the face, and I guess, once in a while, I need to learn the lesson again. In hopes of preventing Hiker from chewing, I put Tabasco sauce on the rope all the way from the snap at his halter to the knot where it was tied to the gate, and I put the rest of the rope over the gate, thinking he would not reach that.

Ray and I are sleeping in my two-man tent, which I bought from Menards for $24 on sale. The poles are weak and it has no fly, but it's good when rain is not expected and when one wants to keep snakes and scorpions out. I'm going to sleep on horse blankets and pads, and Ray is on a self-inflatable mattress.

Glen has his own tent. It's small like mine, a Western Field from Montgomery Wards. His also has no fly, but it has much better poles.

Tomorrow, I'll give Ray the saddle I'm riding. Maybe that will help him some.

CHAPTER THIRTY-THREE

The landord(s) of Hachita

Tuesday, March 27, 1990

We got up at 4:30 this morning.

Not a single car or truck passed by in either direction on the road from the time we camped last night until we left this morning.

Overnight, Hiker had chewed practically all the way through the rope on the other side of the gate and beyond the knot. Only one thin cotton strand still held. A cat could have broken it. I used baling twine to repair it and kicked myself for not putting Tabasco sauce all the way to the end; besides it was Al Severson's lead rope that got ruined.

We started breakfast in the dark, and Glen didn't eat any. Ray and I had only one egg each and pancakes. I brought along leftover pancakes and found out Ray liked them, too. After hauling water again in a pannier, one person on each end, we packed up and left camp at 8:15.

We rode the 23-plus remaining miles into Hachita today. We were able to water twice, the first time about 10 miles out of camp. Where we stopped was an interesting place. The water in the tank was cool, but the water coming out of the pipe from the pump was warm. Just the opposite of the usual where water comes out of the ground at about 57 degrees and warms up in a tank from the air and sun.

We didn't stay long since there was a cold wind. It warmed up considerably today after the sun came up, and then about 10 a.m. it clouded over and a cool wind made jackets necessary. It was the same yesterday.

When it rains, the water doesn't hit the ground. Evidently the dry air makes it evaporate before it can get there.

Along the way today, a rancher named Max Jones stopped in his pickup truck. He had a non-English speaking friend with him. This Mexican looked soft like a merchant: pretty good size, big hat, gray moustache, and ornate belt buckle; obviously a man of means.

Max, it turned out, was a friend of Roger Morrison, the customs officer, and had heard about us from him. Max said Roger had said he was sorry he had not invited us in to sleep in one of his trailers. He had an empty one. As Max talked about the speed of our traveling, he figured we could get to his new ranch, the Thorne Ranch north of the Interstate, by 1 p.m. on Thursday, the 29th. He invited us to stay for lunch when we get there and said he would tell the "boys" to have beans ready for us. Max will not be at the ranch when we get there, he said. He will be at an auction in Deming. Max surely was friendly; some people are just more hospitable than others.

Just before Hachita, we watered at a windmill site and then rode into town at 3:30 p.m. We passed the Catholic Church that Roger and family had come to on Sunday night, then went past the home of a lion hunter who had many hound dogs making noise over us from the back yard, then past a home that had a painted sign on the front porch that read in both English and Spanish: "Anyone who comes into this house at night will be found here, dead, in the morning." Not too friendly.

As we rode past a one-pump gas station on the corner where Highway 9 and Highway 81 intersect, we looked for a campsite. It was pretty bleak; nothing was found. I went inside the gas station to inquire. Besides the counter and cash register, there was a candy machine. Sitting at a small round table was an older woman with Roger Morrison's wife! She was waiting for her daughter to get off the school bus from Lordsburg. Twice a day she drives 47 miles–one way from Antelope Wells–so her daughter can get on a bus for another 46-mile ride for school. She drives 188 miles a day, and her daughter goes 186 miles to and from school. Wow.

The older lady, I found out, is the wife of the Deputy Sheriff who arrested the hikers Roger told me about. She said he had released them immediately. She told me, upon my inquiry, about a place we could camp, and suggested we talk to her son who was working on a pickup in a side bay bout a potential campsite. He had seen us ride up and seemed to ignore us. Then, when I walked by him as I was going into the station, I said hello; his response was very brief and he turned away. I wondered why he didn't ask questions, like "where did you guys come from?" It can't be too often that three men ride up with four pack horses. I agreed to go back and talk to him, anyway.

This time, for some reason, his behavior was just the opposite. He was very friendly and offered the building next door for cooking and sleeping. I tried not to react too negatively as I glanced over at a concrete block building with a fallen roof and broken-out windows. He offered the use of his broom to clean it out. As I looked at it again, I figured we could pile up the old rafters on the floor, put the roof board on one end, and clear enough space of glass, bolts, and old spark plugs to be able to get by. On the good side, we'd be out of the incessant wind.

We put our horses in the back lot, but the only place to tie up was at two telephone poles, too far apart to run a picket line. There also was an old wreck of a combine with junk all around it. Across the street there was some ungrazed, dried up grass where the horses were presently eating. I asked if that land was his also, and he said it belonged to Souzzi. So I asked him where I could find Souzzi in order to ask permission for our horses to graze there. He said his mother could give me the number, and he added that Mr. Souzzi owns much of Hachita.

Usually the biggest landlord in town is a person of some power, and I figured he would like to be asked even though the man in the garage had already given us permission. I called, and when Mr. Souzzi answered, I started to explain our predicament. He interrupted before I could finish asking permission for our horses to graze on his property. He said he would be right down "and show it to me." That seemed peculiar since he could have just said "yes" or "no," and since it was only a vacant lot with junk where our horses were grazing. I couldn't understand why he wanted to show "it" to me.

When he arrived, he turned out to be a little old man in a broken down station wagon. His first comment was, "You really *do* have horses, don't you?" He asked me to get into his station wagon so he could take me and show me where we were going to stay. As we reached the apartment building by the church, he announced that we could have rooms upstairs as well as in the basement.

Now I understood.

I explained I was actually looking for a place for our horses, and that we wanted to camp by them. If only he had listened during our phone call.

I asked again about pasture for the horses and a place to put up our tents. He said he owned the trailer park south of town and there was pasture land next to it. We could use that. He said there was a gate from the trailer park into a pasture of 133 acres. We drove to look at it; the pasture seemed to be only brush and sand, but he assured me there was some grass. There was a fence around the pasture, but Souzzi said he couldn't vouch for it. He would charge us only $15 for the night.

On the way back, he told me he used to be a union official in New York and had hunted all over the world. He retired in Hachita and started buying up property, but the town kept dying.

When I told Ray and Glen where we would be staying and the cost, the fellow from the garage called Souzzi a crook. He evidently felt I got took; he said the vacant lot next to the trailer park belonged to Mays, not Souzzi. Oh well.

From the station looking south past a couple of vacant lots I could see a two pickup trucks with horse trailers parked in front of a place. I could see some cowboy hats bobbing up and down, so I knew we were being watched.

We rode that direction to our campsite, and as we passed by, I saw that these cowboys had a number of horses of many colors in a very small enclosure. The horses were all in great shape and of excellent conformation and good withers. Horses like that can only be roping horses; I guessed this was a place where jackpot ropers keep their horses.

We had not more than reached our campsite and were taking off the packs and saddles when one of the hats drove up in a pickup truck. Under the hat was a roper named Clint Jacobson. He said if we needed anything to let him know and that we could water at his place if needed. We had water at a trailer hook-up, so we didn't need to take him up on his offer.

I was about to ride the fence to see if it was OK, when Clint said he had ridden it only the week before, and found it to be OK. I took his word for it.

As we were cooking dinner, another pickup came up; a woman got out and went up to Glen. I could see by her posture that she wasn't happy, so I ambled over to find out what was going on. It was

Mrs. Mays who ran a show horse operation across the pasture. The gate had been left open and the fence was down. Our horses and mules had come into her place and caused a commotion. She said she closed the gate after chasing our horses back, but the fence was still down.

We said we would immediately take care of it; it wasn't hard to prop up. Some of her horses were blanketed and were in pipe corrals. Goldie likes to snort new horses even more than Bull this year.

After dinner (canned turkey, two onions, four carrots, some potato buds for thickening, and salt, pepper, and Tabasco sauce for seasoning), I went to walk the fence to make certain it was not down elsewhere.

From our camp, the fence went east, then north, and then back east again. At that last corner the fence was cut and two post lengths were pulled aside. The horses could have come out there and easily run into town. It was now dark, and I had to use a flashlight to find my way. Soon I saw some activity among the brush to the east of me.

I walked over and found two men unloading a big truck. When I asked them what they were doing, the one on the truck asked who I was. I explained and said I rented the pasture from Mr. Souzzi. He replied that Souzzi didn't own the property. I asked who did. But the look on his face caused me to also quickly ask if he was the owner. He answered, "Yes, I am."

Now I was embarrassed and I apologized. He said it was OK for us to be here and said we could stay. He explained that he had purchased the land from Souzzi a week or so ago and was building pens to raise pheasants for a hunting preserve he was developing. He said I could close up the fence for the night and open it in the morning.

Then I asked if anyone else would be coming, and he said no. No one would come after him. But not five minutes later two sets of headlights pulled in. One car carried the fellow from the gas station plus a friend who had a load of railroad ties, and in the other was the Deputy Sheriff. Soon they all left.

Now it was so dark I figured the horses would quit roaming, and if there were more holes in the fence we could get the horses before they found them.

I hope they will be here in the morning. The "latest owner" said all the rest of the fence was OK.

Wednesday, March 28, 1990

We got up at 4:45; breakfast at 5:30–eggs and pancakes again. Each lunch has been sausage and cheese sandwiches, a granola bar, and dried fruit and raisins. We heard the horses making noise over by the Mays place again, so I called for them and they all came, Goldie in the lead. I guess they like our feed better than dry grass.

We rode out the streets of Hachita at 8 a.m., then went north alongside Highway 145 heading for the Interstate.

North of Hachita, two horses in a pasture followed us, a chestnut and a buckskin. To my amazement they walked and ran beside us for three miles, and the pasture went on for another half mile. How would you like to go get your horses some three and half miles away at the far end of the pasture? Everything is big out here. Lots of cactus–like Cholla and Yucca and Chaparral.

We found our first water–a place with a windmill-just before the Interstate after being on the road for 17 miles. As we opened a gate to go in, a pickup truck pulled up, and a Mexican ranch hand got out.

We can ride all day and never see a vehicle, and just as we open a gate to trespass, a vehicle pulls up.

Glen used what little Spanish he learned with Portuguese some years ago in Brazil to ask permission to water our horses. The ranch hand said OK.

Usually water storage tanks are steel and 20 or more feet across. From this a pipe usually runs to a trough where the stock drink. At this broken down, abandoned place, on the other hand, the windmill ran steady; the leathers were poor so little water came out. A hole was cut in the side of the tank; there was no trough to drink from. The animals had to stick their heads through the hole to drink. Ray got there first, but Goldie bumped his bit when he tried to poke his head through the hole, so he would not drink. We found a leak on the far side of the tank; the horses drank from a dirty puddle on the ground.

~ ~ ~

At the Interstate, we turned west and rode a gravel road for six miles. Strawberry (Glen's riding mule) must have known camp was coming, so she picked up her pace; we arrived at camp–a large holding and loading corral–at 5 p.m.

There is grazing outside the corral, and we'll be able to enclose the stock tonight. We hung a tarp on the corral fence to cut off the wind as we cooked, and we tied one end of our tents to the corral rail rather than to a stake.

We mixed canned chicken, pea and barley soup (which had soaked for a day), and potato buds in the dutch oven. Yogurt in small cans was our dessert. I got the impression that Glen didn't like the yogurt.

After supper, Ray went up to the truck stop in nearby Separ. There he discovered shower facilities, and he took full advantage. He surely seemed happy upon his return, both from being cleaned up and from his conversation with the Hispanic gentleman who ran the place. It was a good experience for him. His high spirits almost made me wish I had gone to the truck stop, too, but not quite.

Thursday, March 29, 1990

We got up at 5 a.m., put the horses out to graze, and fixed breakfast. Ray has learned the clean-up routine and how to store food. Glen is an envy to watch as he moves smoothly and efficiently.

We rode out, going under the Interstate and railroad tracks, my mind was already thinking ahead toward lunch with the "boys" at the Thorne ranch. Then I realized Ray had fixed lunch for today! We had all forgotten. We are in such a routine.

From Separ we went west of Soldier's Farewell (named because soldiers would follow the stage to that point to protect passengers from Indians) and on up to the Thorne Ranch. We arrived a little after 11 a.m. rather than 1 p.m. Two Mexican hands were doctoring a horse that had fallen into a cattle guard. We tied up our horses and Glen, with his limited Spanish, tried to communicate with them. Then we went to the house, but no one was there, and the cooks had no plans for our lunch!

Since they had some cattle that had been just bought at auction, we stayed and helped them drive the young stock into another corral and then into the chute for branding. They built a small wood fire and heated the branding irons, and Ray and I photographed them in their work. Since they didn't invite us for lunch but drove off when they were done, we rode off and ate lunch about a mile away. It turned out to be a good thing Ray had prepared lunch after all.

Besides watching that little bit of ranch work and enjoying the beauty of their hacienda with the white adobe-like dwelling, we learned that windmills are called pumpalitas.

After lunch we rode another nine miles before a storm came up. We rode down into a swale, tied up to a fence, and decided it would be a good place to set up camp. As it started to sleet, we figured this precipitation might not evaporate before it hit the ground. The wind was strong so we wrapped a tarp around two Yuccas and set up the stove on the leeward side. The horses are really eating now and had watered at a windmill we had passed just a mile or two before reaching camp.

We are at higher elevation, but the storm passed over and around, so the moisture never hit us. The wind continued strong for quite a while.

~ ~ ~

Supper was canned hamburger with hamburger helper and peaches for dessert. We are in a lovely spot, but we are tired and are going to bed early. It's only 7:30 p.m.

CHAPTER THIRTY-FOUR

Stories about personal encounters with Cochise

Friday, March 30, 1990

Up at 5 a.m. We all ate eggs for breakfast. Ray and I also had pancakes, and Ray and Glen had coffee while I had my Tang. I don't drink coffee. People wonder what kind of Norwegian I am.

We hit the trail at 7:30 with eight miles to go to get to White Signal where I want to stop so we can go back to get our rigs. Then we'll trailer around Silver City, which is 17 miles from White Signal.

Ray is riding Tico now since he is slimmer and walks fast, therefore, is not causing as much pain for Ray as the wider, slower, Goldie. This worked well for Ray, but I had to put him back on the saddle he started with since it hurt my back too much to not have my saddle. Really, this other saddle was pressing my prostate, and as I rounded my back to compensate, my back began to hurt. I remember now Ben complained of the same thing in 1983 when he rode that saddle, and I thought he was faking his pain so he could leave the ride early to be with his beloved Virginia. I thought he had heartache, but I guess it really was a backache. I've got to see about getting a sponge rubber seat sewn into that saddle.

As Ray and I rode side by side, I told him I had made some of my bridles, and I even sewed the leather straps which hold my spurs on. I swung my boot out from the stirrup and raised it high to proudly show him, oblivious to the fact my spurs weren't even on! With a slightly puzzled look, Ray asked, "Did you pick up your spurs this morning?" It wasn't until his comment that I realized I'd forgotten them in camp. The laugh was on me. Ray was very nice to me about my mistake. He didn't even chuckle. I remember my dad saying to me when I was a child, "If you didn't have your head attached to your shoulders, you would forget that, too!"

I asked Ray and Glen to ride on as I went back the mile or so to pick up the spurs. When I got there, I was struck with how different an area looks when you come at it from the opposite direction and you are alone rather than with others. The swale looked entirely different—as though I was at the wrong campsite. But I wasn't.

After I picked up my spurs, feeling both chagrined and chuckling at what had happened to me, I hastened to go back and catch up with Ray and Glen. I was further intrigued by how far Glen and Ray got, even at a walk.

Shortly thereafter we spotted a rider and I rode over to him. He was a young boy, riding on a day off from school, gathering heifers with his dad and a hired hand. He asked if I had seen the hand, but we hadn't. The boy's name was Yancey MacCauley. In conversation with him, I found out he was a national 4H sharpshooter. His grandfather owned the ranch and inherited the 23 sections from the great grandfather who had accumulated such big holdings in the 1800's that he was able to give a ranch to each of his 10 children.

Yancey said we could keep our stock at a corral 1-1/2 miles from White Signal by some big cottonwood trees while we went back to Antelope Wells to get our rigs. Later we spotted his dad and he agreed to this arrangement as well.

Ray stayed with the horses and equipment as Glen and I rode into White Signal to find a phone for calling Glen's daughter, Darcy, over in Arizona. We had previously arranged for her to pick us up and take us back to Antelope Wells. The first place we came to was the home of Bob Abercrombie and his wife, Mary. Bob was initially cautious as we requested permission to use his phone, but he brought one out for us.

After I explained who we were, Bob opened up a little and I found out that he was retired from the Soil Conservation Service in the U.S. Department of Agriculture. I told him I had once been a District Supervisor of the Rice County Soil Conservation District in Minnesota, and that's when he invited us in. The Lord brings people together! There are those who might say this was a coincidence, but I don't believe in coincidences, nor do I believe in a secular world vs. God's world—God created everything, it belongs to Him, and He is in charge of all. The Spirit of God is at work in people, and most times He is at work without our knowledge and/or acknowledgment.

Bob then showed us his stock, especially three 4H steers he raised for his grandchildren. He showed us his office with his awards, and his wife invited us in for lunch. We finally got our Mexican beans. Also, meat loaf, fried potatoes, green beans, and a tossed salad.

The most fascinating part was visiting with Mrs. Abercrombie's 89-year-old mother who told how her grandfather had been massacred by the Apaches just south of White Signal when Cochise was on the war path. I had just read about Cochise and that same event this past January.

She said her grandfather and some hired hands had gone to Silver City for a load of feed and had broken a wheel on the way home. So they rode to a ranch and got tools to fix it, and on the way back the Apache were lying in wait for them and killed them. I believe Cochise was an honorable man, but I'd read that a rancher and a wrong-thinking army officer had previously insulted him, so that's why he went on the war path.

Mrs. Abercrombie's mother also told us about she, herself, having gone to Columbus, New Mexico, to teach school when she came of age. Her uncle had given her a six-shooter to take along for protection. There was a cavalry regiment stationed in Columbus, and she said one of the men from this regiment tried to break into her room. She emptied the gun at the noise, making a lot of holes and evidently wounding him, which made it possible to easily identify and later arrest him.

~ ~ ~

After this pleasant interlude of lunch and listening to stories at the Abercrombie home, Glen and I rode back to Ray and the corrals. Both Strawberry and Bull have fire, and they love the rapid pace when pack animals aren't being led.

We gave our uneaten sandwiches to Ray, and then waited for Darcy to arrive. Once again, Ray stayed back as Glen and I went this time to Antelope Wells. I envied Ray's being able to be alone and able to watch and study animals. But I felt the responsibility to drive my rig back.

The trip to Antelope Wells was uneventful. Darcy's little girls came along. At Lordsburg we gassed up and ate. I bought a hamburger, fish sandwich, fries, and drink to bring back for Ray. Glen and I did not get back from Antelope Wells until 10 p.m. Ray really was hungry for the food I brought him, as we prepared to sleep in the trailer gooseneck again.

Saturday, March 31, 1990

We got up at 5 and left the corrals at 7. Ray told us McCauley had come up yesterday when Glen and I were gone and told him, if the horses ate too much of the protein blocks, they would die. Ray got them out of the big corral and into a smaller one, away from the protein blocks. Good for him. He had done all right with strange horses. We left the corrals and drove into Silver City where we gassed up again, ate breakfast in a restaurant, and called our wives.

After re-supplying groceries, we drove to Pinos Altos about five miles away. There we dropped my rig at the post office, and Ray and I began, about noon, by riding up the road Gretchen and I had hiked when in the area on vacation this past January.

Rather than riding with us, Glen drove his rig around to where the Divide crosses Highway 35. He plans to meet us there tomorrow. He is concerned about getting back to his wife as quickly as possible, and he figured his driving to this next spot would save us some time.

After Ray and I rounded Twin Sisters and got to Black Peak, we couldn't find the trail. The only one that was apparent turned left and headed toward Signal Peak. So we retraced our steps and camped at a weak spring where there wasn't much grass; a place called The Homestead, only about 3-1/2 miles from Pinos Altos. Poor signage by the Forest Service is a big problem for us.

Ray came close to getting hurt at one point today when Tico had stepped into his reins which had a knot in the end, and Ray was standing by him, bending over trying to correct it. Hiker came pushing in, and at close quarters and with panniers could have shoved Tico over. In this case, it would have been right on top of Ray. When I saw the accident about to happen, I called to Ray, and he quickly scampered out to safety. God was caring for him.

Ray and I had had a good talk tonight in which he made me realize I wasn't letting him do enough. Now he will do all the cooking. He has a knack for it. He is more careful both about taste and appearance than I am. Also, I found he could hear Glen easier than he could hear me. That's why he seems to enjoy talking to Glen more than to me.

Sunday, April 1, 1990

We got up before 5 and for breakfast ate leftover cold casserole from last night. Not the best—a bit salty—but nourishment, nonetheless. Ray will begin showing off his culinary skills at noon today.

We left camp at 6:30. With me saddling and Ray now packing the panniers, everything is speeded up.

We retraced our steps up to Black Peak. Again we couldn't find the trail or the Continental Divide, so we took the trail to Signal Peak where we ran across Sam Wainer and Steve Kara, hikers we had met in Pinos Altos yesterday. They had lost their way, as well, and were short on water; so were we.

We kept on toward Signal Peak and after traveling about three miles saw a trail parallel to ours and down the slope a bit. It appeared to be going back toward Black Peak. We went down to it and saw a sign saying "three-fourths mile to Black Peak." There was a trail, and both the hikers and we missed it. Three-fourths of a mile would sure have been better than three miles.

We came upon a cabin just before Highway 35 that I thought was a ranger cabin (according to my map), and continued on. But we didn't come to Highway 35 as I expected. Apparently, I read the map wrong; what we saw was not a ranger cabin. But instead of going back to the cabin where we would have found the trail to the Continental Divide again, we plowed on, following a jeep trail which got us lost at times. We also came upon a dry creek bed and finally made our way out to Highway 35. At 7 p.m., Ray went into a cafe and talked a fellow there into giving him a ride to Glen's rig. We had ridden 12-1/2 hours. I continued along the highway leading three horses.

'Frank got smacked solidly in the stomach...his head jerked back...' July 22, 1985. (Chapter 10)

When we all three got together again, I found out Glen had been out looking for us, even having gone back to our rig in Pinos Altos. It was good to see him.

For supper we ate Glen's recipe of Spam, tomatoes, green beans, and rice made to taste Mexican with Tabasco sauce.

Monday, April 2, 1990

We got up leisurely today and left camp at 9:30. Glen is going to ride with us one day and camp with us tonight. Tomorrow he will ride back to his rig and take it around to Beaverhead to meet us there on Wednesday.

We rode seven miles on the Continental Divide in the Aldo Leopold Wilderness, and after lunch and letting our horses drink at a pond, we turned down toward the Mimbres River. It was beautiful. A nice flowing stream and Ponderosa Pine so tall and stately. A feeling came upon me as though I felt like I was in a sanctuary.

At the north fork of the Mimbres we turned north on a faint trail and soon left water behind. Finally, the trail petered out. To find the next trail, we were forced to climb some places in treacherous conditions. I was concerned about Ray, but he seemed, from outward appearances, to be doing well and not overly concerned with the difficult travel. I really love this sort of thing, since it makes the trip more memorable and tests our mettle.

As we came to branches in the dry stream on our left and sharp canyon walls on our right, we chose and chose again. At one point we came upon an area that was more flat and with grass. We let the animals graze and rest for a while. Then pushed on, mostly east but some south, and it began to sleet and then turned to snow! When we could climb no more and were at the top of whatever we were on, we saw to the east that the mountain dropped off sharply, and to the north it was too steep for our navigation.

Then it began snowing hard, and I suggested we go back to the only spot of grass we had seen—and the only flat spot—to make camp. There was a big evergreen tree under which we could cook without getting our feet wet. Ray suggested we follow our tracks back, but the snow soon obliterated every sign. Now what to do. At that point, and to our surprise, Glen's little white pack mule who had always followed, stepped out ahead, and we followed him. We did this for better than a mile around rocks and deadfalls, through brush and rough terrain and came to a stop right at the spot we wanted! It was as if an angel had led the mule who led us. Ray and I suggested to Glen that he change the mule's name to Angel.

We dug a pit and built a fire in it. We were safe and could stay dry. We talked of hypothermia, and Glen gave us a lesson by telling a story of his rescuing some girls who had gotten lost in the mountains and had experienced hypothermia.

God is caring for us.

Tuesday, April 3, 1990

It was still snowing when I got up this morning. I accidentally woke Ray and Glen when I was snapping off branches for a fire. The small twigs on the lower trunk of pine trees always seem to be dry and good for fires. Glen again ate nothing at breakfast today.

He and I agreed that we should head mostly north this morning, looking for another high point to get to Reeds Peak. I figured we had gone too far southwest yesterday afternoon. In not much over a half mile we came to a fence and cut through it because, immediately on the other side, was a trail. Glen followed it southwest thinking we were even with or on Reeds Peak and that the trail went on the west side of the peak. I didn't think so, but followed him, anyway. After about a mile, we parted company. I figured Glen could travel southwest to get back to his rig where the Divide crosses Highway 35, and Ray and I would travel north and east to find the trail by Reeds Peak.

We found no trail going north on the west side of the mountain. There was a trail going north on the east side, though, so Ray and I followed it–including many switchbacks and snow. After a while, I realized we were going east, not north. So we began to climb again, and when we broke out to where I could see what I thought was Reeds Peak, I saw it was straight west of us.

It's tough to figure out where you are going and where you are when you don't know where you start from. Last night filled me full of doubt about where I was. If I did this more than once a year, I'd get better at it. I didn't feel so bad, though, since Glen didn't know where we were, either. But that consolation didn't help me find my way.

At this point I had to get back to where I was sure of my location. Ray and I finally rode all the way out to Highway 35 hoping to find Glen still there but he wasn't.

I began unpacking and unsaddling horses after we had watered them at a pond, and Ray hitched a ride to the cafe where he'd gotten a ride before. The first vehicle picked him up–a girl in a pickup. She made him get in the back. Ray said that when he got to the cafe, the natives there laughed at our lostness. He finally secured a ride for me to Pinos Altos from a Bob Hickman and his high school-aged son, Ron.

They needed to pick up some school work for Bob's daughter near Silver City, anyway. He wanted only gas money. I gave him $40 but he only wanted $30.

To my dismay, Bob drank beer all the way and needed to re-supply in Silver City. Ron only chewed snuff, so he did the driving.

A surprise was that Bob once was a rodeo rider and worked for my friend Jack Brainerd from Rochester, Minnesota. We shared acquaintances as we rode. On the way, he showed me the open pit mine where he worked. The second largest in the nation. He expected the miners there will go on strike, and, as a mechanic, he will go

out in sympathy, likely losing his job. He has 20-plus years in the mine and two children who should go to college.

After getting my rig in Pinos Altos, I drove back to our campsite.

Ray and I are sleeping in the tent tonight. Tico bent a pole while we weren't paying attention, but I got it fixed. It's now a couple inches short.

Wednesday, April 4, 1990

The temperature dropped overnight. When we took the tent down this morning there was frost on it. The aluminum canteen was frozen solid.

What a delight to hear turkey gobblers in the distance this morning. There seem to be a lot of turkeys in this area; it must be their breeding season.

Hiker chewed through Al Severson's other cotton rope last night, and he pawed over the bottom wire of the fence, cutting himself badly. I know from past experience a horse doesn't bleed to death from a cut that far from his heart, but this injury was unsettling, just the same.

It was about a 160-mile drive to the Beaverhead Ranger Station where Glen was waiting for us. We needed to go through Truth or Consequences, so I took the opportunity to find a vet there to help Hiker.

We did find Dr. Bill Cardwell who fixed Hiker up and said we could ride him.

As we headed out north and west, we went through a little village, I think called Cuchilo. We watered the horses there at an interesting old-time store that looked like it might have the same goods that it did at the turn of the century.

We reached Glen at 1:30. He was just going to settle down for a nap in his pickup. The horses received another watering and we turned them in with Glen's animals. The rest of the afternoon we visited among ourselves and also with a road grader crew and a ranger who had horses by the name of Phillip and Tagg.

Glen left at 4:30 for Colorado, and Ray and I are camping for the night in our tent.

Tomorrow we ride south and east to go over Diamond Peak in the Aldo Leopold Wilderness and pick up where we left off yesterday.

CHAPTER THIRTY-FIVE

The mysterious 'Lady in Blue'

Thursday, April 5, 1990

Ray and I ate eggs and pancakes for breakfast and then packed up for a two-day trip. We are taking only the essentials so the pack horses are light. We drove south eight miles to Wall Lake where we also watered our horses since a ranger told us he didn't know how far we would have to go on Diamond Creek Trail before we would find water. Our plan is to go 20 miles up that trail to Diamond Peak and then back by way of South Diamond Peak Trail.

Before we took off, a pickup drove up and stopped. Inside were a lion hunter named Collins and his uncommunicative son. There were six hounds in back of the truck. He said it looked like rain, so he was going home and would hunt another day. He said he thought for sure it was raining on Diamond Peak, where we were headed. He also told me it was next to impossible to find South Diamond Creek Trail from the peak.

Undaunted, we began our ride–18 miles today. All up hill but gradual. We climbed about 2,200 or 2,300 feet. There was no water the first 6-1/2 miles.

We came upon a most interesting site which I photographed: a metal-clad dwelling built against a cliff, and with corrals at the opening of some caves.

The first corral was like a workshop. There was a hitching rail for three or four horses under the overhang of the cliff. To the side and in the front of that was a work bench with many horseshoes, some rusted and others quite new. There were some old hay bales of alfalfa.

An old refrigerator was in the dwelling, but there was no evidence there had ever been electricity. In the yard was a tank for storing drinking water; and on the north side of the house were a screened food cooler, stock tanks and an old pump.

The main cave was about 25 feet deep and 60 feet across the opening. Its roof showed black from continuous fires; it was even thick with pine tar or creosote in some spots. I'm guessing it had to have been a cave belonging to Indian families long ago.

~ ~ ~

We rode to the James Brothers Spring where an old chimney from a fireplace stood. From there to the top, the trail became at times indistinguishable. The grade increased and the canyon narrowed.

We came to a spot where I saw some grass above me. I asked Ray to hold the pack horses as I rode off to explore this area, thinking it might be a good campsite. I explored for 15 minutes and rode quickly back in five.

When I got back, Ray told me he had been worried when I was gone so long. My trouble is that I like to see what is over the next knoll or around the next bend. I must explain myself more, especially to new people who don't have the experience of years of riding in the mountains. I can understand how it might be spooky to be alone, especially when things begin to look a little foreboding–like a person could be permanently lost. I am now so at home in the mountains that I don't think of that possibility. If I do get lost, I keep track of landmarks and ways to find my way back.

I was reminded of Gretchen's reaction when she was in the mountains back in the '60s and was out of sight of any human sign.

My city-person Gretchen is very comfortable around people. Since I grew up on the farm, I am very comfortable not only without people, but also without any sign of them. I am attracted to total wilderness. Back in 1968, when our whole family came to the mountains, the kids and I were having a great time riding one day while she stayed back in the cabin.

When we got back from the ride, I discovered Gretchen had walked for some exercise from the cabin, across a creek and up into the mountains. Unfortunately, she had gotten out of sight of the cabin and that's when she panicked. She said she had frantically started to wonder, "What if I can't find my way back? What if I get totally lost?" With great anxiety, she immediately forgot about her beautiful surroundings, and with trembling found her way back to the cabin.

I can understand panic. I felt it when I was spelunking. Her panic came when she felt separated from civilization.

I need to be understanding that these feelings show themselves in others, as well.

~ ~ ~

We then went to the grassy site above us, found a little (and the only) flat place to set up our kitchen, and put up a tarp over our sleep area, including placing a log at the end so we would not slide down hill during the night, since it was not flat.

The dinner Ray fixed was a good recipe: one can of Spam, four onions, six carrots, tomato paste and seasoning.

I tethered Goldie and let the others loose to graze. After dinner we went to a stream for a bucket of water which was down the slope about fifty yards. Climbing back, I suggested we set our water bucket on the trail and walk toward a rock I had seen as I explored the area earlier. We found an opening in a rock wall which I had noticed while Ray was waiting for me during my earlier explorations. It opened into a large domed area with a hole at the top. The radius of the circular rock interior was about 25 feet. The 10-foot ceiling had a black coating from fires. Someone had taken advantage of the great shelter the dome provided, and had hung a wire from the ceiling hole. The object was higher than we could reach and, from its shape, looked like a good place to dry horse blankets and pads. One above the other. I wondered, though, whether it was a religious symbol of some sort.

We told deer hunting stories then and mused about Indians, as we walked back to camp, now quite late. Back at camp I began filling the nose bags with feed for the horses and I called Bull—no response. I would have heard them come if they had been within the sound of my voice. Then the truth hit me with a thud. The horses were gone.

I hurried to where Goldie had been tethered, and he was gone. The knot I used to tie one rope to another was not adequate. I had run the rope through the snap of the other and only used a bite for the knot. It did not suffice. I knew I had to take action immediately. I grabbed another lead rope (Goldie already was dragging another) and a bridle, and I told Ray to stay put until I got back. Thinking the worst, I said it could be tomorrow before I returned.

Ray asked if I would take feed to catch the horses, but I knew I could catch mine without it. When I found them, it was 8:30 and dark; there was a little light from a quarter moon, but I took a flashlight, anyway. The 12-foot rope Goldie was dragging was fortuitous. In the moonlight the dragging rope caused the dirt to stand out and shimmer at times. I could see by the recently-disturbed dirt from the tracks that the horses had gone on the back trail. They always do. While it was 18 miles back to the trailer, I remembered we had gone through a gate about nine miles back. That gave me some hope.

In the moonlight I could see the trail all right, but whenever it was in the shade of the trees it was blotted out. I needed to conserve my batteries so I could have light in an emergency. As I went along I called for Bull at first. No response. I saw they had taken off at a trot and at times they were galloping. I thought of Ray and wished I hadn't been so brief with him. I also thought about how he must be feeling back in camp alone.

As I moved along, following the horse's tracks, I talked to God for the experience and thanked Him for caring for me. The horses' trail took me across the stream nine times, and not once did I fall on the rocks. I prayed for Ray's safety and peace.

After about four or five miles I left the stream and came upon a flat meadow-like area where some cattle were grazing and green grass was growing. There the horses were. What a lovely sight.

First I came upon Tico and tied him to a tree with the lead rope I'd brought. Then I caught Goldie and tied him to a tree near Tico. Then I caught Bull, brought him over, and transferred the rope from Tico to Bull. I bridled and mounted Goldie to make him carry me back while I led Bull (because Bull is so tall, it's sometimes hard to mount him when riding bareback). I expected Tico to follow Goldie and Hiker to follow Bull.

But Goldie didn't want to go in the lead. I could tell it would have been work for me to force him the whole way. And I soon noticed Tico and Hiker weren't following as I'd expected. Thinking they had missed our leaving (it was dark), I tied up Goldie again and bridled and mounted Bull (who is much more responsive to me), and rode back toward the other two. I wanted Goldie to whinny, which he did; I knew that would draw the other two back. It worked. I then turned Bull toward Goldie, rode up and untied Goldie and rode off. But Tico and Hiker, with the Hiker in the lead, ran back to the meadow again. Once more, I tied Goldie and got him to whinny, and once more, they returned.

I now tied Hiker to Goldie's tail and proceeded with Tico finally following on his own. Horses don't like to be left alone.

Bull was amazing. He knew the trail and followed it without my guiding. Only twice did he miss it; once on a steep hillside. And on that hillside I could not keep my legs on Bull's side, so I hung onto his mane and lay flat on his back with my legs on his hips. It was that steep. Another time Bull missed the trail when it was by a stream. I lost my hat there, and had to dismount to retrieve it. I had him stand on a side hill so it was easier to re-mount.

As I neared camp, maybe a mile away, a most interesting event took place. On my left, a bright, white light was shining. I thought it must be the moon glowing through the trees, but, then, there wasn't this white glow anywhere else. And as I reached the area of light it was on the cliff wall, I saw there were three areas of light, and the center of each was much brighter than the surrounding area and an indentation on the canyon wall like three grottos. It was as though a bright moon was shining through three small holes in a cloud. But the clouds were scattered.

The smallest light, on the left, was about eight feet tall, the middle one was 10 feet, the largest, on the right, was about 12 feet tall. All three were about four feet across. It made me think of the Trinity.

As I passed the wall where these lights shone, I kept focused on them as I rode, twisting my neck to peer until my neck hurt from looking back. When I turned forward, I saw to the right another bright white light on the stream. I remembered seeing a log across the stream this afternoon, making a small waterfall. But now, seated on the log, was the image of a lady in flowing robes. From her shape it was obviously a woman. I could not tell what was on her head; it did not look like a hair-do. Maybe she was a nun.

I am a little surprised that I did not get goose bumps over this experience, but it makes me wonder. I am anxious to share it with Gretchen.[16]

~ ~ ~

I had put my duffle on the trail so I would know where to turn up to camp.

On arrival, I found Ray in bed but awake. It was after midnight. He got up to help me with the horses and we shared experiences.

Friday April 6, 1990

Ray told me this morning about his thoughts while I was gone to get the horses last night. I wonder what I would have done the first time I was in the mountains and quickly left in the dark at the beginning of the night and told that my guide would be "back tomorrow?". It would have been pretty hairy for me. When I left Ray, my concern for horses and our ability to pack out of this place was greater than the sensitivity I should have had for Ray.

~ ~ ~

I was surprised that I slept until 7 this morning. I must have been tired after going after the horses last night. When I got up, I found Ray had gotten up earlier, and he'd fixed breakfast for himself and had mine ready for me. I appreciated that he had kindly let me sleep.

While the horses were grazing, we partially packed up, leaving the tarp up to dry out. Then we fed the horses and tied Tico and Hiker while we went exploring on Goldie and Bull.

We rode up the Diamond Creek Trail to get to Diamond Peak and then to see if we could find the South Diamond Peak Trail. We had not ridden far before we came upon the ravages of some storm on the stream and on our trail. The stream was washed out and boulders had been deposited on the trail. We alternated between trail and creek in our riding. At times we rode over rock and sand-covered ice.

Finally, after traveling about two miles, and before we got to the peak, we came to a dead end. No way could we get around large, downed trees. We had to give up.

We backtracked a little, and when we came to the trail marked "one mile to the Continental Divide," we turned and ended up on the steepest trail I have ever ridden. It's true, I've climbed much steeper grades, but I've never climbed such a steep trail. When it was laid out, some switchbacks should have been put in.

This was very difficult and tiring for Bull. Ray thought it was too hard on the horses, so he got off and walked, leading Goldie.

I got to the top first and followed the trail south a little. It led to a better, more used trail. Then I turned to go back to where Ray was still coming up. He was practically to the top when I got there. He asked if there was a good view. Since I reported it was not, due to the trees that obscured the view, he decided to stop his ascent, commenting that he might just as well have stayed at the bottom.

Sometimes I don't talk enough, but how does one know. I let people figure things out for themselves, rather than care for them. In some situations I ought not do that, and when I finally realize it, I feel bad.

We got back to camp at 11:30, finished packing and loading, and left at noon. We rode out to the meadow–where I found the horses the night before and ate lunch.

Ray and I dismounted and sat on the back trail and let the horses graze. First Tico, who now had Ray's saddle, tried to roll; then Hiker ambled over to do the same. He got his saddle shifted to the side and one pannier right on top of his back. A wreck was in the making. I could see Hiker wanted to buck and kick, but as I hurriedly got closer, I talked him out of it. I then unpacked, re-saddled and repacked.

When we had about four more miles before reaching my trailer, the horses seemed to know it, too. They picked up the pace as we headed out from lunch. The last couple of miles, Tico out-paced Bull, and Hiker had to practically trot continuously to keep up.

As we passed the last fence about one-half mile from the trailer, two of Collins' hounds came up to me and followed us.

When we loaded up, I put the hounds into the pickup truck to give them the five-mile ride back home and let them off by Wall Lake.

On the way, the darkest one stuck his nose into any place where there was food smell. He got a bag of prunes out of my saddle bag and scarfed up the prunes, stones and all.

We're making camp tonight by Beaverhead. Ray is sleeping in the gooseneck and I have my cot set up for sleeping outside. It is a beautiful moonlit night.

Saturday April 7, 1990

We packed up the trailer for the trip to Minnesota and waited to eat breakfast on the road. We went to Truth or Consequences to buy a bale of hay and feed, and then drove to Tucumcari, New Mexico, by 4:30 for the night. We put the horses in a pasture for a while as we ate supper and then tied them to the trailer. We're staying at the Pony Soldier Motel, and they are surely accommodating.

Sunday, April 8, 1990

We got going at 5 a.m. today and made it to a place about 100 miles from Des Moines. We're leaving the horses in the trailer tonight.

Monday, April 9, 1990 (at home)

Drove to Faribault this morning and left the two horses, Tico and Goldie, at Severson's. Al was not there, but I talked to Doris. We then went over to Ray's house outside LeSueur, and I met his wife Ardy and Ray's parents.

We then went to Jordan and left Bull and Hiker at Burdett Steif's place, where I board them–St. Lawrence Farms.

After this, I took Ray to his car in Edina and went home to unpack.

It's good to be home, but I feel like I didn't stay in the mountains long enough this time. I need about a month.

1991

Northern New Mexico

Dulce

Cuba

Jicarilla Apache Indian Reservation

Prewitt

Pie Town

Gila Cliff Dwellings

Beaverhead

CHAPTER THIRTY-SIX

Floors are not bullet-proof

Monday, July 1, 1991

As I write this, we are speeding across Nebraska about 15 miles from Kearney. Lynn Street is driving, and we are making 9.44 miles per gallon. We each pay half the gas costs.

It is quite hot–nearly 100 degrees. Lynn is a good travel companion. We talk about education. Lynn says the problem is not education but families. He is quiet. Also easy-going.

At first only Lynn Street committed to ride with me this year. I felt like we needed a third, so I wrote to A.M. Lips in Florida and told him I'd changed my mind from last October when said I didn't think he should go because of his health. I told him I'd like him on my last ride, and he agreed to come. That would make three of us.

As the time for the ride neared, I ended up with four more! Al Severson and Mert Schwarz started to sound more and more like they wanted to come, and Gary Hanson, who at first declined the invitation, decided he would come. Gary is a construction architect from Northfield whom I met when we built our house in 1983. And Robert Taylor of Silver City, N.M., is going to join us for a few days.

I'm bringing Hutch, one of Burdette Steif's horses with me. Because he is untrained–only halter broke–he was not my first choice, but through a series of circumstances, was the only choice Burdette had for me. I spent a little time training him before bringing him out here. I'm hoping the effort pays off.

My back has been giving me trouble all spring and summer. I hope my chiropractic treatment and the new back belt I'm wearing helps.

After church and lunch yesterday, I tried sleeping beginning about 2 in the afternoon. Couldn't sleep. I lay there with my thoughts racing. Typical of me the day before I leave on a ride. At midnight I awoke and got the pickup loaded, but a severe electrical storm began. I put everything in the cab and waited out the heavy rain. We were planning to leave as soon as we were loaded. Instead we left Lynn's house just a little after 2 a.m.

~ ~ ~

I discovered last year that riding on roads was not as bad as I thought it would be. There was plenty of shoulder room, and many times we would go an entire day without seeing anyone.

So this year, I plan to take our ride along the Divide from Dulce, New Mexico, to the Beaver Ranger Station in the Gila National Forest. We will be starting at the headquarters of the Jicarilla Reservation.

Because the country we'll be going through is dry, I rigged a plastic water tank to carry in the back of my pick-up between the cab and fifth-wheel post. It's about 4 feet long, 3-1/2 feet wide and 3-1/2 feet tall. We'll fill it whenever we can to make sure we have enough water for the horses.

The other thing that will be different this year is the need to do the ride in "leap frog" fashion. We won't be able to leave our rigs at a single spot, ride to our final destination and get an auto ride back, as in the past. Instead, half of us will ride, while the others will drive ahead about 10 miles, leave the rigs at that point and begin riding from there. When the first bunch of us arrives at where the rigs have been left, we will load our horses into the trailers and drive them ahead another 10 or so miles, and we will begin riding again from that spot. It will be interesting to see how this all works out.

~ ~ ~

We made it all the way to Castle Rock just south of Denver today. We will have driven exactly 1,200 miles by the time we get to Dulce tomorrow.

Tuesday, July 2, 1991

We all met in Dulce today. Al Severson had arrived first and had been informed we could not camp at Stinking Lake on the reservation tonight. In fact, he was told we could not ride reservation roads but only on State Highway 537. Not taking kindly to this information, I managed to arrange a meeting with Leonard Altoma, former president and now vice president of the tribe. He reiterated that the tribe did not want us on reservation roads, so we will follow their will.

We're staying the night in the Dulce Sales Corral. Al and A.M. are sleeping in the Suburban and Mert and Gary in his pickup. Lynn and I out on the ground. Bob Taylor will meet us later.

Wednesday, July 3, 1991

I had a tough time sleeping last night. Too much noise from the stockyards, and I am tense. That will change when I get to riding.

I awoke at 4 a.m., got up and took the horses out for pellets and grass. We left camp at 6:30. Mert, A.M., and I were the first to ride. After about a mile, Al, Lynn, and Gary drove by. We rode about another eight miles and found where they had parked and started their ride.

We loaded our horses in the rigs and drove 9-1/2 miles, passing Al, Lynn, and Gary along the way. We stopped at a Northwest Pipeline Co. building and waited for Al, Lynn and Gary to arrive. We ate and loaded up the tank with water. All took a nap but me. Al, Lynn, and Gary rode off again, and we passed them with the trailers, then and parked about 8-1/2 miles down the road.

Mert and A.M. and I rode past Ojita where there was only one house.

We turned on a dirt road to go east a ways to Highway 95. Riding on the roads is not bad. We do not have to ride in the ditch alongside the road like I thought. There are 50 yards between the center of the road and the fence outside the right of way.

We are camping near an oil well tonight.

Kind of a boring day.

Thursday, July 4, 1991

Others seemed to sleep well, but I slept fitfully, so 5 a.m. didn't roll around too early for me. Gas was hissing from the oil well all night.

We ate pancakes and eggs for breakfast. Lynn and I started out at 6:30 riding toward Lindreth. When we neared the town, we could see the trailers, over a mile away, that the others had driven on ahead of us. It certainly adds to the anticipation that a section of the ride is "over."

We drove 10 miles and then rode another 10. This time Gary rode with me.

We all stopped for lunch under some trees by the side of the road at about noon and stayed until 2:30. The trees give much-needed shade and let the breeze flow. I took about a 15-minute nap; the others slept longer. They sure are able to sleep well. Usually I am the one who sleeps easily. Too much to be concerned about, I guess.

This afternoon Al, Mert, and A.M. rode 10 miles into Cuba, and the rest of us drove there. Many Hispanics were celebrating the Fourth of July, including having a parade–mostly with horses. Lynn, Gary, and I filled the horse tank in my pickup truck with water again and found a place at the end of Cuba to leave the trailer. Lynn gave some kids $2 to watch the trailer until Al, Mert, and A.M. got there.

They caught up with us another eight miles out, along Highway 197. It was raining and we had not brought rain covers, so we loaded the horses and drove a mile to Clarac Trading Post. No one was there, so we went on to Johnson Trading Post. A rancher came by, and when we explained to him what we were doing, he invited us to camp at his ranch–about two miles back. There is a lot of sage brush here and not much cactus but the prickly pear is in beautiful bloom.

The trip started with the telling of stories, and it was awkward to move to spiritual matters. Now, after a few days of being together, we are in the routine of saying grace before our meals. I read from the Spiritual Classics just before supper tonight.

This is a very comfortable group of men; everyone pitches in and figures out what to do on their own.

The sunset was beautiful tonight.

Friday, July 5, 1991

Got up at 4, gave horses hay and went to a high point and prayed. Got the rest up at 5. Bacon, eggs and pancakes for breakfast today.

Lynn, Al, and I were the first to ride this morning as A.M., Mert, and Gary finished up packing before driving on ahead. By the time I got done puttering around, Al and Lynn had ridden one-half mile. Takes time to put on my back brace. I caught up to them at the gate where we went onto the road; then we rode nine miles to Torreon.

A.M., Mert, and Gary had driven the rigs there and left them at a store. We filled the water tank, and it was the first time we were charged–but only one cent per gallon. I called Gretchen, but she was out.

As we were pulling out, two Navajo with two children pulled up in a pickup. Having seen my license plates, the driver called out, "You're sure a long way from home!"

I went over and explained what we were doing, and mentioned my name. Then the man asked if I knew Bruce King, New Mexico's governor while I was governor of Minnesota. This man's wife, Dareen Morgan, sitting next to him in the pickup, had been personal secretary to King when he and I left our governor positions in '83. What a small world. Dareen is an excellent potter and is teaching the art to her daughter. A friend had lent them the pickup truck; they were here to dig up a special clay. I look forward to telling Gretchen, who is also a potter, about this.

We caught up with A.M., Mert, and Gary nine miles later. We stopped for lunch at a station and grocery in Pueblo Pintado. A Mr. Hill was the proprietor, and a very articulate Indian woman managed the place. We found out Hill had Quarter Horses and mules, and that he hunted bear and mountain lions in the Cuba and Stinking Lake areas. From the stories he told us, I am tempted to buy one of his mules. But no room in the trailer.

After sitting in the shade of the store for a while, we drove on to White Horse and began our ride toward Prewitt on I-40 west of Grants.

We are camping right on the Continental Divide tonight. I'm glad we were able to get on it, even though it is still very close to the road. Most of the time a person cannot be exactly on the Divide; usually it is only possible to travel–even by horse or foot–to one side or the other.

In camp tonight, I heard a rumble like hundreds of WWII bombers approaching. Before long, hundreds of Indians drove by in campers, cars, and pickups, many of which were pulling horse trailers. There must be a big celebration someplace.

For a long time stragglers drove by. Finally a couple of older men stopped by my trailer where I was standing. They thought we were a part of the party. They drove on after we exchanged pleasantries–they in broken English, and I, well, I didn't even have broken Navaho.

Great sunset.

Saturday, July 6, 1991

Up at 4; turned horses loose and did chores until 5. The tarp was flapping in the wind. I took it down to stop the noise so Lynn could get another hour's sleep. I started the stove after filling it with gas. The others made breakfast once they were up.

I then looked to check on horses. I didn't see Bull and Hutch anywhere. Gary said he saw Bull going south. I couldn't imagine that, so I went out to look for tracks; none showed up going south, so I checked north. None there, either. Al suggested we eat breakfast and then saddle up to look for the missing horses. I verbally agreed, but kept walking, anyway. Instead of breakfast, I really wanted to find my horses. I felt they would get too far during the time it would take me to eat. I walked over to where the canyon edge came close to the road. That narrowed the route they could follow, and I found tracks going north.

After following tracks for about a mile, I found the horses. I climbed on Bull with no lead rope to guide him and galloped bareback the whole way back to camp. Hutch followed. I felt young and free in balance.

~ ~ ~

I started riding with Al and Lynn today. After about six miles, we arrived at Borrego Pass Trading Post.

To Al and Lynn I said, "Let's do a non-typical Al Quie-type-of-thing and go in for a can of pop." They agreed in an instant.

As we rode up, the proprietor, Billy Moore, and his 9-year-old son came rushing out. There certainly was a lot of joy on their faces at seeing us. His wife and one of her friends were in the store, all smiles.

One of the women related, "When we saw you coming from a long ways away, we yelled to Billy, 'Here come some white men on horseback!'" He apparently didn't believe them because he chimed in, "I told them, 'No, they have to be Navajo.' But when the women insisted you were white, I came from the back of the store to see for myself." He told us he could tell from a distance we were white because, he said, Navajo sit on a horse differently than we Anglos.

As we walked inside, Billy told us he had had the store for three months, and the only people who had come by in all that time were Navajo. That's apparently why he rushed out of the store to greet us. He said he had taken the store over from an 86-year-old man whose relatives had told him it was time to hang it up.

Billy and his wife Jennifer buy and sell sheep, goats, mohair, cattle, and horses. They also have a pawn shop. Jennifer gave us a tour. Hanging on the back wall was a brand new walking plow and handle bars that had not yet been attached. There also was a wringer Maytag washer not yet out of the box. They had old guns, even a breech-loading Sharps rifle.

The rug we stood on was a large beauty. Billy said it was valued at about $10,000. I stepped off quickly. Too valuable for my feet! We were a happy occasion for them, and visiting their store was fun for us.

~ ~ ~

After we left the trading post, now a convenience store, we came upon an Indian boy riding his pony and what looked to be about a 4-week-old colt following. The boy was quite shy, but Lynn talked to him. He was looking for his sheep. Al gave him a drink from his canteen.

As we rode on, we saw his sheep, being cared for by the boy's dog. I trust they connected later.

We rode into Prewitt, and Al lined up a corral for us to drop our horses overnight. When we looked at it, though, it appeared too dilapidated–so I went to the trading post in Prewitt to inquire about leaving our horses at the rodeo grounds. That is where they are tonight.

While at the trading post, we met Joe "Blackie" James and his wife, Birdie. They invited us out to their place six miles away. The others were excited to go. At first I was concerned about losing time on our ride, but then I reconsidered. I decided we could ride toward Thoreau to Highway 53 (about 40 miles), and then trailer to Joe's ranch tomorrow.

We all went into Grants where we got two motel rooms just for showering. A.M. and Al treated us to dinner in town, and then it was back to Prewitt.

Sunday, July 7, 1991

Got up at 3:45 today. Seems to get earlier and earlier.

We ate breakfast at a truck stop (biscuits and gravy for me), and we got to the Prewitt rodeo grounds at 5:10. It did not take long to get things together, and we headed out for our day's ride. It was beautiful in the mountains today, and we saw our first running stream of water for this year. After "leap-frogging" for about 40 miles, we stopped at a bar by the road, drank pop, and called Birdie James to make sure they were ready for our visit. Then we rode back to our rigs and drove out seven miles by dirt road to the James ranch.

As Joe showed us around, it was difficult to move on to see all that he had–he is such a talker. In one way, the ranch yard was like a junk yard. It appears Joe never traded off a piece of equipment, car, truck or tractor in his life. (He said the dealers would never give him enough for his old equipment and vehicles whenever he was buying new, so he just kept the old.)

They invited us in for fry bread and beans, which were excellent. Birdie has a right to brag about her culinary skills.

They are a unique couple. He is 73; this is his second marriage. I'll bet he is tough. Joe and Birdie make a good pair, though; their different eccentricities play to each other.

As we visited about rugs and jewelry (it was obvious they had acquired much), Lynn asked about the value of guns at pawn shops. Joe, who was sitting at a large table in the dining room, turned and moved the drapes that were in easy reach. There, on one side of the window, was a single action rifle. I reminded the men that western people keep their guns loaded. Joe affirmed that fact and passed the gun to Lynn. He then reached around to the other side of the window and pulled out a shotgun. After passing that around, Lynn asked about pistols.

Birdie left the table, picked up a 41-caliber pistol and returned. "This is loaded," she said, and handed it to me. Looking for assurance, I said, "None in the chamber, though." She said, "Yes." I didn't know if she meant, "Yes, there are none in the chamber," or "Yes, there are bullets in the chamber." I held it up and all holes in the cylinder were filled.

I passed it to Joe, who pointed it right at me as he pulled the hammer back slightly in order to rotate the cylinder! I said, "Joe! You are pointing the gun right at me!"

Then he pointed it at A.M. who had slid behind me for protection. I said, "Point it up or down, Joe, not at a person." I couldn't imagine a guy with all those guns doing such dangerous things.

To me, he seemed so focused on trying to look at the gun that he didn't realize where he was pointing it. He moved it again and this time pointed the gun right at Birdie.

Trying to ease the situation, I laughed and said, "I don't know what you think of your wife, but you had better not point the gun at her, either." So he pointed it at the floor as he tried to turn the cylinder. I don't know what he did next, but the pistol went off, sending a bullet through the floor!

Birdie snapped at Joe, "If that bullet had hit my china closet, the next one would have been for you!" Joe didn't seem to be bothered.

After dinner, we went into another room where Birdie played the piano and Joe the fiddle. For a time, we sang familiar songs together. We then went outside to see Joe's stud and mare since it was still light out.

It's now about 9:30; I'm sleeping tonight in their house. Two shot guns at the door and two rifles at each window of the bedroom.

CHAPTER THIRTY-SEVEN

Tragedy strikes!

Monday July 8, 1991

I didn't wake up until 5:45 today–probably because I had been sleeping indoors. I went outside to stroll around a bit, and Lynn, who also slept indoors, went to see his horses. I had seen them off in the distance, in the corner of the pasture, and figured they were all right.

But when Lynn returned, I could tell by his pace and the look on his face that something was horribly wrong. He said some of the horses had been cut in wire, and it looked like Gunther (Mert's favorite horse) was dead!

We quickly roused the others and ran out to the corner of the pasture where the horses were. Sure enough, they had gone through the wire fence that divided two pastures. I'm guessing they'd been scared by a mountain lion, they all took off (except my two), and they hit the fence together. If one had been in the lead, he would have ripped out the fence and gotten cut with the others going through unscathed. But they all were cut in some way. And Gunther had his jugular cut and lay there dead. What a tragedy!

We could see by where the blood was on Schatzi's hip that Gunther had laid his head and neck over Schatzi.

How sad for Mert. He loved that horse for so long. He was a great friend. Mert cussed him out at times, and then loved him. He was so careful, never wanting Gunther to be lonesome or anxious. He babied Gunther, a large buckskin Quarter Horse who was a fast walker and always ready to go, and who took a lot before getting tired. He was one grand, great horse who will never be forgotten by us.

How does a person handle such a grief? I felt bad. Mert finally cried. We decided the news should be broken to the Joneses. They felt so bad; Joe immediately told about his favorite horse that broke his leg. It is interesting how we try to help others by sharing a story about how something bad has happened to us. Perhaps it is an effort to let another know that we have gone through similar circumstances and that we understand. Instead, I wonder if it belittles the grief of the moment.

Death brings grief. The closer the object of love is, the deeper the grief and regret when it dies. About all I seem to be able to do is just keep quiet and "be there" for someone who is grieving.

All this before breakfast.

Talk turned to burying the horse. Many options were discussed, as we tried to consider Mert's feelings. Mert, in his grief, finally said, "Do what you usually do with dead animals. Drag him out and leave him for the buzzards if that is the custom."

But Joe showed a sensitive side. He apparently recognized the importance of this horse to Mert. "Even though that is the custom here, I will bury your horse."

Joe's bulldozer had not been operated for 17 years, and the last time the backhoe, which was two miles away, had been used was two years ago. These people must just stop and leave their machinery right where it is when they are done with a job. Joe, Al, and A.M. got the backhoe going, but it ran on only three cylinders, and it took until noon to get the hole dug. Then they put a log chain on a tractor, hooked the chain onto Gunther, dragged him to the hole and pushed him in.

Gary and I went on a ride with Mert so he wouldn't have to watch the burial. He will be going back home this afternoon. I don't blame him. Gary will accompany him.[17]

I fixed stew when we got back, we took it into the house where we ate it with the leftover fry bread from yesterday (not as good as when fresh).

We left after lunch. Rain was threatening and we wanted to leave before the dirt roads got slick.

When we got to the highway, six or seven miles later, we stopped to see Mert and Gary off.

I then asked Al and A.M. if they were ready to head out and camp. Al said he had been having shortness of breath all morning. I decided right then and there to go the 50 miles to Grants and stay at a motel.

We are the only customers at the Stagecoach Motel tonight.

We drove out to the rodeo arena corrals and found a woman in charge–Janie Holtan–who gave us permission to leave our horses there overnight. It must have been a slow night for Janie because she spent a lot of time chatting with us, sharing much of her life story, and tales of the infamous characters of the area. She first told us she was Jewish and married, as she said, to "one of us." She and her husband left Pennsylvania 35 years ago to make a new life in California. They made it all the way to Grants without a mishap, and then their car broke down. It took $500 of their $1,000 to put in a new motor, and in order to get the rest of the way to California, he took a job. The uranium mining was just beginning and he got a job in the mines. "They were hiring any warm body," she laughed. She said they agreed to stay for a year, and at the end of the year he decided they ought to stay longer because the pay was so good. Janie didn't agree, so she left him and went back to Pennsylvania.

But it took her only four days to realize that this dry, god-forsaken place (Grants) had magnificent sunsets and clear, clean dry air that she couldn't breathe in Pennsylvania. So she came back, was reunited with her husband, and they have been here ever since. Her husband became Superintendent of Mines. Now the uranium mine is closed, with 7,800 people laid off. The environmentalists closed them down, she said.

We then talked about her daughter's barrel racing, the Indians, Joe "Blackie" James (so nicknamed, she said, as he never bathed), and Gus Raimy, who was recently linked to several murders in the area. He had been a Texas Ranger, and he claimed he only killed people who "needed killing." She said the locals think the last two people were killed by Raimy's grandson, not by Raimy. He died before going to prison at 100 years of age.

Tuesday July 9, 1991

Up at 4, ate breakfast at a truck stop, picked up horses and drove about 70 miles through the "El Malpais" (Spanish for the "badlands of lava rock"), and then began our "leap frogging"–Al riding with me today and Lynn and A.M. taking the first stint at driving ahead. We rode to Pie Town where we ate and were filmed by a crew who was shooting a photo history of Pie Town, 50 years after a first history book had been written. The town was named because a local person made money simply by making pies for workers and anyone else interested in buying them.

We rode 20 more miles, which took a long time, looking for the rigs left by Lynn and A.M. Al and I thought they must have left the rigs elsewhere; I started riding back to get help from someone, and Al rode on, found the rigs, then turned around to come and get me.

The road to Horse Springs was terrible. We could only drive 15 miles per hour. Everything in the town was in disrepair, and the town's one house looked abandoned. There were two old cars parked in front, so I knocked on the sagging screen door, taking a chance there might be someone around who could direct us to a place to stay for the night. A man about 55 years old, in an undershirt and with a belly hanging over his belt and thin gray hair, came to the door. I asked him about camping there and he said "No," since he didn't own the place. So we moved on to Old Horse Springs. It was bigger, meaning it had more abandoned buildings.

The Mexicans here are very accommodating. They gave us permission to camp, but we had to be very careful with our horses, since there was so much barbed wire lying around. We set up camp–in this old, broken-down, practically-a-ghost town–late.

Wednesday, July 10, 1991

We took pictures this morning and drove west to where a dirt road began to run south. We had between 40 and 50 miles to go to Beaverhead. Lynn and A.M. started to ride, and Al and I drove eight miles ahead where we left the rigs and started riding. The road followed a wide valley, dry and rocky. It's a wonder people can make a living in this area.

A woman drove by in a pickup and stopped. After talking a while and letting her know what we are doing, Lawana Hite invited us to stop at their ranch, the Triangle C. I didn't want to stop because the ranch was 12 miles out of our way, and the extra time it would take to get there would give us too short a day. I may live to regret my decision not to accept Lawana's invitation. I tend to wonder later what I might have missed whenever I can't see over a hill or around a curve, or when I've declined an invitation to visit someone's place.

We continued on, not stopping to do more than eat a quick lunch at noon. The other guys drove ahead as I rode 10 miles alone on Hutch; then I met up with them and got Bull so I could ride him the remaining 40 miles into Beaverhead. The others drove ahead to meet me there.

When riding alongside the road with Hutch today, we came to a cattle guard. (steel rails across the road at a fence so animals cannot cross but cars may). No gate was nearby. Usually there is one so if you wanted animals to be able to travel through, you could. In every other instance on these rides there has been a gate next to cattle guards we've encountered. I had no pliers, the barbed wire was wound tight with no ends sticking out to grasp with my fingers. So I was unable to unwrap the wire to make an opening in the fence.

There was, however, a wooden beam—about six inches wide—on each side of the cattle guard, and I decided to coax Hutch to go across on one of the beams. First, I tied his stirrups upon top of his saddle since there would be so little room between the beam he'd be walking on and the fence post. Then I brought Hutch up to narrow beam on the right side of the cattle guard, put my hand on his neck and urged him to walk across on the beam. As he took his first step, his hoof clicked on the steel v-shaped barricade leaning from the cattle guard to the fence post. This frightened him. When metal horseshoe hit metal barricade, he quickly backed off. I reassured him and again put my hand on his neck. Then I walked at his left side, stepping right on the cattle guard to keep him from stepping off the beam.

He crossed on that narrow wooden beam, putting one hoof in front of the other! Any misstep and a leg would have gone down between the guard rails and he could have broken his legs. When he got across he gave a huge sigh of relief. I gave him great praise; not many horses would have that confidence in a man to try such a thing. I get goose bumps when I think of what could have happened.

~ ~ ~

We took pictures when I arrived at Beaverhead, the end of Riding the Divide.

I was elated that I'd accomplished my goal, but I must say, it was anticlimactic. Beginnings are exciting, endings are not.

Much was exciting in the 3,500 miles I'd ridden in nine summers. But now at the end, it is over. Physically I feel great. Without riding in the West in the summer, would I ever feel this good again?

Al and A.M. left on Highway 59 toward Truth or Consequences, and Lynn and I will continue on into the Gila Wilderness tomorrow. We are camping tonight south of the Beaverhead Ranger Station at a spot where Ray Seaver and I ended last year.

Thursday, July 11, 1991

We got up late–5:30. After chores and eating breakfast, we laid out all our gear for the pack trip into the Gila. This will be kind of a layover day as we wait for Bob Taylor to arrive. I first met Bob when I was doing some vocational education work while in Congress. He was heading a vocational research center in Columbus, Ohio. We quickly discovered our shared interest in horses; I went on a ride with him once on his farm in Ohio. We stayed in touch over the years; he now lives in Silver City in the winter and Crede, Colo., in the summer.

We talked to the ranger, filled our tank with water and drove into Winston to look around. What a disappointment. There was little to see. We bought a spatula from the store keeper–right out of her kitchen since she had none in her merchandise. We drove back slowly–42 miles–and checked out the trailhead for tomorrow. When we returned to camp, Bob Taylor was there. He had brought champagne to celebrate the completion of my multi-year ride. He is talkative and worried about one of his horses.

Off to bed. It is about 9:30.

Friday, July 12, 1991

Got up at 4:45, and got the horses from a small, nearby pasture. It was dark when I got them this morning, and dark when I put them in last night. I left them in this same place last year where they could graze and lie down some if they wanted to.

Lynn and Bob got up at 5:30. I was already packed up by then (I decided to pack Bull today and ride Hutch), so I made breakfast of pancakes and bacon while Lynn and Bob packed their gear. The canned bacon was more than we could eat, so we used it to make sandwiches with cheese for lunch. We got everything into six panniers, taking six pounds of feed per horse per day for the next four days, and started at the trail head we'd scouted yesterday, six miles west of Beaverhead. Our plan was to get to the Cliff Dwellings today.

The climb up to Black Mountain was not too steep, but very rocky at first. How the horses could take it, I don't know. I got off and led Hutch for a ways; he didn't like it and balked at times. And then there was Bull–pretty insulted about being packed, and he objected at the start by doing a powerful bucking job.

We stopped at the look-out tower on Black Mountain, where we met its occupant, a guy named Rusty who had a cute black lab. He said he was in the process of spotting a fire. Another was burning, which, he said, was a good thing because it is natural. There was a small corral there, so we put the horses in and watered them while we ate lunch.

Bob was very worried about his horse not drinking and not having loose enough stools. His concerns proved unnecessary later today; I never realized a person could give such exclamations of joy over his horse "going to the bathroom."

Going down Black Mountain on the other side was as rocky as going up. Again, very, hard on the horses. Then I began worrying about Bob's horses because they looked very soft.

We really had difficulty finding the trail and did quite a bit of scouting back and forth. We came to a tank (which, in New Mexico, is a dammed-up low area) that held muddy water. Glad the horses could drink it.

We tried to find the correct trail to get to the Cliff Dwellings; but just couldn't. We found what are called antelope corrals, making us think there should be a trail nearby, but we didn't find a trail past them, either. We then tried to find a spot where we could get down to the river and failed at that. All we encountered were cliffs which prevented us from progressing. It seemed we were stuck at this higher level. We got down two tiers but ran into worse of cliffs. The land was so rocky, even with little patches of dry grass, and it revulsed us.

At 5:30 we gave in, realizing we could not get down. We were short of water, so we decided instead to try and find the dam (tank) we had been by earlier. We found it at about 7:30 tonight with very tired horses. We're camping here tonight.

By the end of today, Bob's pack horse was finding it more and more difficult to do the work. He was right to worry about her. When we were unpacking, she squatted like she was going to go down. We kept her up as we unpacked her, and then I suggested that Bob lead her. I could see Bob's saddle horse was going into colic as well, so I led her over to Bob so he could lead her, too. Lynn and I ate, and then we led Bob's horses for him for a while, so he could eat. Bob led both his horses until after dark—in fact until about 10 p.m.

We are at a high point from where, at dusk, we could see a herd of elk.

We'll try again tomorrow to find our way to the Cliff Dwellings.

CHAPTER THIRTY-EIGHT

Trying to make it last

Saturday, July 13, 1991

Lynn had turned his horses loose last night, and I did the same with Hutch, but I kept Bull tied until I was sure he was relaxed. I was concerned about Hutch because I couldn't hear any action in his stomach. I heard him pawing during the night so he might have been hurting some.

At 3:30 this morning I heard a noise, and when I got up I saw Bob's pack horse was down. I got Bob up so he could walk her again; he did, for better than an hour.

Our sleep was fitful. I was concerned that Bob's horse would die. Also, that we were about out of water for ourselves. I had tried straining the water from the dam yesterday through a T-shirt, but it came out muddy. I boiled water this morning to make breakfast pancakes.

Bob decided, because of his sick horses, that he'd better quit the ride. I then figured that, instead of trying to find the trail to the Cliff Dwellings, we would all go back down together. I didn't want to take the chance of Bob being by himself and getting lost. That would be disastrous. And besides, I didn't want to worry any longer about not having enough water.

When we got back to the lookout tower, it was hard on my pride to admit to Rusty that we had not been able to find the trail to the Cliff Dwellings.

We went back down the mountain the way we had come up, and even though the way was rocky, the horses seemed fine when we got out. Especially Hutch. He has certainly turned out to be dependable, sensible, and stable, and now I can say he is experienced. He never blows up whenever we are in a tight fix. He has good stamina and an amazing recovery rate on steep mountains and climbs like we were on today. Considering all the scary objects, mountain streams, rocks or jumps we've encountered, he's never refused me. I like his stride, too. We can cover distance rapidly at a fast walk and at both a slow and fast trot, and now he has a balanced, lazy canter, too. He's a real gentleman.

~ ~ ~

We said our goodbyes to Bob, and he contributed the food and feed he'd bought. I gave him a lead rope.

Lynn and I then trailered around so we could ride in to the Cliff Dwellings from the east instead of the north.

We parked our trailers near a dirt road, and we rode about a mile to the end of it where we found the Trail's End Ranch. There were five adobes on the spread, a barn, and a shed. The east fork of the Gila River ran in front of the ranch house. Lynn got off and found the caretaker, Roland Stone. He was using his air compressor to try to blow a squirrel out of a rock pile he had built.

Roland told us the Nature Conservancy had purchased the ranch some years ago and then gave it to Albuquerque Academy. He said the ranch had once been owned by a fellow who was a friend of a gangster from Oklahoma. Together they had built a still and irrigated the property so they could raise potatoes to make vodka. Remains of the still and barrels are still in the cave which Roland showed us. The most recent owner was a geologist from Alaska, who still lives on five acres he kept for himself.

Roland has been caretaker for about 3-1/2 years. He rides a motor bike around the ranch and drives to Silver City every week in an old 4-wheel drive pickup. I know he is an interesting person with varied experiences since he had his dismantled airplane near the garage or shed. Roland invited us to stay the night when we return in a couple of days.

After our goodbyes, we rode off. He ran after us to say he might be gone when we return, and where he would leave the key to the gate.

~ ~ ~

On our way once again to the Cliff Dwellings, we rode past an arroyo at which we should have turned right. We retraced about a mile, and when we came to some salt blocks, we climbed out of the arroyo and proceeded over the top. When we hit a fence, Lynn proposed that we go back again. I didn't want to go back down in the arroyo again, travel a ways, and climb out of there again. But I also did not want to sound obtuse by rejecting his suggestion outright, so I said, "OK, but first let's rest the horses, and while they rest, I'll walk and take a look at what's ahead."

I walked up the rocky hill and was thinking of "doing something" to the old rusty fence so we could get through. That's when I came upon a place where someone else must have found themselves in the same predicament. The old, abandoned fence wires had been cut. I then walked on to check my directions and figured out that in the terrain ahead, we could intersect the trail we had been looking for. I then found the least rocky route to take and went back and told Lynn that all was well; we would soon be on the trail again.

We hit the trail shortly thereafter and followed it to a grove of Ponderosa Pine where we ate lunch. After lunch we rode by a dam, made a steep decline into the Middle Fork of the Gila River, and then, 1-1/2 miles later, arrived at the Cliff Dwellings Visitor's Center. At last. We tied up in back at the hitching rail, filled our canteens from the drinking fountain, and Lynn called home (he seems anxious to get home as soon as possible, even early).

In the Center, I bought a book, *No Life for a Lady*, by Agnes Morley Cleaveland, thinking I might have a moment to read in camp (wishful thinking). The book caught my eye because a sketchmap inside the cover has the Continental Divide running through it. And listed are several landmarks, like Horse Springs and Pie Town, where I'd been. I was impressed that this woman author had grown up on a ranch and could work cattle. Flipping the pages of the book, I saw that her recordings started in 1884 and ended in 1937. I thought, "This is my kind of book!" It made me think of Barbara Cole and Bob Abercrombie's 89-year-old mother-in-law. I like meeting people who have faced hardship and made joy out of life, especially when they've lived in country that most think is hard life. But that kind of country has a certain beauty, a certain kind of freedom and character.

Also at the Center, Lynn and I learned about horse trails from a big map, and about the Cliff Dwellings from a brochure.

Then we rode near the Cliff Dwellings, tied to trees, and climbed to see the view. It always amazes me whenever I visit the Cliff Dwellings. No one really knows why the dwellers came and why they left. Some corn cobs were even found near fire pits when the dwellings were discovered.

It started to rain a little, so we did not stay long, but did talk to a volunteer ranger who, we learned, was an art major from Slippery Rock College in Pennsylvania.

Then we rode up the West Fork of the Gila. We made camp just as it was starting to rain again; we are on some sand, so our boots won't get wet.

There is good grass across the stream, but the horses won't go over. So I took Bull by the halter and led him to the water. He walked over as I urged him, and the others followed. The tarp kept us dry.

I have never felt better. All my pains are gone. Just good healthy tiredness. If I never go on another of these trips (which is a good likelihood), I will never feel this good again the rest of my life. If I can get someone to ride with me, I'll go to the Big Horn Mountains–maybe next August while Gretchen is at her reunion.

Sunday, July 14, 1991

After breakfast of four pancakes each, coffee for Lynn and Tang for me, we packed up and climbed up out of the West Fork of the Gila River Valley, heading toward The Meadows. We passed a turn-off and went on until we came upon two log cabins that were evidently being used by rangers. That's when I looked at the map and realized we had gone way too far. We retraced our steps and when we got to the cliff overlooking The Meadows, Lynn and I took pictures.

I was concerned because I could see a storm brewing in the southeast sky. The rain came quickly.

The drop down to The Meadows was a steep 1,000 foot cliff. We walked down the switchbacks and led our horses, in rain coats and hat covers, while our uncovered saddles got wetter and wetter. Midst thunder, lightning, and hard rain, the trail got treacherously slippery. I wondered if Bull would hold me by the reins if I slipped off the trail. Lynn said it was the most precarious descent he had ever made.

Normally I'd think such a descent would be impossible for any thing but a mountain goat. It was an extremely steep trail two feet wide, cut into the bank with switchbacks. It had a footing of dirt, stone and rock, and the water was coming down so hard it ran into the trail and then tumbled down to the trail again as the trail switched back. We had little traction. It was dangerous as we slipped and skidded our way down.

When we came out at the bottom, our presence frightened the horses of three women who were there in their saddles, waiting out the storm. When they got their horses under control, I rode over. From San Angelo, Texas, they were doing the same as we were, but without pack horses. One was a school teacher, another was her assistant principal who was just "along for the ride," and the third was a secretary who likes horses. She said she likes to ride in Wyoming where she spent a summer in the Tetons, exercising rangers' horses. The rain quit and they rode off to wherever their trailers were parked.

We set up camp quite near the river and put everything under a tarp. I am aware of the danger of setting up camp near a river in a canyon. But there was no debris in the trees, so I figured a flood would not come.

Then it began to pour and this rain lasted for three hours. I enjoy storms. To me, they bring the opportunity to experience peace. Many people compare peace to a smooth, serene, untroubled river on a warm, sunny day. But to me, peace is much more like a trusting songbird who continues singing despite the storm swirling around him. The peace of God transcends all understanding and is not dependent on our circumstances.

During one break in the storm I started a fire and tried to dry my clothes some. The horses seem to be doing great. Maybe they are at peace like the songbird.

Monday, July 15, 1991
We got up early today and started breakfast in the dark.

Today is our last day to ride. I packed Hutch today so I could give Bull one last day of the privilege of being my saddle horse. He has made it all the way from Canada to Mexico. Despite his arthritis in his left ankle for which I give him medication, he has finished as strong as he started.

What a joy to have this horse who thinks like me. He senses where I want to go and goes there. He helps me find trails. He is courageous and always willing to be the leader. We have come to know each other so well. When I'm around he seems always to be aware of my presence.

Bull has always been anxious to get going after long trips in the trailer. When he protested being a pack horse at the beginning of this trip, he bucked hard. If he had done that with me riding him, he would have thrown me. But he never has, and he has never hurt me.

~ ~ ~

We rode several miles down the Middle Fork today. No words can describe the majesty of the scenery. There were tall rock walls of varied colors, a beautiful stream, Ponderosa Pine, Pinion Pine on top, Juniper, Alligator Juniper, Gambel Oak, Live Oak.

We struggled at times with the trail today. The trail to the East Fork was steep. We let the horses rest often, so they did well.

When we came into the adobe canyon again, I spotted some geodes–some rough rocks that have colorful hollow interiors. Not all rough rocks are hollow, but the broken ones reveal themselves. I'd been keeping my eye out for them for days and spotted two small nice ones. I'd like to have stayed longer or ridden back to look some more, but Lynn wasn't interested. He is pretty anxious to get home. I'd be willing to stay another day to explore.

~ ~ ~

We rode into Trail's End Ranch and the pickup was gone so we knew Roland was gone. Plus, he'd forgotten to leave the key, but I figured a way to get through the gate.

After we unloaded by the bunkhouse we turned the horses out to graze. I broke out some trail mix from my saddle bag since Lynn likes to eat something as an "appetizer" before his meals. He heated water for coffee and Tang if I wanted it.

Just then we saw a young, slim Asian fellow walking down the road. It turned out to be a Korean by the name of Martin. In conversation, we learned he was the new head of security for Albuquerque Academy. He also works with their computers. Martin, now 41 years old, was raised in America by foster parents. He had come out to meet Roland for the first time and bring two new fire extinguishers. He didn't have a key and had waited two days for Roland. Being a city person, he was lonely. He was a jolly fellow. We invited him to eat with us; he was hungry.

After dinner I suggested we go and explore for caves. Finding none at the lower level in the red rock, I scaled the 100-foot rock wall (or maybe it was only 75 feet at that point), figuring the caves might be at a higher level in the more yellow and gray rock level.

I was pretty proud of my accomplishment when I reached the top: climbing a stone wall looking for firm hand holds and foot steps, kicking or throwing away the loose rocks and getting higher and higher, deciding whether I should chance one more step, questioning, "Is there a way to get over or around this impassable spot?", trying to remember the moves, too, so that I could come back the same way. And then reaching the top, realizing what I had just plotted from the level below, and that I might have found the only way up the face of that wall for a long distance–maybe miles. (Anyway, for the mile we had followed the wall.)

And sure enough, the caves were at this higher point. They were not a tourist attraction. They looked like they had never or seldom been seen. I also was closer to-and across the draw from–a herd of elk we had seen at about the same place from our trailer three nights ago.

It was fun walking around up there, exploring and looking down over the edge. In fact I was a little like a small boy who got away from his parents. He doesn't want them to worry about him and knows they will after a while. I wondered whether Martin and Lynn were waiting for me by the creek or if they had walked back.

In some respects, I'm a loner. That's not to say I don't enjoy being around people (or I wouldn't have invited people to go with me on these rides). And it isn't that I am anti-social. I do gain energy from being around people. It's just that when you are with a crowd of people, or even just a group, there is so much going on that you don't have time to be alone with God.

Out in the wilderness I'm alone, but I am not. What an odd person I am! Out here, "alone" is sort of like having a person you normally see only in a group whom you now have all to yourself for sharing and listening.

~ ~ ~

I finally came to the point where I figured Lynn and Martin would worry too much, so I decided to go back. I also needed to make sure I could find the spot for my descent, so I'd make it down before dark. This meant I didn't make it over to the farther caves where it looked like people (probably Indians) had lived.

When I got to the bottom, Martin was just coming to look for me. Roland had returned by the time Lynn and Martin returned to the dwelling. When I told Roland about the place where I scaled the wall, he affirmed that it was the only spot it could be done.

Lynn is sleeping in the big house tonight, but I wanted to sleep under the stars, so I am outside. What a time to pray and meditate. I went back through the gate with both my horses and laid my sleeping bag out by the East Fork of the Gila.

Tuesday, July 16, 1991

About 12:30 last night, Bull and Hutch were spooked and their snorting woke me up. I opened my eyes, and as I lay on the ground in my sleeping bag, I saw Bull standing by my head and Hutch by my feet. They continued snorting and looking off across the stream. I turned my head in the direction they were looking and saw a herd of elk coming down the mountain toward the river. They all came into the stream by me and drank.

Then an elk came over to where I was lying in the grass and stared at us for a while. I lay completely still, looking at his huge frame, wondering what he was thinking about. Then he snorted and walked away. I guess I got my answer!

I hope I always remember this final experience of this great ride.

At 5 a.m. Lynn was out loading Roland's truck with panniers and pack saddles. It was easier to do that than to pack the horses and move the gear up the mountain to my truck that way. After transferring the gear, we brought the pickup back and rode and led the horses to the trailer. I bought five gallons of gas from Roland to make sure we had enough to get out of the mountains.

When I said goodbye to Martin and Roland, they said they had never met a politician like me, and if they could they would vote for me. They don't have a very good impression of politicians. I'm glad I could help someone gain some respect for those who serve in political office.

~ ~ ~

We drove out about 7 a.m. heading for Beaverhead. Again, I looked around at the splendid terrain. After nine summers of riding along the Continental Divide, you might think I would tire of the mountains, or at least become so accustomed to them that I'd lose appreciation for their beauty and majesty. I didn't. My love for the mountains is stronger today than when I embarked on this adventure.

Riding the Divide was indeed a mountain top experience. It was exhilarating to be "throned on the cragged heights." To nearly touch the sky. To be so near heaven.

But you can't *stay* "on top." Each day, at the end of our rides, we necessarily descended to the valley, because it was there we found level places for setting up camp, water for cooking, and grass for our horses. It is in the valley where real life occurs.

And while in the valley, it is hope that sustains. Including a hope for return to the majesty of the mountains. But for me it is more than hope. I know for *certain* I'll return.

EPILOGUE

July, 2003

I never tire of the mountains. My nine summers of riding along the Continental Divide so increased my love of the West that in the 20 years since my first ride, I have made it a point to ride in a mountainous or wilderness area each year (until 2001).

In this, the year I'll turn 80, I went back to the Scapegoat Mountains and Bob Marshall Wilderness Area. To my surprise, pain was not greater with this old body, but some sounds were not as vivid. I did not hear a Western Jay scolding, nor did I instinctively become aware of a predator (like a Grizzly) hiding off the trail.

My grandson, Sam Quie, 18, (Ben and Virginia's son) was with me, and will soon head for the Air Force Reserve. He and I now have stories to tell, and he and his dad, I'm sure, will compare experiences, noting what 20 years have done to the "old man."

Also along on this ride was Chip DeMann of Dundas, Minnesota, his 13-year-old son, Gus, plus a friend, State Senator Morris Westfall, from Halfway, Missouri. Chip is now an old salt on these trips, and the others were new. Deja vu of previous trips.

Spanish Bull is no more. The memories of this great companion continue to be vivid, and I occasionally find someone willing to listen to my stories about this faithful horse. I purchased him as a yearling, and he is the only horse I have not sold, since owning my first horse on the farm.

I now ride a four-year-old Missouri Fox Trotter gelding, Nugget (officially, "Playboy's Southern Gold"). Because of my relationship with Bull, I'm a better trainer now than I ever was, and I've taught Nugget what Bull taught me. He did great on the ride this month. I find it pure joy when a horse and I learn to communicate well and respect each other. What a spectacular creature created by God and developed by humans. Prey and predator in union with one another.

A heartwarming moment for me is when I've had a long working session with a horse, and I lead him back to the pasture where his buddies are grazing or just hanging out. He goes through the gate, and I remove all restraint. He heads for the other horses as I step back and close the gate. Then he stops, looks back at me, then back at the others, and with a second turn, back to look at me. Then he returns to stand by my side. What a thrill when a horse prefers to be with me. I scratch and rub him and know it can't be forever.

This relationship I have with horses continues to be an area of internal struggle for me. As I re-read each year's journal entries from the nine rides, I noticed my repeated concern about Gretchen's feelings. They are with me today. I know without question, however, that she is more important to me than mountains or horses. It's just that God made us different. At times, each of us does what is enjoyable for ourselves, not feeling that the other must participate. Gretchen's trip to Italy to attend nine operas will be among her cherished memories.

I believe there are times when one needs to spend some time fulfilling dreams; these experiences can draw us closer to God.

A benchmark in my spiritual life was the prayer experience described in Chapter 22 of *Riding the Divide*. My view of God did not change through this experience. But it did change my view of my relationship with Him, as well as my realization of who He is and how He works. God is never silent or sleeping. Everything that happens is part of His plan.

He speaks to us–and confronts us–through circumstances. He speaks through other people, especially wise and God-fearing people. He speaks to us–in a most authoritative way–through the Scriptures.

When I was in the mountains for those nine rides, I really learned to be quiet and listen to God speaking through these three means. It helps in understanding others if we remain still, listen and learn to "read" them. Similarly, we must listen and learn to "read" the mountains and horses to know how to relate to them. And we definitely get an understanding of God by listening as He speaks through Scripture, others, and circumstances.

Sometimes He reveals our true nature through circumstances. There were so many times on the rides that I was confronted with the fact that I can be an impatient man. While I learned I was able to pick up the skills of "mountain men" (remember, as someone who was "green" at the start, I needed to be taught how to pack–and then my pack flew apart when we'd barely started!), I quickly became aware that other people riding with me were more giving and caring of their colleagues than I was.

I am thankful for each one who rode with me, thankful for Gretchen's willingness to let me fulfill this dream, and thankful that God drew me closer to Him through these experiences.

And I thank you for taking time to read about my adventures!

End Notes

Epigraph

1. The author of our epigraph is unknown. While Julia W. Henshaw quotes the verse in her book, Wild Flowers of the North American Mountains (New York: Robert M. McBride and Co., 1917), she does not identify the author.

Continental Divide Map

2. For those who may not know, the Continental Divide is a line of summits in the Rocky Mountains, separating streams that flow to the Pacific Ocean from those that flow eventually to the Atlantic Ocean.

Chapter 1

3. A mantie is a pack cover–usually made of canvas or cotton duck–and used to protect the things inside the pack from water or dust. We wrapped bundles of our gear and equipment in the canvas, tied the packs in equally weighted pairs, and slung them with rope from the pack saddle. We weighed the pairs each morning to make sure they were balanced.

Chapter 2

4. On a typical morning, we would be up around 5 a.m. to let the horses out to graze. Then we would fix breakfast over a fire built from wood that had been prepared the night before. After cleaning up from breakfast, we would begin packing everything, weighing the packs and securing the pack saddles. One person would prepare our lunch. About 8 a.m. we would give the horses some grain, give them a good brushing, and check for any soreness. Then we'd saddle up and take off.

   In the evening, when we arrived at our chosen campsite, the first thing we would do is put up the "kitchen" tarp and then get all the packs under it. We piled pack saddles in one location and covered them with tarp. Then we began preparing the evening meal and put the horses out to graze. (Each campsite needed to be flat and have grass, water, and trees.)

5. Because horses like comfort and dislike anxiety, new trails and new experiences do not draw them. If they decide to leave where they are because of danger, hunger, thirst or loneliness, they will return "from whence they came"—i.e., the backtrail–either from pleasant memory or because they are thinking, "the devil I know is better than the devil I don't know."

6. Mike Dudley tells me he still has his mule Buford, who is probably 30 years old by now!

Chapter 3

7. A pig tail is a strong rope anchored to the rigging with a small loop of breakable twine; only the replaceable loop will break in case the last pack animal pulls back too hard.

Chapter 4

8. In later years, sons Fred and Dan, who spent time in this vicinity, often wondered if this man was the Unabomber.

Chapter 7

9. Generally I would wait until about the third day out on a ride before letting the horses run free at night. I would usually hobble them the first couple of nights because, if they were loose, they might be tempted to go back to the horse trailers. By the third night they usually wasn't an issue. Other times that we hobbled the horses rather than let them loose depended on how they were getting along with one another and with us.

Chapter 10

10. We used boxes–or panniers–to pack our breakable items and to better organize small items. They were hung from the pack sad-

dle by loops or hooks, and, again, we weighed the boxes each day so each pack horse would be carrying two panniers of equal weight.

Chapter 12

11. I first learned about using washing machine covers as fry pans from a friend, Cecil Garland, whom I met in the 1960s. Cecil owned and operated Garland's Town and Country Store in Lincoln, Montana, and, as president of the Wilderness Society, came to Washington, D.C., to lobby for legislation promoted by the Society.

In 1970, my son Fred and I went on a pack trip with Cecil around and onto Scapegoat Mountain (as referenced in Chapter 15). On that trip, we saw three airplanes that had crashed in past years, listened to the coyotes around us at night, and learned that washing machine lids make fine frying pans. Cecil also took us down steeper mountain sides than I ever thought possible with horses.

I also learned that, in earlier years, Cecil was a mountain lion hunter. He told us he once had a partnership with a man in Nevada who was an outfitter for mountain lion hunting trips. Cecil and his partner would guarantee the hunter his lion, and in order to do that, Cecil would go into the Montana mountains around Lincoln, capture lions and ship them to Nevada.

To capture a lion, Cecil's dogs would tree it, and Cecil would climb a nearby tree, carrying with him a long pole with a noose on the end. He would somehow stretch across and get the noose around the neck of the lion in the neighboring tree. I can only imagine the struggle he had getting the lion down, binding it, loading it onto his pack horse, and traveling miles to the trailhead where he had a crate waiting in his truck.

Thank goodness Cecil changed to be a protector of certain wildlife and the wilderness.

Chapter 13

12. A sawbuck (or crossbuck) saddle has two cinches (double rigging), which can make it a little more stable on the horse's back. It doesn't allow as much adjustment as a decker saddle does,

however, since you have no choice in where the cinches are placed, nor on the angle of the crossed bars that are on top of the saddle (to which pack sling ropes are attached).

A decker saddle has a D-ring on the top to which pack sling ropes are attached. The D-ring can be adjusted by a metal worker so the saddle will fit the horse better, and the single cinch can be moved forward or backward. It has a padded cover, called a half breed, with a board at the bottom to spread the load.

Chapter 17

13. When we got out of the wilderness last year, I asked a friend in the Forest Service in Lincoln about this cabin. The ranger told me he knew nothing about the cabin, and, after checking, we found no trace of it in the Forest Service records.

14. While catching up on the news after the 1986 ride, I read that a Russian satellite had fallen out of orbit and burned in the earth's atmosphere. Checking dates, I discovered this happened about the same time the guys and I were watching the "falling star." I wondered at the time why it lingered so long, making it possible for all of us to see. We probably had been looking at the burning-out-of-control satellite.

Chapter 30

15. I followed through on my promise to Nancy Zeller, the nurse I met August 9, 1989, in Lake City, Colorado. Two months after the ride, I wrote to Mark Hubbel, executive director of Prison Fellowship in Oregon, asking his help in arranging a visit with Nancy's son who was being held at the prison in Pendleton in eastern Oregon. When I arrived in mid-October, Mark gave me the details of the time and place for my visit to Pendleton, but he also warned me that the prisoner I was about to meet had been the leader of an in-prison protest of Native Americans, and that the authorities were concerned.

I'm sure the authorities thought I was being naïve, but I had no fear meeting this young man. In fact, his association with the Native Americans, I reasoned, would give me a starting point for discussion.

When we met, I first asked Nancy's son about his involvement with the Native Americans, wondering why he had led such a rebellion. I wasn't being accusatory with my questioning; I was sincerely interested.

He told me that even though his dad was Native American, he was not interested in practicing the Indian religion. He said he led the rebellion simply because he thought it was unjust that the Indians were unable to practice their religion in prison.

He must have recognized that I was genuinely interested in him and understanding of where he was coming from, because he then listened intently as I shared stories about the Holy Spirit working in my life. When I asked him whether he was interested in knowing Jesus Christ, he said, "Yes. I would like to follow Jesus." So we talked about Bible passages that teach how our sin separates us from God, and how Jesus' sacrifice bridges the gap. We also talked about the importance of being guided by the Holy Spirit.

Several years later, Nancy wrote me a letter telling me that she and her work as a nurse were to be featured in Life magazine. She also brought me up to date on her son: "He is a believer, is married with children and is living a very stable, caring and competent life." Praise God.

Chapter 35

16. When I got home after the 1990 ride, I told Gretchen about the image of the blue-clad woman reclining on the log in the small stream the night of April 5. She was as intrigued as I about the incident. Periodically the encounter would come to mind, and I continued to wonder about it.

    Then, in the fall of 1998, Gretchen ran across an article in her Christianity and the Arts magazine titled, "Mystery of the Lady in Blue." It was written by Sr. Sheila A. Smith, O.S.U., a widely published author living in Albuquerque, New Mexico. As we read the article together, Gretchen and I were astounded at how similar my vision had been to the woman described by Sr. Smith.

    As Sr. Smith tells the story, in July of 1629, about 50 Jumanos natives journeyed south–as they had since 1620–from their home in the Manzano Mountains of New Mexico to the adobe church at Isleta Pueblo in Mexico. Each year these natives had come to ask for baptism. This mystified Fr. Benavides, for as far as he knew, they had had no instruction in the faith (a pre-requisite to baptism). Fr.. Benavides was forced to turn these Indians away each year because a shortage of personnel meant he did not have anyone to send back with them to teach them. That is, until that particular year, when several missionaries had arrived from Spain.

So Fr.. Benavides sent two of these missionaries to minister in the Indians' village of Salinas, New Mexico. Before sending them on their way, however, he asked the Jumanos who had sent them, and how did they know to come to Isleta for a priest?

The Indians' leader replied that a "Lady in Blue" had taught them the faith of Jesus Christ and had sent them to Isleta.

When the two priests arrived with the Jumanos at their homes in Salinas, they found an entire village waiting to be baptized.

Meanwhile, in Agreda, Spain, there was a nun, Sr. Maria de Jesus, who was sharing with her confessor how, at the end of her prayer time, she "felt" herself returning to her convent chapel, exactly where she had been hours earlier at the beginning of her prayer time. She said she knew her body had not moved, but she felt her spirit had been elsewhere.

This Sr. Maria, who had made solemn vows in 1620 as a cloistered nun, was totally given to God. She was aware of God's special love for the native people of America, especially those of New Mexico, and she said God had granted her lifelong wish to be a missionary to them by mystically transporting her to New Mexico. There she miraculously found herself speaking and understanding the Indians' language, which she had not studied and did not know. After sharing the faith with them for several hours, she said she would leave. Sr. Maria said she experienced over 500 such visits to the American Southwest.

The confessor wrote a letter to the bishop-elect of Mexico City in an attempt to confirm the nun's accounts of supernatural journeys to New Mexico. In the letter, the bishop asked if a Spanish woman wearing a blue cloak had been seen in any Indian villages.

Fr.. Benavides had heard rumors of a "Lady in Blue" visiting other places besides Salinas, and he wondered whether Sr. Maria of Agreda might be she. So he traveled to Spain in 1630 to visit Sr. Maria himself. When there, he found that Sr. Maria was able to accurately describe the people, pueblos, plants, animals, landforms, and climate of central New Mexico. She even described baptisms at which Fr.. Benavides had been present, adding that the Indians could see her, but not the Mexicans. Fr.. Benavides believed Sr. Maria was indeed the Lady in Blue, but how could she travel so quickly between two continents?

The author of the Christianity and the Arts magazine article, Sr. Smith, responds to that question: "God gives many gifts for service. One of the most extraordinary is bilocation, in which one's presence is perceived in two places at once. When one's heart is totally given to God, faith can open the way for God to break through the ordinary, and work in extraordinary ways."

She continues: "If the 'legend' of the Lady in Blue were only a legend, we could easily dismiss it as merely an interesting story. But being documented not only by Fr.. Benavides, but also by numerous reports from tribes ranging from Texas to California, it makes us ponder the workings of God in human history...

"Only God knows. (So) we might more profitably ask if there is a message for ourselves in these events. Do we live in a world where everything is clear-cut? Or do we find our world, our governments, our communities, and even ourselves to be more of a mixture of 'weeds and wheat?' Perhaps our stability and source of hope lie in seeing both the past and the present with eyes of faith. If looking at history with the advantage of hindsight can show us that God is ever-present in human events...then can we not also believe that God walks with us today, despite all the constrictions of our times? Perhaps it is precisely this view of faith that can strengthen our hope and enable us to grow in, and draw good from, circumstances in which we least expect to find God."

Chapter 37

17. When one is as close to a horse as Mert Schwarz was to Gunther, the grieving process over losing such an animal is very similar to that we experience when we lose a beloved human. In 1993, two years after Gunther was tragically killed, Mert took his granddaughter to New Mexico, and while there, they visited Gunther's grave.

Acknowledgments

Al would like to thank:

Son and daughter-in-law, *Fred Quivik* and *Mindy Quivik*. Thank you for the extensive time each of you gave to editing the manuscript. I especially appreciate your interest in the project, reflected by your honest comments that motivated me to make changes in the manuscript, your excellent questions that probed my thinking, and your painstaking attention to the details of grammar and sentence structure.

My friends and acquaintances who accompanied me on the rides. Your friendship and companionship gave these rides an added dimension that I will treasure all my life.

Bill Bontrager, '87
Ellen Bontrager, '87
Martin Bostetter, '87
Darrell Cade, '84
Bob Cashin, '83, '87, '88
Dean Cates, '83, '86
Doug Coe, '83, '84, '86, '87
Dennis Casano, '83
Mike Dudley, '83
Gary Hanson, '91
Jeff Hoeffner, '83
Suzy Erickson Johnson, '86
Monroe Larson, '87
Marlin Levison, '83
Rob Linner, '84
A.M. Lips, '83, '84, '85, '86, '87, '88, '89, '91
Bill Manee, '84
Malcolm Marsh, '84
Rick McIlhenny, '84

Pastor Paul Nelson, '85
Hank Pederson, '87
Jerry Potter, '86
Scott Pritchard, '86
Tom Pritchard, '86
Graham Purcell, '88
Ben Quie, '83
Fred Quivik, '84
Frank Rawlins, '85
Glen Roberts, '88, '90
Mert Schwarz, '84, '85, '86, '87, '88, '89, '91
Ray Seaver, '90
Al Severson, '83, '84, '85, '87, '88, '91
Dave Singer, '89
Bill Starr, '83
Lynn Street, '84, '87, '91
Dick Whitmore, '88

These people, now deceased, also rode with me:

Jonathan Coe, '83   Claire Erickson, '86   Jerry Franz, '85, '86
Norm Madson, '87   Robert Taylor, '91

My wife *Gretchen*. Without your encouragement, I may not have embarked on this project. Thank you for your ever-present love.

Carol would like to thank:

Al. Thank you for giving me the opportunity to work on this project with you.

Helen Peterson. Thank you for the role you played in bringing Al and me together.

My husband *Bob.* Thank you for your patience throughout the process, for believing in me, for being a sounding board, for your suggestions and encouragement, and for being my all-around techno-geek.

The rest of my immediate family, *Nicole, Krista, Jonathan, Tanya* and *Evan.* Thank you for your patience, encouragement and willingness to see that my sometimes-cranky nature is just that: "sometimes."

Bonnie and Gordy Addington. Thank you for sharing your "Cross Lake Retreat Center" so I could finish the writing.

Cheryl Henry. Thank you for your prayer support.

The *St. Anthony Park Branch* of the St. Paul Public Library and *St. Anthony Park Lutheran Church.* Thank you for giving us meeting space during the months we poured over Al's journals.

Biographical sketches

Al Quie

Al Quie, the third child of Nettie and Albert Knute Quie, was born September 18, 1923, at Longfurrow Farm near Dennison and Nerstrand, Minn. Like most farm children, Al learned to do chores at a young age. He was given his first pony when he was eight years old.

Al graduated from Northfield High School in 1942, and shortly after became a pilot in the U.S. Navy during World War II.

He graduated from St. Olaf College with a degree in political science in 1950, and married his college sweetheart, Gretchen Hansen of Minneapolis, on June 5, 1948. The two have five children, 14 grandchildren and one great grandchild.

In 1954, while operating the family farm, Al was elected to the Minnesota State Senate. He served there until February, 1958, when he was elected to the United States Congress, representing Minnesota's First Congressional District. Al was successful in his bid for governor of Minnesota in 1978.

After 28 years in public service, Al decided not to run for re-election as governor. That is when he was able to take time to fulfill his life-long dream of riding horseback along the Continental Divide from Canada to Mexico.

Al has served on many boards including Prison Fellowship Ministries, Lutheran Brotherhood Mutual Funds, Lutheran Health Systems, Tentmakers, Vesper Society, Nobel Peace Prize Forum, Search Institute, Council on Crime and Justice, Urban Ventures, AGORA, the Commission on Excellence in Education that wrote "A Nation at Risk," and Word Alone. Several of these are currently on his agenda. He also is a sought-after speaker, and serves as mentor to many individuals.

Al is a member of Minnetonka Lutheran Church and is a voting member of the Evangelical Lutheran Church in America Church-Wide Assemblies.

Carol Pettitt

Carol Pettitt has been a free-lance writer in St. Paul, Minnesota, since 1983. She was born and raised in North Dakota and graduated from the University of North Dakota in Grand Forks with a Bachelor of Arts degree in journalism. As a member of a family of horse lovers, some of her growing up years were spent riding the same trails as Al in the Badlands of western North Dakota. She and her family attend First Evangelical Free Church in Maplewood, Minn.